Green Acres S

Going Places
With Children
in Washington, DC

16th Edition

Editor
Kathie Meizner

Production Editor
Karla Thomas

Director of Development
Joan Adler

Layout and Editing
Lisa Baydush

Cover Art
Jennifer O'Connell

Photographs
Leathia West

Editorial and Production Assistance
Lee Baydush, Diana England, Susan Greif,
Jane Meyers, Virginia Murphy, Parker Orr,
Donna Perlmutter, Gary Rubin, Dawn Smith, Meg Thale

Much appreciation to the parents and teachers of the Green Acres School community for their assistance and support throughout this project, to Brenda Robinson for her marketing and distribution work, and to the students of Green Acres School for their creative artwork! The editorial staff would especially like to thank their families for their patience with the many volunteer hours devoted to this project.

First edition 1958, Second edition 1961, Third edition 1963,
Fourth edition 1965, Fifth edition 1968, Sixth edition 1971,
Seventh edition 1974, Eighth edition 1976, Ninth edition 1979,
Tenth edition 1982, Eleventh edition 1984, Twelfth edition 1988,
Thirteenth edition 1992, Fourteenth edition 1995,
Fifteenth edition 1998, Sixteenth edition 2003.

Text Copyright 2003 by Green Acres School.
All rights reserved.
ISBN 0-9608998-6-3

Cover design by Jennifer O'Connell

Photography by Leathia West

Illustrations by students of Green Acres School

Metro map courtesy of
Washington Metropolitan Area Transit Authority

Published by:
Green Acres School
11701 Danville Drive
Rockville, Maryland 20852
Telephone: 301-881-4100
Fax: 301-881-3319
E-Mail: GASDEV@GREENACRES.ORG
On-Line: www.greenacres.org

About Green Acres School

Green Acres was founded in 1934 by a group of parents and teachers who believed that children are naturally curious about their world and learn best in an informal, flexible environment. This group created a school that balanced children's social, emotional, physical, and creative development in an atmosphere of intellectual rigor. They created an environment with a low student-teacher ratio, and an ethnically, racially, and economically diverse student body. Their primary goal was to help children learn to think and be creative in their thinking. Today, Green Acres School continues that progressive tradition.

Located in a Washington suburb on a 15-acre wooded campus, Green Acres School provides a full curriculum for pre-kindergarten through eighth grade. In addition to an outdoor amphitheater, stimulating play areas, science lab, art and music studios, and a gymnasium/performing arts center, the school provides an integrated curriculum with a focus on the whole child. Through hands-on problem solving, Green Acres cultivates in students a lifelong love of learning. A former students sums it up:

"I believe that my time at Green Acres was instrumental in giving me the ability to believe in myself, to think with an open mind, and to pursue my ideals and dreams."

Introduction

Green Acres School is almost 70 years old – and *Going Places with Children in Washington DC* is 45. We have a great deal to celebrate with our anniversaries: seven decades of the very best in progressive education, and nearly half-a-century of letting our community know about splendid adventures in history, nature, and the arts in and around our nation's capital.

Going Places is the longest running and most comprehensive guide to family outings and explorations in the Washington area, with over 400 descriptions of family-tested places to visit and sights to see. From the solemnity and richness of the national monuments and museums to the delight of local gardens and parks to rainy day play, there is something here for everyone, any day of the year.

 The 16th edition of *Going Places* includes a number of new sites, and guides to on-line information. Cross-reference lists provide easy ways for readers to find activities and places of interest. Please note that admission to sites listed in this book is free unless otherwise indicated, and that new security measures are now in place at many sites in DC. Be sure to double-check security policies as part of your visit planning.

A number of museums were either closed for renovation or unavailable for public tours in 2003. Among these are:

- FBI — tours suspended until further notice.
- The White House — tours available only through Congressional representatives.
- National Institute of Standards and Technology Museum — not open to the public.
- Pentagon — not open to the general public.
- Marine Corps Air-Ground Museum — closed permanently. The National Museum of the Marine Corps is beginning site clearing and construction.
- The Newseum — will reopen in a new location in 2006.
- Smithsonian American Art Museum; National Portrait Gallery — renovations through 2005
- Goddard Space Flight Center — closed indefinitely to the general public

Table of Contents

1. **Starting Out**   **1**

    Websites: Maps, Virtual Tours, Events   1
    Information and Visitors Centers   3
    Sightseeing/Tours   6
    Public Transportation   10
    Publications to Take Along   13

2. **Main Sights and Museums in Washington, DC**   **14**

    On The Mall   14
    The White House   31
    On Capitol Hill   32
    Around Town   38

3. **Main Sights and Museums Around the Beltway**   **68**

    Maryland   68
    Virginia   80

4. **The Great Outdoors**   **99**

    Hiking, Fishing, Biking, and Boating in DC   99
    Hiking, Fishing, Biking, and Boating in Maryland   103
    Hiking, Fishing, Biking, and Boating in Virginia   116
    Battlefields and Historical Sites   124
    Regional Parks and Playgrounds   127
    Nature Centers, Planetariums, and Sanctuaries   144
    Historical Farms   156
    Pick Your Own   161
    Gardens   165

5. **Arts and Entertainment**   **169**

    Performing Arts   169
    Children's Books and Toys   184

6. **Sports and Recreation**   **192**

    Spectators   192
    Canoeing, Kayaking, and Sailing   195
    Equestrian   198
    Golf and Miniature Golf   199
    Skating, Boarding, and Blading   200
    Snowboarding and Skiing   204
    Swimming and Splashing   206

7. **Indoor Recreation**   **210**

    Indoor Play and Arcades   210
    Climbing and Laser Tag   213
    Make Your Own Crafts   215

8. Day Trips in the Region   **216**

Baltimore Inner Harbor   216
Around Baltimore   223
Annapolis   232
Harper's Ferry   237
Gettysburg   239
Maryland   242
Virginia   250
Pennsylvania   255
Theme Parks   257

9. Field Trips   **262**

10. Quick Guide to Special Interests   **267**

New for the 16th Edition   267
Appropriate for Preschoolers   268
Of Special Interest to Teens   269
Airplanes/Space   270
Aquariums   271
Arboretums/Gardens   271
Batting Cages   271
Battlefields/Forts   272
Biking   272
Birthday Parties   273
Boating   274
Canoe and Kayak Rentals   275
Carousels   276
Children's Museums   276
Disk Golf   276
Equestrian   276
Fishing   277
Golf Courses   278
Miniature Golf   279
Nature Centers   279
Observatories/Planetarium   280
Railroads   280
Ships   281
Swimming   281
Tennis   282
VA TimeTravlers Site   283
Zoos   284

12. Annual Events for Children and Families   **285**

Spring (March-May)   285
Summer (June-August)   288
Fall (September-November)   291
Winter (December-February)   294

1. Starting Out

Three important keys to successful family trips
— whether for the afternoon, the weekend or longer —
are planning ahead, stopping for rest and food, and finding
the balance among traveling, seeing, learning and
entertainment.

Take care of the environment and of yourself wherever you go
— the places you visit today with your children will be part of
their legacy to their children and other generations.

And, of course, begin with *Going Places* — this book is a
treasure box of ideas for you to begin your planning.

Websites: Maps, Virtual Tours, Events

One good place to begin an adventure away from home is to
check out current information about services, hours, and
special events on line, either from home or at your local
public library.

This section provides a list of excellent web sites for visitors in
our region. In addition, nearly every entry in *Going Places*
lists a web site that provides updated information about the
site you intend to visit, as well as information on special
services for visitors.

- Visit **www.cr.nps.gov/nr/travel/wash/intro .htm** for
  a wonderfully eclectic on-line tour of National Historic
  Places in Washington.

- The National Park Service on-line guides to the National
  Monuments are easy to use and provide helpful tips for
  visitors. See **www.nps.gov**.

- The Washington D.C. Convention and Visitors
  Association has an official tourism website that
  provides a comprehensive introduction for visitors,
  including information about transportation and places
  to eat and stay. See **www.washington.org**.

- The Conference and Visitors Bureau of Montgomery
  County, MD has an excellent guide to events, history,
  and sights in the county. See **www.cvbmontco.com**.

- Visit **http://DCpages.com/Tourism** for a 360-degree
  look at 10 buildings and monuments on the National
  Mall.

- Go to "America's Homepage" at **ahp.gatech.edu /dc_map.html** for links to a collection of tours of the landmarks on the Mall along with other resources — including a terrific collection of historic documents.

- The Maryland National Capital Park and Planning Commission websites, **www.mc-mncppc.org** and **www.pgparks.com**, are terrific guides to the parks and park facilities in Montgomery and Prince Georges counties in Maryland.

- Find online maps to bike trails and routes throughout the metropolitan area along with suggestions for recreational rides at the Washington Area Bicyclist Association, **www.waba.org**, and Bike Washington, **www.bikewashington.org**.

- A guide to historic Alexandria, Virginia can be found at **oha.ci.alexandria.va.us** with photos and background information on many of the sites listed in Going Places.

- Maryland state parks are described in detail at the Department of Natural Resources, **www.dnr.state .md.us**.

Information and Visitors Centers

Visitor centers can be treasure troves of information and ideas about places to visit, activities for families, and entertaining facts to add to the enjoyment of sightseeing. Some of the most useful general visitor's centers are listed here.

Alexandria Convention and Visitors Bureau

Ramsay House Visitors Center, 221 King Street, Alexandria, VA (703-838-4200, 703-838-5005, 24-hour recorded information) - **oha.ci.alexandria.va.us.**

This Visitors Center is the restored home of William Ramsay, Scottish merchant and city founder. Stop here for information on historic Old Town Alexandria. You can also pick up annotated maps, lists of galleries and shops, and tour information.

- Open daily, 9-5, except Thanksgiving, Christmas, and New Year's Day.
- The free DASH weekend shuttle runs 15 minutes between King Street Metro Station (Orange line) and Old Town's Market square.
- No wheelchair access. Strollers permitted, but must be carried up steps.

Special activities include Candlelight Tours of historic homes in Old Town Alexandria, the second weekend in December for children age 12 and older; the Scottish Christmas Walk, a parade of Scottish clans with each family dressed in its traditional tartan finery, the first Saturday in December; and a George Washington Birthday Parade around February 22.

Annapolis Conference Center and Visitors Bureau

26 West Street, Annapolis, MD (410-280-0445) - **www.visit-annapolis.org**. *Directions: Take Route 50 east to Exit 24, Rowe Boulevard; go through two traffic lights and stay in the right lane as the road forks; go through one light and follow signs for visitor center on the right. Parking available in Gotts Court Parking Garage.*

While not a destination in and of itself, the Visitor's Bureau is brimming with free information about the city of Annapolis and many sites in Anne Arundel County. Because there is plenty to see in this area, a stop here can help you plan a visit to meet your family's needs.

Get information about the U.S. Naval Academy, museums, boating, arts festivals, field trips, historic homes, and workshops for kids. Directions are provided to picnic areas, kid-friendly local restaurants, athletic fields, parking, and playgrounds.

- Open daily, 9-5.
- Wheelchair Accessible.

Baltimore Visitor Center

451 Light Street, Inner Harbor, Baltimore, MD (877-225-8466, 1-877-Baltimore) - www.baltimore.org; vc@baltimore.org.

Baltimore is less than a one-hour drive or train ride from Washington, DC. See Chapter 6, "Day Trips," for suggested sights to see, and request a visitor information packet online.

- Open Monday-Saturday, 9-5; Sunday, 10-5.

Special activities include Kids on the Bay the third Saturday in October with mermaids, fish casting, Tales of the Sea, singing, dancing, and face painting, as well as maritime, scientific, and other educational programs.

Ellipse Visitors Pavilion

On the corner of E and 15th Streets, NW (202-523-3847) - www.nps.gov/whho/ellipse.

- Daily from 8–3 except for Thanksgiving, Christmas, and New Year's.
- Metrorail Blue and Orange line (McPherson Square) and Red Line (Metro Center).
- Tourmobile Sightseeing stop.
- Facilities include: restrooms, phones, first aid, water fountains, concessions, information, and sales area.

Maryland Tourism

217 East Redwood Street, 9th Floor, Baltimore, MD (800-634-7386 or 1-800-MDisFun) - www.mdisfun.org.

Call or write to receive a free travel kit, which includes a state map, a calendar of events, and a Destination Maryland Travel Guide.

National Park Service - National Capital Region

1100 Ohio Drive, SW, Washington, DC (202-619-7222) - www.nps.gov.

Senate and House Visitors Galleries

United States House of Representatives, House Office Building, Washington, DC (202-224-3121, 202-224-4910-public group tours) – ***www.house.gov****; United States Senate, Senate Office Building, Washington, DC, 202-244-3121 -* ***www.senate.gov.***

Elected officials will often meet with their young constituents and even have a picture taken with the group on the steps of the Capitol, but you must arrange this in writing before your trip. If you are planning to visit Washington in the busy spring season, be sure to make arrangements six months prior to your visit. Gallery passes are required to attend sessions of either legislative body.

Smithsonian Institution Information Center

See page 27.

Virginia Tourism Corporation

901 East Byrd Street, Richmond, VA (800-847-4882, 800-Visit-VA) - ***www.virginia.org****.*

Washington, DC Convention and Visitors Association

1212 New York Avenue, NW, Suite 600, Washington, DC (202-789-7000) – ***www.washington.org****.*

Get free maps of Washington, brochures on major attractions and special exhibits, hotel information, and a calendar of events.

Sightseeing/Tours

Real life tour guides can greatly enhance your experience of a visit to Washington and neighboring historic places. The stories and facts shared by well-informed tour guides can provide a memorable introduction to the sites, and a multi-stop tour can help you squeeze in a few more sites during a day's visit.

A Tour de Force

*North Nash Street, Arlington, VA (703-525-2948) - **www.atourdeforce.com***.

Enjoy specially designed, historically oriented tours of Washington, DC neighborhoods, monuments, and museums. Each tour is filled with stories of the people who have made Washington such a great national capital city. No two tours are alike.

- Daily tours, including holidays.
- Call to arrange convenient meeting spots.

Anecdotal History Tours

*9009 Paddock Lane, Potomac, MD (301-294-9514) - **info@dcsightseeing.com***.

These tours provide an unending supply of interesting tales, anecdotes, and stories about Washington, DC. Tours of interest include: *The Curse of Lafayette Square*: A leisurely stroll in front of the White House. *A Walk Through Adams Morgan:* An historical hike through this colorful Victorian and early 20th century neighborhood. *Georgetown Homes of the Famous and Infamous*: A two-hour walk through Georgetown. *Lincoln's Assassination*: A walk in the footsteps of America's most beloved President

- Reservations are essential; check web site for tour times.
- Tickets $10-$15 for individuals.

D.C. Duck Tours

*Union Station, Washington, DC (202-966-3825) - **www.dcducks.com***.

Take a land/water tour on an amphibious vehicle. The "Ducks" are the same ones that were used to carry troops and supplies in World War II and are fully restored and Coast Guard approved. The fully-narrated tour spends one hour on land and 30 minutes on the water. Children are sure to be thrilled when the "bus" drives into the Potomac River!

- Reservations are not required. Tours are offered April through October and depart hourly from Union Station.
- Children, $13; Adults, $26.
- Metrorail Red line (Union Station).
- The 90-minute tour covers the White House, the Capitol and other sites before driving *into* the Potomac River.
- Duck Tours are also available at the Baltimore Inner Harbor.

Old Town Trolley Tours of Washington, DC

Tours depart from Union Station, Washington, DC (202-832-9800) - www.trolleytours.com.

Old Town Trolley Tours offers a wide-ranging tour of 100 points of interest in Washington, including Georgetown, Embassy Row, the Washington National Cathedral, Capitol Hill, Dupont Circle, and the Mall. Passengers can get off and re-board at their leisure at 18 stops. The ride in an old-fashioned trolley car makes sightseeing all the more enjoyable. Out of town visitors - check to see if the trolleys stop near your hotel. Evening tours are available by reservation.

- Trips daily every 30 minutes. The complete route takes two hours and 15 minutes.
- Adults, $26; children 4-12, $13; children under four, free.
- Metrorail Red line (Union Station).
- Wheelchair access, but wheelchairs must be collapsible.
- Available for field trips and birthday parties.

Potomac Riverboat Company Cruises

205 The Strand, Alexandria, VA (703-684-0580, 703-548-9000) - www. potomacriverboatco.com. The dock is located behind the Torpedo Factory Arts Center, North Union and Cameron Streets in Old Town, Alexandria.

The **Admiral Tip** offers a 40-minute narrated cruise along the waterfront of historic Alexandria. The **Matthew Hayes** is a 90-minute narrated cruise past Washington's monuments. **Miss Christin** provides roundtrip transportation to Mount Vernon, home of George Washington - upon arrival at the estate, you will take a land tour of the grounds, gardens, and museums.

- Open daily April-October, except Mondays. Morning, afternoon, and evening tours are available. Departure times vary with the day and season.
- Tickets may be purchased at the dock.

- **Admiral Tip**: Adults, $8; seniors, $7; children, $5.
- **Matthew Hayes**: Adults, $16; seniors, $15; children, $8.
- **Miss Christin** (fare includes admission to Mount Vernon): Adults, $26; seniors, $24; children, $13.
- Wheelchair access, but wheelchairs must be collapsible. Parking for strollers.

Spirit Cruises

*Pier 4, 6th and Water Streets, SW, Washington, DC (202-558-8013, 866-211-3811 toll free) - **www.spiritcruises.com**. From the Washington Beltway (I-495) take George Washington Parkway east to I-395 North. Pass over the 14th Street Bridge then take the Maine Avenue Exit. Cross over Maine Avenue and turn left onto Water Street. Pier 4 is located at the end of 6th and Water Street.*

Both **Spirit of Washington** and **Potomac Spirit** operate from Pier 4 in Washington D.C. **Spirit of Washington** offers two-hour lunch cruises, three-hour dinner cruises, and two-and-a-half-hour evening and moonlight cruises. Sights along the route include the capitol and historic monuments, Fort McNair, National Airport, and the Potomac skyline.

- **Potomac Spirit** tours to Mt. Vernon, George Washington's estate, are five-and-a-half hours long, and operate mid-March to November. Cruises depart at 8:30 a.m. and return at 3 p.m.
- **Spirit of Washington** operates daily March-December, except on Mondays.
- Daily lunch and dinner cruises.
- Costs vary with the day of the week and the meal being served.
- A five-minute walk from the Waterfront Metro Station. (M Street, left on 6th Street-go one block, left on Water Street-Spirit Cruises directly ahead.)
- Call for information on wheelchair access. Strollers are permitted.

Special activities a holiday cruise in December and a New Year's Eve cruise; Gospel Lunch cruises on Saturdays once a month March-November, Big Band Senior Dinners are scheduled during the April-May. Please call for exact dates or see web site.

Tourmobile Sightseeing Incorporated

Landmark Services Tourmobile, Inc., 1000 Ohio Drive, SW, Washington, DC (202-488-5209, 202-488-5218, groups) - www.tourmobile.com.

Tourmobile is a concessionaire of the National Park Service, offering a convenient way to get from one main attraction to another. The open-air vehicles, accompanied by guides, stop at 22 major sights along the Mall, Union Station, MCI Center, Ford's Theatre, FBI Building, Lincoln Memorial, John F. Kennedy Center and Arlington National Cemetery. The Arlington National Cemetery tour includes the Kennedy Family Grave Sites, the Tomb of the Unknowns, the Arlington House, and the Robert E. Lee Memorial. For an additional fee, you may add Mount Vernon and the Frederick Douglass Historic Site to your tour. You are allowed unlimited stops along the route and re-boarding is free throughout the day. This is an efficient and energy-saving way to see numerous attractions. Several Tourmobile stops are located near Metrorail stations.

- Hours of operation: June 15-Labor Day, 9-6:30; remainder of the year, 9:30-4:30. Closed Christmas. Board every 15 to 30 minutes, depending on the season, at any stop. The complete tour, without the swing to Arlington, takes about 90 minutes.

- Adults, $14; children 3-11, $7. June 15 through Labor Day, for a slightly higher fee, you may also purchase a ticket, after 4 (or after 2 the rest of the year), that can be used for the remainder of that afternoon and again the next day.

- Handicap accessible buses are available - call for information.

Washington Walks

(202-484-1565) - www.washingtonwalks.com.

Washington Walks offers two-hour, easy walking tours of the city. Don't miss **Capital Hauntings**, a tour of ghostly hauntings, and **I've Got a Secret**, a tour of surprising, little-known secrets about Washington.

Public Transportation

Many of the sites listed in Going Places are easily accessible by public transportation, and many others are accessible with a bit of planning. Whether you have a single destination — or are planning a day in Washington, Alexandria, Baltimore, or Harper's Ferry — you may want to leave the car and parking hassles at home, and try the region's extensive public transportation system.

DASH

(703-370-DASH).

- DASH operates buses along four routes within the City of Alexandria, Virginia, connecting several Metrorail stations with locations throughout the city, including the Old Town shopping and restaurant area.
- Base fare is 85¢ with a 25¢ surcharge to the Pentagon Metrorail station.
- DASH operates from approximately 5:30 a.m.-midnight, Monday-Saturday, with reduced Sunday hours.

MARC Trains

(800-325-RAIL, recorded message) - *mtamaryland.com.*

This commuter rail service links DC with Baltimore and points in Maryland and West Virginia. All three services have their Washington, DC terminal at Union Station. These trains operate on weekdays only, about every half hour during the commuter rush and approximately every hour otherwise. Weekly and monthly tickets are available.

MARC and VRE tickets to Washington are good for travel on one another's trains that leave Washington before noon and arrive in Washington after noon.

Tickets are available by mail.

- Children under six may ride free with any passenger paying the full fare (limit two children per full fare passenger).
- The Camden Line from Baltimore includes stops at College Park and Riverdale.
- The Penn Line includes stops at BWI Airport and New Carrollton.
- Along the West Virginia Line, which eventually stops in Duffields, West Viriginia, the MARC makes stops in Silver Spring, Kensington, Gaithersburg, Germantown, Boyds, and Harpers Ferry.

Metrorail and Metrobus

*Washington Metropolitan Area Transit Authority, 600 5th Street, NW, Washington, DC (202-637-7000) - **www.wmata.com***

Parking in many downtown areas is expensive and difficult to find. Avoid frustration by using Metro, Washington's subway and bus system.

Metro is an excellent (although not inexpensive) alternative for getting to and around downtown Washington. Children will enjoy the Metrorail train rides and the spacious vaulted underground stations. Call for information on special bus/rail passes or on routes for any part of the Metro system (see inside back cover).

Take Note...

If you can get a seat in the first car of the train, children can press their noses against the glass and see the tunnels up ahead illuminated by the train's lights!

Metro parking lots, adjacent to many suburban stations, are convenient places to leave your car while riding Metro. In order to pay a discounted parking fee at some lots, you must obtain a bus transfer at the beginning of your return rail trip when you enter the station. Many Metro parking lots fill early on weekday mornings, but space is available on weekends at no cost.

Entrance to Metrorail is by farecard, which can be purchased at any Metrorail station. The amount charged depends on the distance traveled and the time of day. Be sure to keep your farecard until you exit the Metrorail system. Each passenger (including children age five and over) must have a farecard; two children age four and under ride free with a paying passenger. The farecard vending machines will take bills in denominations from $1-$20. The highest fares are charged during weekday rush hours - 5:30-9:30 a.m. and 3-8 p.m. There are substantial fare savings during non-rush hours. Discounted transfers are available for riders going from rail to bus.

Metro has elevators and train space for wheelchairs, features to assist the blind, and devices to assist the deaf. Information regarding reduced fares for persons with special needs may be obtained by calling the Handicapped Services Unit, 202-637-1245. Metro TTY-teletypewriter for the deaf and hearing-impaired is 202-638-3780. For the para-transit system called "MetroAccess," dial 301-588-8181.

- Metrorail opens at 5:30 a.m. Monday-Friday, and at 8 a.m. Saturday and Sunday. Metrorail closes at midnight Monday-Thursday and Sunday nights, and at 2 a.m. Friday and Saturday nights.

- The five Metrorail lines are designated by color: Red, Blue, Yellow, Orange, and Green. Transferring between the lines is possible at several points.

- Metrorail pocket guides are available from the Washington Metropolitan Area Transit Authority or at any Metrorail station.

- Metrobus routes dovetail with Metrorail, and together they provide a comprehensive transportation system for both city and suburbs. Exact fare ($1.10 in DC) is required on Metrobus because operators do not make change. There are no transfers from bus to rail.

- Metro offers interactive trip planning on its Web page: www.wmata.com!

Northern Virginia Transportation Commission

*4350 North Fairfax Drive, Suite 720, Arlington, VA (703-524-3322, 202-637-7000, Metro) - **www.vre.org**.*

Contact this organization for information on other mass transit options in Northern Virginia. Some are designed to serve commuters, others may be of interest to visitors to Washington, DC.

Ride-On Buses, Montgomery County, MD

*Montgomery County Transit Information Center (301-217-RIDE, 301-217-2222, TTY/TDD) - **www.dpwt.com**.*

The blue and white Ride-On buses are part of the transportation network in Montgomery County, MD. They stop only at the blue and white Ride-On signs. Day passes are available, and Metrobus transfers are valid on Ride-On buses.

- Children under age five ride free.

- Exact change is required ($1.10 at peak times; 90¢ non-peak).

Virginia Railway Express

*(800-743-3873, recorded message) - **www.vre.org**.*

This commuter rail service links DC with Virginia. The trains operate weekdays only, coming into Washington in the morning and leaving Washington in the afternoon and evening. Use a credit card to purchase tickets at the stations or via the Internet.

- Youth tickets are half-price, but *must be purchased in advance* and are not available at the platform. See the website for details.
- VRE and MARC ticket to DC are good for travel on each other's trains that leave DC before noon and arrive in DC after noon.
- VRE connects with Metrorail at Franconia/Springfield; Alexandria/King Street, Crystal City, L'Enfant Plaza, and Union Station.

Publications to Take Along

There are many events guides and calendars for the region. These two are especially useful for basic information:

- **The Washington Post**: The Friday Weekend Section column "Saturday's Child" highlights children's programs and family activities, and the rest of the Weekend section is a great source for information about current exhibits, festivals and music events.
- **Washington Parent** (www.washingtonparent.com) and **Washington Families** (www.washingtonfamilies.com) are free monthly publications about raising children in the Washington area. Each includes a calendar of events, along with special features on activities with children.

Among the many guides to Washington, D.C. historic sites, two useful, unusual ones stand out:

- **A Literary Map of Washington D.C.**, published in 2000 by The Women's National Book Association Washington Chapter in partnership with the Library of Congress Center for the Book, the poster-sized map brochure features authors who lived, worked or are buried in the Washington area along with literary establishments and landmarks. The map is $7.95 and sold in local bookstores and tourism centers, or contact WBNA/ Amy Barden at 703 578-4023.
- **On This Spot: Pinpointing the Past in Washington, D.C** (National Geographic, 1999), by longtime residents Douglas E. Evelyn and Paul Dickson, is a fascinating and entertaining look at Washington historical events and places, both familiar and little known.

2. Main Sights and Museums in Washington, DC

Washington D.C. is home not only to the three branches of the United States government and to the monuments and museums surrounding the National Mall, but to a wonderful collection of historical and cultural resources of its own. As the capital city of our country, Washington is host to embassies and organizations from around the world — and it is a city rich in the fine and performing arts, in natural resources, and in recreational opportunities. The sights and museums in this section express the rich diversity of the city, from the National Mall to Capitol Hill and to the city beyond.

On The Mall

The Mall is the heart of Washington, home to many of the monuments, museums, and main attractions that draw visitors to the nation's capital. The Mall is almost two miles long and there is no such thing as a quick walk from one end to the other, especially in the heat of the summer. A good stroller is a must for young children, as are comfortable shoes for everyone else.

On a fine day, pick two or three museums to visit for an hour or two. Take a break at the carousel near the Air and Space Museum, in the two marvelous sculpture gardens near the Hirschhorn and at the National Gallery, and at the outdoor fountain at the East Wing.

If time is short, a good way to squeeze in all the main attractions is to save the Washington Monument, and Lincoln, Jefferson and FDR memorials for the cool of the evening, when they are dramatically lit. They are impressive, historical and together give a powerful sense of the wisdom and courage of four U.S. Presidents. Take a minute at the Lincoln Memorial to contemplate, and to stand in the place where Marian Andersen sang and where Martin Luther King Jr. delivered the words, "I have a dream." Then choose from among the Smithsonian's treasures: The Spirit of St. Louis and the Lunar Lander at the Air and Space Museum; the impressive Alexander Calder mobile at the East Wing of the National Gallery; Dorothy's ruby slippers from the movie "The Wizard of Oz" at the American History Museum, and the dinosaurs at the National History Museum. If you are visiting with older children, be sure to take time for a memorable tour of the U.S. Holocaust Memorial Museum (see page 62).

A visit to the Smithsonian Information Center, located in the Castle, will provide you with an orientation to all 15 Smithsonian locations in Washington, including the zoo (see page 27).

Admission to all museums and monuments on the Mall is free. Parking on Mall streets is very limited; use Metrorail if at all possible. Otherwise, try your luck or find a nearby parking garage.

When traveling with children, picnics are often your best bet. Find a shady spot on the Mall, such as near the Washington Monument or the Reflecting Pool, and take a break from sightseeing. You can picnic on the benches or the grass. The gardens adjacent to the Arts and Industries Building also make for a lovely picnic spot.

Arthur M. Sackler Gallery

*1050 Independence Avenue, SW, Washington, DC (202-357-2700, 202-357-4880, tours) - **www.asia.si.edu**.*

In an underground quadrangle formed by the Arts and Industries Building and the Freer Gallery, this museum of Asian art is connected to the Freer by underground exhibition areas. The Sackler Gallery houses one of the finest collections of Asian art, including ancient Chinese jades and bronzes and important Chinese paintings. It also offers a schedule of interesting loan exhibitions.

Recommended for children is **ImaginAsia**, a hands-on art project for adults and children, which takes place on selected Saturdays. Call for information.

- Open daily, 10-5:30. Closed Christmas.
- Metrorail Blue and Orange lines (Smithsonian, Mall exit).
- Recommended for children age ten and older.

Constitution Gardens

*Between the Washington Monument and the Lincoln Memorial on Constitution Avenue, NW, Washington, DC (202-426-6841) - **www.nps. gov/coga**. Park on Ohio Drive along the river. On evenings, weekends, and holidays, parking is available on Constitution Avenue.*

A large mall area, on which temporary government buildings once stood, has been transformed into a memorial to the Founders of the United States. The informal design includes a six-acre lake with a landscaped island (the site of the 56

15

Signers of the Declaration of Independence Memorial). The unusual design was intended to create the effect of a park within a park. This is a pleasant place to stop and take a break from sightseeing. Take a stroll, play some outdoor games, and give the children a chance to stretch their legs, but please do not feed the ducks and seagulls.

- Open daily, 24 hours.
- Picnicking, Restaurant/Snack Bar, Wheelchair Accessible.

Special activities include a naturalization ceremony held on September 17, Constitution Day.

Franklin Delano Roosevelt Memorial

*Ohio Drive, West Potomac Park, NW, Washington, DC (202-426-6841) - **www.nps.gov/fdrm/home.htm**. Follow Independence Avenue (heading west) past the Washington Monument and the Tidal Basin. A short distance past 17th Street, there is a traffic light at the intersection of Independence and West Basin Drive; turn left, crossing Independence. Follow West Basin Drive; the memorial entrance will be on the left.*

This memorial creates the sense of a secluded garden. Surrounded by shade trees, waterfalls, and quiet alcoves, the memorial is divided into four outdoor galleries separated by walls of red South Dakota granite, featuring quotations from Franklin Delano Roosevelt.

- Open daily, 8 a.m.-midnight.
- Metrorail Blue and Orange lines (Smithsonian, Mall exit). It is a 15-20 minute walk from the metro.
- Tourmobile stop.
- Ranger Talks and Tours available upon request.
- Wheelchairs available upon request (first come, first served). Handicapped parking at front entrance of the memorial (West Basin Drive, just off Ohio Drive).

Freer Gallery of Art

*Jefferson Drive at 12th Street, SW, Washington, DC (202-357-2700, 202-357-4880, tours) - **www.asia.si.edu**.*

Chinese jades, bronzes, and paintings, Buddhist sculpture, Japanese screens, early Biblical manuscripts, miniatures from India and Persia are exhibited at the distinguished Asian collection at the Freer. Exhibits are continuously rotated since only a fraction of the catalogued artwork can be displayed at one time. The Freer is also noted for its collection of important work by American artists, especially James Whistler. Whistler's "Peacock Room," with its lavish golds and blues, will particularly fascinate children.

ImaginAsia, a hands-on art project for adults and children, takes place on Saturdays in the spring, weekdays in the summer and Saturdays in the fall.

- Open daily, 10-5:30. Closed Christmas.
- Metrorail Blue and Orange lines (Smithsonian, Mall exit).

Hirshhorn Museum and Sculpture Garden

*Independence Avenue at 7th Street, SW, Washington, DC (202-357-2700, 202-357-1618) - **hirshhorn.si.edu**. Located on the National Mall between Jefferson Drive and Independence Avenue at the corner of 7th Street.*

This monumental collection of 19th- and 20th-century paintings and sculpture, displayed in an unusual circular building, offers children an exciting introduction to art. Many of the paintings are massive, vivid, and often very colorful - making a direct impact on viewers, young and old. Exhibits from the comprehensive permanent collection (nearly 14,500 paintings, sculptures, and works on paper) and changing loan shows provide opportunities to study major modern artists such as Rodin, Calder, Eakins, and Matisse. Diverse art movements, including realism, pop, and abstract expressionism, can be studied in depth.

The building's architectural design immediately fascinates visitors. Special exhibitions and early 20th-century paintings are displayed in windowless outer galleries on the second and third floors. Sculptures fill inner ambulatories, which offer comfortable chairs in which to relax and view the central courtyard and fountain through window-walls. Or you can relax on benches in the outdoor sculpture garden and plaza. Contemporary paintings and sculptures are displayed in the lower-level galleries.

Be sure to obtain a family guide to the museum at the Information Desk. This series of sturdy, colorful cards including facts and activities related to an artwork shown in a color photograph. The format encourages children to tell stories about what they see and offers information of interest to adults.

- Open daily, 10 a.m.-5:30 p.m. Closed Christmas.
- Metrorail Blue, Orange, Green, and Yellow lines (L'Enfant Plaza - Smithsonian Museums exit to Maryland Avenue and Seventh Street SW).
- Walk-in tours: Monday-Friday, 10:30 a.m. and noon; Saturday-Sunday, noon and 2 p.m. Sculpture garden

tours in May through October, Monday-Saturday,
12:15 p.m. Call in advance for groups, 202-357-3235.

- Web site lists special parent and child programs.
- Wheelchair access through swinging doors on plaza.
  Sculpture garden accessible from the Mall. Sculpture
  tours for the blind and visually impaired, and sign-
  language tours are available by appointment, 202-357-
  3235.
- Infant backpacks are available without charge.
- Recommended for children age ten and older.
- Restaurant/Snack Bar.

Special activities include Saturday Young at Art Programs,
offered for children ages 6-9 and their parents. Pre-
registration is required; call 202-357-3235 x116. Each
program combines an interactive gallery visit with presentations about an artist and exhibition. Children then create
their own special art during a hands-on workshop.

Jefferson Memorial

*Located on the southern edge of the Tidal Basin, Washington, DC
(202-426-6841) - www.nps.gov/thje/home.htm. Parking on Ohio Drive
and limited parking at memorial.*

The pillared rotunda is a tribute
to our third President, Thomas
Jefferson, who was also the
author of the Declaration of
Independence. Like the Lincoln
Memorial, it is impressively lit at
night. Park Service rangers are
available to provide visitor
services and present interpretive
programs every hour.

> ## Take Note...
>
> This is a great place for a
> recreational break from
> sight-seeing. Rent pedal
> boats and go boating in
> the Tidal Basin! In the
> spring, see the famous
> cherry blossoms in
> bloom.

- Open daily, 8 a.m.-11:45
  p.m. Closed Christmas.
  Park Service rangers on duty 8 a.m.-midnight.
  Interpretive programs presented hourly.
- Metrorail Blue and Orange lines (Smithsonian), but this
  is a long walk for children.
- Tourmobile stop.
- Elevator for wheelchairs.

Special activities include a wreath-laying ceremony on
Jefferson's birthday, April 13, and the Cherry Blossom
Festival usually held in early April (call the National Park
Service, 202-619-7222, to obtain date).

Korean War Veterans Memorial

*Independence Avenue and Chester French Drive, NW, Washington, DC (202-426-6841) - **www.nps.gov/kwvm**. Park during non-rush hours and weekends on Ohio Drive off Independence Avenue or on Constitution Avenue.*

A group of 19 stainless-steel statues, created by World War II veteran Frank Gaylord, depicts a squad on patrol and evokes the experience of American ground troops in Korea. Strips of granite and scrubby juniper bushes suggest the rugged Korean terrain, while windblown ponchos recall the harsh weather. This symbolic patrol brings together members of the U.S. Air Force, Army, Marines, and Navy; the men portrayed are from a variety of ethnic backgrounds. A granite curb on the north side of the statues lists the 22 countries of the United Nations that sent troops or gave medical support in defense of South Korea. On the south side is a black granite wall displaying etched faces of American soldiers, sailors, airmen, and marines.

- Open daily, 8 a.m.-midnight.
- Tourmobile stop.
- Handicapped parking next to the Lincoln Memorial.

Lincoln Memorial

*Located on Memorial Circle, between Constitution and Independence Avenues, SW, Washington, DC (202-426-6841) - **www.nps.gov/linc**.*

This classical Greek memorial to the Great Emancipator, Abraham Lincoln, is one of the most beautiful sights in Washington. Thirty-six marble columns, representing the 36 states of the Union at the time of Lincoln's death, surround the impressive seated statue of Lincoln. Passages from two of his great  speeches, the Second Inaugural Address and the Gettysburg Address, are carved on the walls. At the foot of the memorial is the 2,000-foot-long Reflecting Pool, which mirrors the Washington Monument at its other end. Try to visit the Lincoln Memorial twice - once in the daytime and once at night.

- Memorial and Lincoln Exhibit in lower lobby open daily, 8 a.m.-11:45 p.m. Closed Christmas.
- Metrorail Blue and Orange lines (Foggy Bottom).
- Tourmobile stop.

- Handicapped parking next to the memorial. Special ramp and elevator for wheelchairs.
- Exhibits, bookstore, restrooms, and concessions.

Special activities include a wreath-laying ceremony and reading of the Gettysburg Address on Lincoln's Birthday, February 12, and a wreath-laying ceremony in honor of Martin Luther King, Jr. in January.

National Air and Space Museum

6th Street and Independence Avenue, SW, Washington, DC (202-357-2700, 202-357-1400-recorded information, 202-357-1505-TTY) - nasm.si.edu.

This great aerospace center has 26 exhibit areas, a puppet theater, film theater, and planetarium. The central display on "Milestones of Flight" includes: the Wright brothers' Flyer of 1903, the X-1, first plane to break the sound barrier, Lindbergh's Spirit of St. Louis, and the command module of the Apollo 11 moon-landing mission. In another section, children can walk through the Skylab orbital workshop and examine the astronauts' living and lab quarters. Each gallery explores a different theme: helicopters, satellites, World War I and II planes, rockets, and more. Many exhibits use motion pictures or a moving display to explain a particular subject.

Take Note...

The Steven F. Udvar-Hazy Center at Washington Dulles International Airport - **www.nasm.edu/ nasm/ext** - will provide space for the display and preservation of the National Air and Space Museum's collection of historic aviation and space artifacts. The December 2003 opening celebrates the 100th anniversary of the Wright Brothers' first flight at Kitty Hawk. Among the 200 aircraft and 135 spacecraft on display in the building, situated on 176.5 acres south of the main terminal at Dulles Airport, will be an SR-71 Blackbird reconnaissance aircraft; an F-4 Phantom fighter; and the "Enola Gay," along with the Space Shuttle "Enterprise."

To avoid crowds, go early on a weekday morning or late in the evening during extended summer hours. Purchase film tickets when you arrive as the day's showing can be sold out quickly.

- Open daily, 10-5:30. Extended summer hours from 9-5:30 from the Friday before Memorial Day through Labor Day. Closed Christmas.
- Metrorail Yellow, Green, Blue, and Orange lines (L'Enfant Plaza, Maryland Avenue exit, and Smithsonian exit).

- Tourmobile stop.
- Highlight tours daily at 10:15 a.m. and 1 p.m.; no reservations. Tour groups should schedule in advance, 202-357-1400.
- Films shown daily on the museum's five-story-tall IMAX movie screen and a presentation at the museum's Albert Einstein Planetarium (nominal fee for both).
- Wheelchair access through ramps on both sides of building.
- Restaurant/Snack Bar.

National Aquarium, Washington

U.S. Department of Commerce Building, 14th Street and Constitution Avenue, NW, Washington, DC (202-482-2826, office, 202-382-2825, recording) - **scr94.ameslab.gov/TOUR/aquarium.html.**

It's an unlikely spot, but you'll find the oldest aquarium in the United States on the lower level of the U.S. Department of Commerce Building. Over 1,200 creatures of the deep reside there in 70 tanks, ranging in size from 50-6,000 gallons. Included are rare sea turtles, American alligators, and tropical clownfish. Children enjoy the "Touch Tank" where they can hold hermit crabs and horseshoe crabs. You can also see a slide show in the Mini Theater. A real draw for your child may be the shark feedings on Monday, Wednesday, and Saturday at 2 p.m. or the piranha feedings, Tuesday, Thursday, and Sunday at 2 p.m. Even though some tanks are a bit high for the younger ones to peer into by themselves, this small aquarium is a fun outing for all ages.

- Open daily, 9-5. Closed Christmas.
- Adults, $3; children 2-10, 75¢; children under two and aquarium members, free.
- Metrorail Blue and Orange lines (Federal Triangle).
- Restaurant/Snack Bar.

Special activities include Shark Day, held in late July or early August.

National Archives

Constitution Avenue between 7th and 9th Streets, NW, Washington, DC (202-501-5000, recording) - **www.archives.gov**. *The newly renovated National Archives building will open to the public in 2003.*

This is the repository of America's records and documents. Permanently on display (and also available on-line) are the nation's three great charters of freedom: the Declaration of Independence, the Constitution, and the Bill of Rights. These documents are kept in sealed glass and bronze cases, which are lowered every night into a bomb-and fireproof vault 20 feet below floor level. Other documents are displayed on a rotating basis in the Exhibition Hall.

For information about the film series, lectures, exhibits, and special programs for children and adults, call the Office of Public Programs, 202-501-5200.

- Open daily, 10-5:30. Extended summer hours set each year. Closed Christmas.
- Metrorail Yellow and Green lines (Archives).
- Reserve tours weekdays at 10:15 a.m. and 1:15 p.m. Write or call 202-501-5205.
- Especially appropriate for teenage children.
- Wheelchair entrance on Pennsylvania Avenue at 8th Street.

National Gallery of Art

East Building, 4th Street and Constitution Avenue, NW, Washington, DC (202-737-4215), West Building, 6th Street and Constitution Avenue - **www.nga.gov**.

One of the world's great art museums, the National Gallery contains major collections of European and American paintings and sculpture. Among its Renaissance and Dutch paintings are masterpieces by Raphael, Rembrandt, and Titian. The gallery hosts major loan shows from around the world in addition to its own special exhibits.

The **West Building's** main foyer is huge and awe-inspiring. Loud whispers can be heard around its circular indoor fountain. For a tour of the main collection, children do well with an audio tour. For a small fee, recorded tours are also available for most major exhibits.

It's a quick trip on the lower-level "people mover" from West to East buildings and a pleasant place to take a break. Visitors pass a waterfall encased in glass as they travel between the two buildings. This is a scenic, indoor lunch spot.

The **East Building** is a feast for the eyes; children love the geometric shapes and unusual visual spaces created by architect I.M. Pei. Look for isosceles triangles in the architecture, they're everywhere. Mostly 20th-century art and special temporary exhibitions are displayed here, along with Henri Matisse's cutouts - the massive Alexander Calder mobile, and the Joan Miro tapestry in the vast open space.

Major special exhibits require a pass for admittance. These passes are distributed free of charge for each day beginning at 10 a.m. Some passes may be reserved in advance or purchased through Ticketmaster, 202-432-SEAT or 800-551-SEAT.

Free concerts are performed in the airy West Garden Court Sunday at 7 p.m., September through June. At other times, the court and other open spaces in the West Building offer visitors a peaceful place to rest.

Take Note...

The 6.1 acre sculpture garden adjacent to the West Building offers benches and shady walkways, featuring 17 works by post-World War II artists. The garden's central plaza encircles a pool with a fountain in the warm months which also serves as an ice-skating rink in the winter.

For information about the Sculpture Gardens Ice Rink and Pavilion Café call 202-289-3361. Skate rentals and lockers are available at the rink.

- Open Monday-Saturday, 10-5; Sunday, 11-6. Extended summer hours set each year. Closed Christmas and New Year's Day.
- Metrorail Red line (Judiciary Square, 4th Street exit); Yellow and Green lines (Archives).
- Tourmobile stop.
- Introductory tours: East Building, Monday-Friday, 10:30 and 1:30; Saturday-Sunday, 11:30, 1:30 and 3:30. West Building, Monday-Friday, 11:30; Saturday, 10:30 and 12:30; Sunday, 12:30, 2:30, and 4:30. Group tours should be arranged four weeks in advance. A variety of school tours are available.
- Parking spaces for handicapped visitors next to East Building entrance, located on 4th Street between Madison Drive and Pennsylvania Avenue. Wheelchair access is at both the East Building main entrance and the Constitution Avenue entrance to the West Building. Wheelchairs are available. You may borrow strollers at the coat check areas of both buildings.
- Restaurant/Snack Bar.

National Museum of African Art

950 Independence Avenue, SW, Washington, DC (202-357-2700) -
www.nmafa.si.edu/geninfo/genifo.htm.

Located in the Smithsonian Quadrangle building next to the
Arthur M. Sackler Gallery and the Smithsonian Arts and
Industries Building, this underground structure is devoted to
the collection, study, and display of the traditional and
contemporary arts of the entire African continent. Its
exhibitions are drawn from the museum's collection of 7,000
African art objects in wood, metal, clay, ivory, and fiber.

The museum offers ongoing drop-in workshops designed to
encourage parent-child interactions as they learn about the
arts and cultures of Africa. Each workshop involves exploring
in the galleries and a hands-on art activity. These programs
are free, require no registration, and are intended for children
age 4-8.

- Open daily, 10-5:30. Extended summer hours. Closed
  Christmas.
- Metrorail Blue and Orange lines (Smithsonian, Mall or
  Independence Avenue exit).
- The museum is a barrier-free environment.
  Wheelchairs are available upon request from the
  security officer at the Security Desk in the Pavilion.

Special activities include story telling, films, lectures, and
musical performances.

National Museum of American History

*14th Street and Constitution Avenue, NW, Washington, DC
(202-357-3129) -* ***americanhistory.si.edu***.

Massive and modern outside,
spacious and fascinating inside,
this Smithsonian building is the
home of the original Star-
Spangled Banner and the
gowns of our nation's First
Ladies. The diversity of
the collection makes this
museum appealing to
children and adults of all
ages.

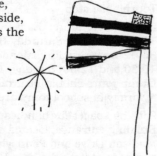

The **Hands on Science Center**, a part of
the larger Science in American Life exhibit, features
both "wet" and "dry" experiments. At the lab bench, children
test for food additives, separate DNA from a cellular solution,
measure the ultraviolet light absorption of their sunglasses

24

and sunscreen, find chemicals using 1890's lab instruments, and explore the conservation of the Star-Spangled Banner.

The **Hands on History Center** brings history to life by giving children the opportunity to try out objects from times past. They can gin cotton, operate a treadle sewing machine, and learn about how children lived in the 1780s.

Parents should note that both the Hands on Science and Hands on History Centers are for children age five and older, that children must be accompanied by an adult, and that younger children are not allowed into these rooms even as observers.

- Open daily, 10-5:30, except Christmas.
- Metrorail Blue and Orange lines (Smithsonian, Mall exit; Federal Triangle, 12th Street exit).
- Walk-in tours: check at the Information Desk for starting times and locations of the Highlights, Ceremonial Court, and Field to Factory tours. Generally, the first tour starts at 10 a.m. and the last at 1:30 p.m. Call in advance for groups, 202-357-1481. Demonstration centers are offered in various exhibit halls, Monday-Saturday. Tours are suspended and the Hands-On rooms closed for three weeks in August/September.
- Hands on History Room, Tuesday-Sunday, noon-3. Hands on Science Center, Tuesday-Sunday, 10-5. Check for ticket availability when you arrive at the museum.
- Fast-food cafeteria on the lower level; ice cream and sandwiches served in the first floor café.
- Excellent bookstore specializing in Americana, and music store with a wide selection of recorded popular music, sorted by period and tradition, with listening stations.
- Security Information: All visitors' bags are checked at entrances.
- Wheelchair Accessible.

Special activities include special family days, events and concerts throughout the year. For more information, check the web site or call 202-357-2700.

National Museum of Natural History

*10th Street and Constitution Avenue, NW, Washington, DC
(202-357-2700, 202-357-1729, TTY) - www.mnh.si.edu.*

It's hard to decide where to begin a visit to this incredible Smithsonian center for the study of humans and their natural environment. The fossils (highlighted by reconstructions of dinosaur skeletons), mammals (animals in lifelike settings), 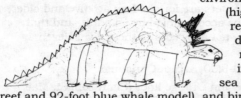 sea life (a living coral reef and 92-foot blue whale model), and birds are all worthwhile choices. Children are dazzled by the gem and mineral collections that include the world-famous Hope Diamond in the newly renovated Hall of Geology, Gems, and Minerals. Consider using the museum's new GO Interactive Audio Tour, a self-paced tour using a hand-held, touch screen computer, which allows visitors to select either a guided tour or a random-access tour.

For children (and adults) with a buggy curiosity, you'll not want to miss the Insect Zoo with its giant centipedes, tiny fruit flies, working anthills and beehives, and other insect communities. A museum guide may even let you touch or hold some of the inhabitants. Well-marked exhibits and an enthusiastic staff make this display a highlight for children.

 The museum's new entertainment complex features an 80,000-square-foot, multi-story Discovery Center, an IMAX Theater with a 3-D screen, a new attractive café and new museum shops. A high-technology science room opened in 2002, and the Discovery Room re-opens in late 2003.

On the fourth floor of the Discovery Center the interactive Immersion Cinema with its wraparound screen offers an informative and entertaining storytelling exploration. For ticket information, call 202-275-2371.

- Open daily, 10-5:30. Extended summer hours determined annually. Closed Christmas.
- Metrorail Blue and Orange lines (Smithsonian, Mall exit; Federal Triangle, 12th Street exit).
- Wheelchair access at Constitution Avenue entrance.
- Restaurant/Snack Bar.

National Museum of the American Indian

*3rd Street S.W and Independence Avenue, SW, Washington, DC (202-287-2020) - **www.nmai.si.edu**. Located next to the National Air and Space Museum on the Mall, across from the National Gallery of Art East Building.*

This new museum, expected to open in 2004, will be a center for ceremonies, performances, and educational programs, as well as an exhibition space for the arts, history, and material culture of the indigenous peoples of the Western hemisphere and Hawaii.

Smithsonian Information Center, "The Castle"

*1000 Jefferson Drive, SW, Washington, DC (202-357-2700 voice, 202-357-2627, 202-357-1729-TTY, 202-357-2020-English, or 202-633-9126-Spanish) - **www.si.edu/visit//infocenter/sicastle.htm**.*

For the visitor who wishes to be introduced to the 14 Smithsonian museums and the National Zoo in Washington, the Castle is the place to start. This aptly named building was the first of the Smithsonians, designed by James Renwick, Jr. and completed in 1855. Today, it houses the Smithsonian Information Center. There are two orientation theaters that continuously show a 20-minute video overview of the Institution, "touch screen" programs in six languages on the Smithsonian museums and on other capital highlights, two electronic wall maps, and scale models of famous Washington monuments. The "touch screen" programs and electronic maps are very appealing to children.

> ## Take Note...
>
> The Smithsonian carousel, located near the Arts and Industrial Building and the Air and Space Museum, provides a pleasant way to take a sightseeing break while visiting the National Mall. Operates daily, year-round - weather permitting.

To receive a packet of information to help plan your visit to the Smithsonian, write to Smithsonian Information or e-mail info@si.edu.

- Open daily, 9-5:30. Closed Christmas.
- Metrorail Blue & Orange lines (Smithsonian, Mall exit).
- There are a limited number of on-street parking spaces for visitors with disabilities.
- Wheelchair access (northwest entrance). To receive "Smithsonian Access," a guide for visitors with

disabilities, write: Smithsonian Information,
Smithsonian Institution, Room 153, MRC010,
Washington, D.C. 20560.

- Security Information: Hand-check of all bags, purses,
  and containers.

- The Commons Dining Room is open to the public for
  brunch Monday-Saturday 11-2 and Sunday 10:30-2.
  Reservations are recommended, 202-357-2957.

Special activities include Black History Month celebrations
throughout February. Exhibits and special events focus on
the lives and contributions of African Americans.

U.S. Botanic Garden

*Independence Avenue and First Street, SW, Washington, DC (202-225-
8333-general information) - **www.usbg.gov**. Main entrance to the
conservatory is on Maryland Avenue SW.*

The United States Botanic Garden is the
oldest botanic garden in North
America. The garden highlights the
diversity of plants worldwide, as well
as their aesthetic, cultural, economic,
therapeutic, and ecological
significance. The complex includes the
Conservatory, the Frederick Auguste
Bartholdi Park with its historic fountain of
sea nymphs and monsters, the newly
created three-acre site of the National
Garden, and the D.C. Village Production
Facility - a nursery and greenhouse complex
responsible for producing all the USBG plants
as well as many for Capitol Hill. Public
programs offered include classes,
information on gardening and botany,
tours for school children, and special exhibits.

- Conservatory 10- 5; Bartholdi Park is open to visitors
  dawn until dusk.

- Metrorail Orange or Blue lines (Federal Center).

- Wheelchair accessible; Sign Language interpreters
  available by advance reservation 202-226-4082.

- Recommended for children age ten and older.

Special activities include major flower shows throughout
the year.

Vietnam Veterans Memorial

*Constitution Avenue between Henry Bacon Drive and 23rd Street, NW,
Washington (202-426-6841) - **www.nps.gov/vive/home.htm**.*

This memorial to Vietnam Veterans was dedicated November 13, 1982. The design by Maya Ying Lin, then a 21-year old architecture student, consists of two black granite walls set in the ground in a shallow V. The walls are inscribed with over 58,000 names of the dead. At the entrances, books are available to assist visitors in finding specific names.

> ## Take Note...
>
> *The Wall* written by Eve Bunting and illustrated by Ronald Himler, provides an excellent introduction for children ages 5-12 visiting this monument.

Frederick Hart's life-size sculpture of three soldiers and the Vietnam Women's Memorial designed by Glenda Goodace are also part of this memorial.

Set in the peaceful, contemplative surroundings of Constitution Gardens, the Vietnam Veterans Memorial imparts a powerful sense of loss. People touch and make rubbings of the names and leave tokens of every description. Be prepared to answer difficult questions from children about the Vietnam War.

- Open daily, 24 hours. Park Service rangers on duty 8 a.m.-midnight.

- Metrorail Blue and Orange Lines (Foggy Bottom). Park during the day on Ohio Drive off Independence Avenue or on Constitution Avenue during non-rush hours and on weekends.

- Wheelchair accessible parking on Constitution Avenue between 20th and 21st Streets, during non-rush hour times and on weekends. Additional handicapped parking is on off of Independence Avenue and Ohio Drive on the Lincoln Memorial Circle near French Drive. Facilities include bookstore, restrooms, and concessions.

Special activities include wreath-laying ceremonies on Memorial Day and Veterans Day.

Washington Monument

*15th Street near Constitution Avenue, NW, Washington, DC (202-426-6841)
- **nps.gov/wash**.*

An impressive obelisk rising 555 feet is our nation's memorial to its founder. A 70-second elevator ride takes visitors to the 500-foot level for a magnificent view of the city.

Exhibits at the 490-foot level and a small bookshop are available for browsing upon leaving the monument. The stairwell inside the monument is closed to the public, but the elevator slows and the opaque elevator doors become clear - so that visitors can see some of the commemorative stones at several points on the way down.

- Open daily 9-4:45, except Christmas.
- Free timed tickets are handed out at the Washington Monument kiosk at 8 a.m. To reserve tickets in advance ($1.50/ticket fee) call 1-800-967-2283 or reservations.nps.gov (24 hours to five months in advance).
- Metrorail Blue and Orange lines (Smithsonian, Mall exit).
- Tourmobile stop.
- Call to arrange for tours and to walk down the monument.
- Wheelchair ramp and elevator. Strollers must be parked before going up in the monument.
- Security Information: No backpacks, large bags or strollers. No food or drink (open and unopened). Allow up to 30 minutes prior to ticket time to go through security.

Special activities include military band concerts held at the Sylvan Theater on the grounds of the Washington Monument on Sunday, Tuesday, Thursday, and Friday evenings in the summer at 8 p.m.; a wreath-laying ceremony on Washington's Birthday, February 22; and a kite festival in March.

30

The White House

The White House has been the home of our President since John Adams moved from Philadelphia in 1800. The private family quarters upstairs are not open to the public, but a visit to the handsome state rooms is always rewarding. Visitors should contact their Senator or Representative for information about tours of the Executive Residence, or call the White House Visitor information line in advance of their visit.

The White House and Visitor Center

*1600 Pennsylvania Avenue, NW, Washington, DC (202-456-7041-tours, 202-456-2200-special events) – **www.whitehouse.gov**.*

- Metrorail Blue and Orange lines (McPherson Square, Federal Triangle, or Metro Center); Red line (Metro Center).
- The White House Visitors Center, located at 1450 Pennsylvania Avenue, is open from 7:30-4 daily except for Thanksgiving, Christmas and New Years Day.
- The Visitor's Center offers a 30-minute video and provides information.
- Tours are scheduled from 7:45 a.m. to 10:30 p.m., Tuesday-Saturday.
- Tourmobile stop on the Ellipse.
- Public restrooms and telephones are located at the Visitors Center.
- Wheelchair access at northeast gate; wheelchairs are available. Strollers are not permitted in the White House. A stroller parking area is outside the visitors' east gate.

Special activities include the annual Easter Egg Roll festivities held on the White House lawn and the Ellipse on the Monday after Easter (open to children under age eight accompanied by an adult). Tours of the gardens and the House are offered one weekend in October and one in April. The House is decorated for Christmas in early December with candlelight tours held in the evenings following Christmas. The National Christmas Tree Lighting and Pageant of Peace take place each December at the Ellipse across from the White House, at which the President lights the national Christmas tree and officially opens the holiday season. Also at the Ellipse are Twilight Tattoos in July and August, with performances by the U.S. Army Drill Team, Army Band, and the 3rd U.S. Infantry with their Fife and Drum Corps.

On Capitol Hill

Just across from the Capitol are the impressive buildings of the Supreme Court and the Library of Congress. Nearby is the Folger Shakespeare Library amidst streets lined by charming 19th-century townhouses. The Capital Children's Museum, an entertaining, hands-on museum for children, is near Union Station. Union Station offers a large food court and several restaurants, as well as shops and movies.

Capital Children's Museum

*800 3rd Street, NE, Washington, DC, located at the corner of Third and H Street, NE, (202-675-4120, 202-675-4149, tour information)-**www.ccm.org**.*

The only museum in Washington with children as the exclusive focus, the Capital Children's Museum is a "hands-on" museum that helps children learn through doing. Children can try on Mexican outfits, make tortillas and hot chocolate, paint with yarn, climb a pyramid, sit on the beach, crawl through under-street pipes, climb on a fire engine, and visit different shops.

- Open Tuesday through Sunday, 10-5. Closed on Mondays from Labor Day through Memorial Day except for certain Monday holidays, as well as Thanksgiving, Christmas, New Year's Day, and the week following Labor Day.

- Adults and children, $7; children under two and members, free. Memberships and special rates available. Sundays before noon, $3.50; Senior Citizen, Military, and AAA discounts available.

- Metrorail Red line (Union Station). Go to the first level of the parking garage and follow the signs to the museum (however, be cautioned that it is a long walk to the museum).

- Vending machine food and drink, and tables and chairs available. Picnic tables on the grounds.

The Capitol

*Located at the east end of the Mall on Capitol Hill, Washington, DC (202-225-6827) - **www.aoc.gov** and **www.uschs.org**.*

Take a 45-minute guided tour of the U.S. Capitol and see all the areas in the Capitol open to the public: the Rotunda, Statuary Hall, original Capitol, Old Senate Chamber, Old Supreme Court Chamber, crypt area, and beautifully decorated Brumidi corridors. The Whispering Gallery is fun for children. To visit the House and Senate Galleries, you must obtain a pass from your Senator or Congressman.

- Tours begin at the Rotunda, daily, 9-4:30 starting every 15 minutes Monday through Saturday. First come, first served ticket distribution at 8:15 a.m. daily. One ticket per person in line - including children of any age. Tickets are not available in advance.

- Open on Federal holidays.

- Metrorail Red line (Union Station); Blue and Orange lines (Capitol South).

- For information about the Capitol, contact the U.S. Historical Society, 200 Maryland Avenue, NE, Washington, DC 20002-5796 or call 202-543-8919.

- For tour information, contact Capitol Tour Guides, 202-224-3235. (No self-guided tours available).

- Visitor services are coordinated at the west front of the capitol facing the mall.

- Tour lines form at Independence Avenue and 1st Street S.W. across from the Botanic Gardens.

Take Note...

United States House of Representatives, House Office Building Washington, DC 20515 (202-224-3121; 202-224-4910, public group tours) **www.house.gov**

United States Senate, Senate Office Building, Washington, DC 20510 (202-244-3121) **www.senate.gov**

Out-of-town school groups (or individuals) should write or call their Senators or Representatives before coming to Washington. Elected officials will often meet with their young constituents and even have a picture taken with the group on the steps of the Capitol, but you must arrange this in writing before your trip. If you are planning to visit in the busy spring season, be sure to make arrangements six months prior to your visit.

- Senate and House open only when in session and by advance reservations with your Congressional representative.

- Wheelchair access on east side; elevators inside. Special areas in both galleries for wheelchairs.

- Security Information: Helpful to call 202-225-6827 to check security concerns. No cans, bottles, aerosols, liquids or backpacks or large bags allowed, and entry is prohibited for visitors with these items.

Special activities include military concerts held on the steps of the Capitol from June through August, Monday-Wednesday and Friday evenings at 8 p.m. (see Capitol Concerts on page 171).

Eastern Market

7th and North Carolina Streets, SE, Washington, DC (202-546-2698).

This farmers market, built in 1871, is still a lively produce market. Children enjoy the outdoor event on Saturdays; there is much to look at and much to buy. A number of vendors sell an array of fruits, vegetables, and flowers; other colorful stalls are crowded with jewelry, cotton clothing, wooden toys, African-American art, pottery, and more. Inside, tasty food counters are located downstairs. If the lines are long, try the casual food establishments across the street. Art exhibits and marvelous pottery are located upstairs.

- The outdoor farmers market is open all day Saturday from 10-5. The inside market is open Tuesday-Saturday, 7-6. On Sunday, there is an outdoor flea market, 9-4.

- Metrorail Blue and Orange lines (Eastern Market, walk north on 7th Street until you see the market).

- Limited wheelchair access. Strollers are allowed, but the market is crowded during the summer and on Saturdays.

Folger Shakespeare Library

201 East Capitol Street, SE, Washington, DC (202-544-7077 Box Office) - ***www.folger.edu***. *From the Washington Beltway (I-495) take the Baltimore-Washington Parkway (Route I-295). Turn left onto 6th Street. Make a left on Pennsylvania and then right on 3rd Street. The Folger is the second building on the left. To reach the front of the building, turn left on East Capitol Street. Located one block from the US Capitol, between 2nd and 3rd Streets on East Capitol Street SE.*

The **Folger Shakespeare Library** houses a unique collection of rare books and manuscripts relating to the humanities of the Renaissance and focusing on Shakespeare. Don't miss the **Elizabethan Theater**, used throughout the year for plays, lectures, concerts, and poetry readings.

- Open Monday-Saturday, 10-4. Closed Sunday and Federal holidays.
- Metrorail Blue and Orange lines (Capitol South) or Red line (Union Station).
- Walk-in tours, 11 a.m., Monday-Saturday, and an additional 1 p.m. tour on Saturdays. Special activities for children's groups can be arranged through the docent program. Children's guides to the exhibition are available at the visitor's desk at no cost.
- Wheelchair access in rear of building, between 2nd and 3rd Streets. Enter behind the Folger and ring bell at the entrance to notify security staff.
- Recommended for children age ten and older.

Special activities include a series of Saturday Family Programs for children 8-12, and 12+ and their parents with activities ranging from paper making to fencing; Shakespeare's Birthday Open House in April features food, games, balloons, and free performances for kids of all ages; Shakespeare Festivals in the spring feature dramatizations acted by children, for children age eight and above.

Library of Congress

1st and East Capitol Streets, SE, Washington, DC (202-707-8000)
- www.loc.gov.

The Library of Congress, the largest literary treasure house in the world, offers a splendid example of Italian Renaissance architecture, with its domed main reading room and beautiful exhibition hall in the Thomas Jefferson Building. The Library's three buildings house 105 million books, maps, manuscripts, photographs, prints, motion pictures, microfilms, and documents. Permanent exhibitions of interest to older children include a Gutenberg Bible and a 15th-century illuminated Bible manuscript. Public exhibitions drawn from the collections change frequently.

- Madison Building and exhibits open 8:30 a.m.-9:30 p.m., Monday-Friday; 8:30-6, Saturday. Visitors Center - Jefferson Building open 10 a.m.-5:30 p.m., Monday-Saturday; other exhibition areas open weekdays, 10-5.
- Public tours are offered at 10:30, 11:30, 1:30, 2:30 Monday-Saturday in the Great Hall of the Thomas Jefferson Building, and at 3:30 Monday-Friday. Special tours for 10-60 participants available by reservation.

Constituent tours (contact your representative's office)
Monday-Friday at 8:30 and 2.

- Metrorail Blue and Orange lines (Capitol South).
- Tourmobile stop.
- Recommended for older children and teenagers.
- Wheelchair access at 101 Independence Avenue.

National Postal Museum

2 Massachusetts Avenue, NE, Washington, DC (202-633-9360) -
www.si.edu/postal. *Located next to Union Station.*

Housed in an historic 1914 Beaux Arts building, the National
Postal Museum is the perfect place to engage school age
children in a trip through history. Everyone is fascinated by
the railway postal car where 600 pieces of mail had to be
sorted in an hour, the early mail planes hanging from the
ceiling in the central court area, the unusual homemade
mailboxes from rural America and around the world, and
vehicles used in mail delivery - a stagecoach, a mail truck on
a sled, and a Model T with wild snow tires.

Many interactive kiosks are available, including one allowing
children to use a computer to address a postcard and receive
information about the postcard's destination. The visitor
inserts the postcard into a high tech postage meter in order to
find out the postcard route.

The final highlight of many trips to the National Postal
Museum is the newest state-of-the-art interactive exhibit with
three-dimensional holograms. Make your own personal ID
card, which records your photograph, personal preferences
and tastes as you travel through the gallery to learn about
direct mail. Adults enjoy the zip code database where they
can punch in a zip code and learn about the habits of the
people living in that area. A final memento as you leave this
gallery includes a discount coupon at the museum store.

Student tours for preschool through grade six may be booked
three weeks in advance by calling the Education Department
or filling out a reservation form on-line. Self-guided groups
may visit any time and may request pre-visit materials by
telephone or on-line.

- Open daily, 10-5:30. Closed Christmas.
- Metrorail Red line (Union Station, First Street exit).
- To schedule a guided tour, call 202-357-2991.

Supreme Court

1st Street and Maryland Avenue, NE, Washington, DC (202-479-3030) - ***www.supremecourtus.gov***. *Located at One First Street, NE, across from the US Capitol and the Library of Congress.*

This dazzling white marble building dates from 1935 and houses the highest Court in the land. It is a powerful symbol of the 3rd branch of our democratic government. The spectacle of the Court in session is most impressive. Note the bronze doors at the west entrance, depicting scenes in the historic development of law, and the Great Hall with the marble busts of all the former Chief Justices.

- Open weekdays, 9-4:30. Closed weekends and Federal holidays.
- Seating for oral arguments is on a first come, first seated basis. Lines form on the plaza in front of the building. Seating begins at 9:30 a.m. and 12:30 p.m.
- Metrorail Red line (Union Station); Blue and Orange lines (Capitol South).
- Tourmobile stop.
- Free lectures offered every hour, 9:30-3:30, except during Court sessions. Visitors information line, 202-479-3030, provides current Court sitting information.
- Wheelchair access at Maryland Avenue entrance.
- Security Information: Supreme Court Police Officers are on duty and there are two security checkpoints.
- Restaurant/Snack Bar.

Around Town

The African-American Civil War Memorial ⚡16⚡

*10th and U Streets, NW, Washington, DC (202-667-2667) - **www.afroamcivilwar.org**.*

The Memorial design features low semi-circular walls bearing plaques with just over 209,000 names of members of the United States Colored Troops as well as the names of the white officers that led them. These walls surround a bronze sculpture depicting soldiers from the various armed forces along with a family of women, children and elders. The sculpture serves as a reminder of the efforts of African-American Civil War soldiers to free their families from slavery.

- U Street-Cardozo Metro.
- Wheelchair Accessible.

Special activities include First Saturday drills and Civil War Reenactments, Founder's Day, Martin Luther King Jr. Day, Black History Month, Veterans Day, and other special events.

Anacostia Museum and Center for African American History and Culture

*Southeast Gallery, 1901 Fort Place, SE, Washington, DC (202-287-2060 recording, 202-287-3306 main office) - **www.si.edu/anacostia**. From the Washington Beltway (I-495) take I-395 North over the 14th Street Bridge. Stay in the right hand lane to cross over the Case Bridge, stay to the left and proceed on I-395 (Southeast/Southwest Freeway) and cross over the 11th Street Bridge. Follow signs to Martin Luther King Jr. Avenue (MLK), SE. Take Martin Luther King Avenue exit to Morris Road, which becomes Erie Street and then Fort Place. Stay to the right at Fort Place, the museum is on the right.*

This museum, run by the Smithsonian Institution, documents the experiences, culture, and heritage of African Americans and people of African descent through paintings, sculpture, and historical documents. Films, slides, and touchable artifacts often accompany exhibits and make for a stimulating museum experience for all. Exhibitions change frequently and include a variety of projects and activities that stress participation from preschool to adult groups. Guided tours are available on Saturdays by reservation. Pre-tour materials are provided for scheduled groups, and teaching kits are available to educators.

- Open daily, 10-5. Closed Christmas.
- Call to reserve a group tour.

- Metrorail Green line (Anacostia). Take the LOCAL exit and turn left to the W2/W3 bus stop on Howard Road. The W2 and W3 buses stop in front of the museum.
- Monthly programs; call for schedule.

Special activities include film programs and oral history discussions.

Basilica of the National Shrine of the Immaculate Conception

*4th Street and Michigan Avenue, NE, Washington, DC (202-526-8300) - **www.nationalshrine.com**. The shrine is adjacent to Catholic University.*

This is the largest Roman Catholic Church in the Western Hemisphere. It is an ideal location to introduce children to the majesty and elegance of religious art.

- Open daily Monday-Saturday, 9-11 a.m. and 1-3 p.m.; Sunday 1:30-4 p.m..
- Donations are accepted.
- 45 minute group tours by special arrangement.
- Metrorail Red line (Brookland/Catholic University).
- Strollers are permitted.
- Security Information: Security guards on duty.
- Wheelchair Accessible.

Special activities include seasonal displays, summer organ recital series, and periodic free concerts.

B'nai B'rith Klutznick National Jewish Museum

*1640 Rhode Island Avenue, NW, Washington, DC (202-857-6583) - **www.bbi.koz.com**. From Maryland, take Route 29 to 16th Street; turn right on Florida Avenue; left on 17th Street; located on the corner of 17th Street and Rhode Island Avenue. From Virginia, take I-395 over the 14th Street Bridge; turn left on Massachusetts Avenue to Scott Circle and take Rhode Island Avenue to corner of 17th Street.*

This museum encompasses a wide range of Jewish cultural, artistic, historical, and traditional ritual and ceremonial items. Life-cycle events and holidays are featured. Rotating special exhibitions are of particular interest, as are lectures, children's activities, and young members' events.

- Open Sunday-Friday, 10-5. Closed Saturday and holidays.
- Suggested donation, $2 per person.
- Metrorail Red line (Farragut North); Blue and Orange lines (Farragut West).

- Docents available for walk-in tours of the permanent collection. Call 202-857-6583 to arrange guided tours for groups of ten or more.
- Gift shop offers a wide variety of high quality books, gifts, and ritual items.
- Wheelchair access on Rhode Island Avenue.
- Recommended for children age ten and older.
- Wheelchair Accessible.

Special activities include Family Fun Day in the winter.

Bureau of Engraving and Printing

14th and C Streets, SW, Washington, DC (202-874-2330)
– www.moneyfactory.com.

Millions of dollars are printed here daily. The Bureau also prints stamps and other official government financial papers. Visitors watch all the processes involved in producing currency - printing and cutting sheets of special papers and, most impressive, stacking and counting the bills. A recording gives explanations and background information.

> ## Take Note...
>
> The BEP for Kids! section of the website presents information about the anti-counterfeiting features of our currency.

- Call the Tour Office, 202-874-2330 or toll free 1-866-874-2330, for updates on public tours and visitor hours.
- Metrorail Orange and Blue lines (Smithsonian).
- Tourmobile stop.
- The gift shop carries a variety of cast-off currency in the form of souvenirs.
- Some wheelchairs available. Strollers are not permitted on tour route.
- Security Information: Photo I.D. required. No backpacks or sharp objects allowed.

City Museum

Mt. Vernon Square, 1307 New Hampshire Avenue, N.W., Washington, DC (202-785-2068) – www.citymuseumdc.org.

Local neighborhood stories and the history and culture of the District of Columbia are the focus of this brand-new museum, operated by the Historical Society of Washington D.C. in the historic D.C. Central Library Carnegie Building. Changing gallery exhibits devoted to specific Washington D.C. communities along with exhibits examining the cultural, historical and recreational life of the city over the past 3 centuries, along with a multi-media presentation on the history of D.C. are among the principal features of the museum.

Corcoran Gallery of Art

17th Street and New York Avenue, NW, Washington, DC (202-639-1700, 202-639-1786 cafe) - corcoran.org.

The Corcoran Gallery is the oldest and largest private museum of art in the nation's capital. Founded in 1869 by William Wilson Corcoran, the museum is dedicated to encouraging American excellence in the fine arts.

Spacious entrance atriums and a grand staircase welcome visitors to this museum, famous for its American art collection with outstanding examples from the Colonial period to present times. Gilbert Stuart's famous portrait of George Washington, well-known landscapes of the Hudson River School, and monumental historical paintings are familiar to many children. In the European galleries, look for the fine selection of French Impressionist paintings. The museum is also known for its extensive collection of modern photography.

The Corcoran School of Art and Continuing Education Program offers children and adults a variety of classes on drawing, painting, sculpture and American crafts.

- Open daily, 10-5; Thursday, until 9 p.m. Closed Tuesday, Christmas, and New Year's Day.
- The café is open for lunch Wednesday-Saturday, dinner on Thursdays, and Sunday Gospel Music brunch.
- Adults, $5; senior citizens and students, $3; families, $8; free admission for children under 12.
- Free admission on Mondays, and Thursdays after 5.
- Tickets required for special exhibits, admission fee for special exhibits varies.
- Metrorail Orange and Blue line (Farragut West-17th Street exit); Red line (Farragut North-K Street exit).
- Walk-in tours daily at noon (except Tuesdays), 7:30 p.m. on Thursday; and Saturday-Sunday at 2:30. Special tours for children's groups can be arranged by calling 202-639-1730.
- Wheelchair access on E Street, call prior to visit.
- Recommended for children age ten and older.

■ Restaurant/Snack Bar.

Special activities include exhibitions emphasizing contemporary art, photography, and Washington regional art. Special events, dance performances, concerts, and story telling are frequently scheduled in conjunction with these exhibitions. The Sunday Tradition program encourages families with children ages 5-12 to investigate the various styles of art represented in the galleries. Contact the Office of Education, 202-639-1727, for specific information or e-mail familyprograms@corcoran.org.

Daughters of the American Revolution Museum

1776 D Street, NW, Washington, DC (202-879-3238)
www.dar.org/museum.

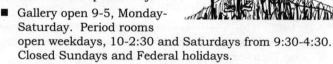

The Museum, located in DAR headquarters, features two galleries with changing exhibitions of American decorative arts and 33 period rooms. Visit the New Hampshire Attic, where dolls, toys, and children's furniture from the 18th and 19th centuries are displayed. Then visit the parlors, kitchen, and dining rooms, all furnished with fine period objects.

■ Gallery open 9-5, Monday-Saturday. Period rooms open weekdays, 10-2:30 and Saturdays from 9:30-4:30. Closed Sundays and Federal holidays.

■ Metrorail Red line (Farragut North); Blue and Orange lines (Farragut West).

■ Special program tours are offered for elementary school classes. Teachers should call 202-879-3240 at least four weeks in advance to schedule a visit.

■ Wheelchair access on C Street, call prior to visit.

Special activities include "Colonial Adventure," offered the 1st and 3rd Saturdays from September to May for children age 5-7 years; call 202-879-3240 for reservations.

Decatur House Museum

*748 Jackson Place, NW, Washington, DC (202-842-0920) - **www.decatur house.org**. Take the Washington Beltway (I-495) to Connecticut Avenue south. Turn right on 17th street. Turn left onto H street. The museum is on the right at the corner of H Street and Jackson Place.*

This elegant, Federal-style townhouse faces Lafayette Square across from the White House. It was designed by Benjamin Henry Latrobe for Commodore Stephen Decatur, an early American naval hero. Decatur and his wife moved into this home in 1819, but they lived here only 14 months before the Commodore was mortally wounded in a duel. There followed a succession of distinguished residents. In 1871 General Edward Fitzgerald Beale and his wife moved into the house and introduced a number of Victorian features. The first floor, in the Federal style, is furnished as it might have been during the Decatur's residency. The second floor is furnished in the Victorian manner and includes parquet flooring in the drawing room.

- Open Tuesday-Friday, 10-3; Saturday, Sunday, and holidays, noon-4. Closed Thanksgiving, Christmas, and New Year's Day.
- Call to make reservations for groups larger than 10 people and for school and children's programs 202-842-0918.
- Metrorail Red line (Farragut North) - K Street exit; Blue and Orange lines (Farragut West) - 17th Street exit.
- Gift shop.
- Partial wheelchair access.

Special activities include three open houses, walking tours, family programs, lectures, workshops, and Holiday events throughout December and January. Interactive programs and tours are available for groups of children and schools.

Discovery Creek
Children's Museum of Washington

*4954 MacArthur Boulevard, NW, Washington, DC (202-364-3111) - **www.discoverycreek.org**.*

Discovery Creek is a living laboratory for science, history and art exploration. Most programs are planned around the 12-acre wilderness of the Potomac Palisades Parkway. The museum offers high-quality science workshops for children. The staff is knowledgeable and excellent at teaching large groups of children. The

43

workshops and classes incorporate live animals, art projects and a guided walk in the woods.

Discovery Creek offers wildlife, craft activities, hikes, summer and winter camps, adventure programs, birthday parties, and family field trips at the Glen Echo Stable. Special exhibits change every few months.

- Open to families on weekends. Saturdays from 10-3 and Sundays 11-3.

- Ages 2-64, $4; seniors, $3; members, $3.

- Groups visits for 10 or more can be booked Tuesday-Friday.

- Climbing wall available the first weekend each month.

Dumbarton Oaks Gardens and Museum

*3101 R Street, NW, Washington, DC (202-339-6401) - **www.doaks.org**.
Museum entrance at 1703 32nd Street, NW.*

Dumbarton Oaks Gardens, an oasis in bustling Georgetown, is spectacular in the spring, beautiful in the fall, and pleasant in the winter. The estate's ten acres of terraced hillsides, formal and informal plantings, and curving footpaths are artfully landscaped, expertly maintained, and enjoyed by children and adults. After viewing the gardens, follow Lover's Lane (on the east border of the gardens) to Dumbarton Oaks Park, a 27-acre wooded, natural area best known for its pools, waterfalls, and spring wildflowers.

The museum features Pre-Columbian and Byzantine art: the Byzantine Gallery presents the luxury arts of the Roman Empire with a few choice objects from the western Medieval and Islamic traditions, while the Pre-Columbian Collection displays some of the finest artistic achievements of the native peoples of the New World.

- Museum is open Tuesday-Sunday, 2-5. Closed Monday and Federal holidays. Gardens open daily, 2-5, except for holidays and inclement weather. Gardens open until 6 from March 15-October 31.

- Suggested $1 donation at museum. Admission to gardens March 15-October: adults and children over 12, $5; senior citizens, $3; children under 12, free. No admission charge to gardens from November-March 15.

- Nearby Montrose Park (see page138) has many pleasant picnic spots.

- Tours available by appointment for groups of 12 or more.

- Visitors with disabilities should call 202-339-6410 in advance of a visit for accessibility information.

Explorers Hall, National Geographic Society

*17th and M Streets, NW, Washington, DC (202-857-7000, 202-857-7588, recording) - **www.nationalgeographic.com/explorer**. Located at 17th and M Street.*

Explorers Hall has great appeal to children of all ages. The museum houses a wide variety of temporarily traveling exhibits as well as permanent interactive exhibits. "Passport Fridays" are live presentations. See the website for topics, times, and dates.

- Open Monday-Saturday, 9-5; Sunday, 10-5. Closed Christmas.
- Metrorail Red line (Farragut North); Metrorail Blue and Orange lines (Farragut West).

Ford's Theatre, Lincoln Museum, Petersen House

*511 10th Street, NW, Washington, DC (202-426-6924) - **www.fordstheatre.org**. From the Washington Beltway (I-495) take I-395 north towards Washington D.C., over the 14th Street Bridge past the National Mall. At F Street turn right and then right onto 10th Street. The Theatre is located between E and F Streets.*

The museum, located in the basement of the theater, provides a self-guided tour that follows Lincoln's career as a lawyer, campaigner, President, and finally, as the victim of an assassin's bullet. Among the memorabilia on display are the clothes Lincoln wore that fatal night. Talks by Park Service rangers describe the events that led up to the assassination.

To complete the story, visit the Petersen House directly across the street at 516 10th Street, NW, 202-426-6830. The wounded President was carried into the bedroom of the house where he died the next morning.

- Open daily, 9-5. Closed Christmas. Theater closed to visitors during matinee performances (Thursday, Saturday, Sunday). Call to verify museum hours on matinee days.
- Self-guided tours when no performance is in progress. Call 202-426-6924 to check times.
- Metrorail Red, Blue, and Orange lines (Metro Center - 11th Street exit); Yellow and Green lines (Gallery Place - G Street exit).
- Talks are held 15 minutes past each hour from 9-5 by National Park Service rangers in the orchestra of the theater. When the theater is closed, talks are held in the museum.

- Wheelchair access to theater and museum, but not to balcony or house where Lincoln died. Strollers are permitted, but must be carried up and down stairs.

Franciscan Monastery

14th and Quincy Streets, NE, Washington, DC (202-526-6800)
- www.myfranciscan.com. From the Washington Beltway (I-495) take I-395 north to 12th Street exit. Turn right onto Constitution Avenue. Turn left onto Louisiana Avenue and then left onto North Capitol Street to Michigan Avenue; go east (right) on Michigan Avenue, past Catholic University; right on Quincy Street. Monastery is at the top of the hill. Parking across the street on 14th and Quincy.

Called the Memorial Church of the Holy Land, this unusual church is located in a 44-acre woodland. The grounds include one of the largest rose gardens in the country. Along the garden walks are the 14 Stations of the Cross with replicas of shrines in Bethlehem and Lourdes. Children like the catacombs beneath the church.

- Open daily, 9-5.
- Metrorail Red line (Brookland/Catholic University), then take the H2/H4 bus to 14th and Quincy Street NE.
- Hourly tours of the Church and Catacombs are Monday-Saturday (excluding Tuesday), 9-4 (no tour at noon); Sunday, 1-4.
- Wheelchair accessible everywhere but catacombs.

Frederick Douglass Home (Cedar Hill)

1411 W Street, SE, Washington, DC (202-426-5961) - www.nps.gov/frdo. Take South Capitol Street from the Capitol to the Southeast Freeway; then cross the 11th Street Bridge; go south on Martin Luther King, Jr. Avenue; east on W Street. Parking available on-site.

The noted orator and anti-slavery editor Frederick Douglass spent the later years of his life at Cedar Hill. The character of the fervent abolitionist is reflected in the furnishings of the house and in information given on regular tours which cover 14 of 21 rooms. One point of interest is the "Growlery," a small, one-room structure, separate from the house, to which Douglass often retreated. Most of the furniture and artwork is original to the house and is typical of that found in any upper-middle-class white or African-American home of the late 19th century. The handsome brick house with its commanding view of the Federal City is spacious and comfortable by the standards of the late 19th century.

- Open daily, 9-4; from mid-April to mid-October, 9-5. Closed Thanksgiving, Christmas, and New Year's Day.
- $3 per person; $1.50 for senior citizens, age 62 and older; free for children age 6 and under.

- Reservations required 1-800-967-2283.

- Metrorail - Green Line (Anacostia Station). Connect to a B-2 (Mt. Rainer) bus; there is a bus stop directly in front of the home. Continue down W Street to 15th Street; the Visitor Center is a half-block from the stop on the right.

- Films about Douglass' life are shown on the hour, followed by National Park Service guided tours of grounds and home. All tours begin at the Visitor Center.

- Groups need to make reservations well in advance.

- Wheelchair accessibility is limited.

- Recommended for children age ten and older.

Special activities include an annual Christmas open house in December, events commemorating Frederick Douglass' birthday, and Black History Month in February. The Annual Oratorical Contest for area students is held in mid-January.

Hillwood Museum and Garden

*4155 Linnean Avenue, NW, Washington, DC (202-686-5807, 202-686-5807; TDD-202-363-3056) - **www.hillwoodmuseum.org/**. Take Tilden Street east from Connecticut Avenue to second left onto Linnean Avenue. The entrance gate is on the right.*

The home of American businesswoman and cereal heiress Marjorie Merriweather Post boasts among its treasures 90 jeweled items crafted by Faberge. The twenty-five acre estate in the middle of Washington D.C. is home to one of the world's the most remarkable collections of 18th and 19th century Russian imperial art outside of Russia, a fascinating collection of French decorative arts, and an impressive house and gardens. A film about Mrs. Post's life precedes the tour and is an excellent introduction to the founder's life and her collections of art.

Reservations are required for all visitors, and a refundable donation must be made for each visitor at the time the reservation is made.

- Tuesday through Saturday, 9:30-5. Closed January and on national holidays.

- Self-guided tours and docent-led tours available daily. Young persons audio tour of the Russian collection.

- 20-minute walk from the Van Ness/UDC Metro station.

- Recommended for older children and teens.

- Café open from 9:30-4:30 for breakfast, lunch, and tea. Reservations for lunch are a good idea — call 202-686-8505 x8811.

Interior Department Museum

1849 C Street N.W., between 18th and 19th Streets, NW, Washington, DC (202-208-4743, 202-208-4659) - www.doi.gov/museum/ interiormuseum. Take the Washington Beltway (I-495) to the Constitution Avenue exit, go North on 18th Street N.W. two blocks, turn left on C Street to the entrance on the right.

The breadth of the Interior Department's activities is evident in the variety of the exhibits here. Native-American artwork, dioramas, and natural history specimens help to tell the Department's story. National parks, mining, geological research, and pottery are among the topics explored in the museum's well-crafted displays. Exhibits, featuring hundreds of photographs, and historic and contemporary artifacts, present an overview of the Department's past and current activities. New to the Museum is a permanent exhibit on protecting fish, wildlife, and their habitats.

- Open weekdays, 8:30 a.m.-4:30 p.m. and on the third Saturday of each month from 1-4 p.m. Closed on Federal holidays.
- Reservations for guided tours and appointments to view the New Deal murals must be made two weeks in advance by calling 202-208-4743.
- Metrorail Blue and Orange lines (Farragut West - 18th Street exit).
- Stroller and Wheelchair access at E Street entrance.
- Security Information: All adult visitors must show photo identification at the building entrance.
- Restaurant/Snack Bar.

International Spy Museum

800 F Street, NW, Washington, DC (202-393-7798, 866-937-6873-toll-free) - www.spymuseum.org. Located on F Street between 9th and 8th Streets, across from the National Portrait Gallery.

The International Spy Museum has a fantastic collection of espionage artifacts from around the world and provides an entertaining look at the role that spies play in current and historical events. The School for Spies exhibit looks at the motivation and skill required for a career in espionage, along with a chance for visitors to try out their proficiency in observation and analysis. In the "Spies Among Us" exhibit, visitors may be intrigued to find chef Julia Child along with singer Josephine Baker and movie director John Ford.

- Open daily from 10 a.m. except Thanksgiving, Christmas and New Year's.
- Closing times vary.
- Adults, $13; seniors, active duty military, and the Intelligence community, $12; children 5-18, $10; children under five free. Tickets are available until one hour before closing and may be purchased in advance. Self-guided tours are available at special rates for student and youth groups grades five and above. Annual pass is $35.

> ## Take Note...
>
> The Coldwar Museum, **www.coldwar.org**, is an on-line collection of exhibits about CIA and DIA activities during the mid- to late-20th century Cold War era. A timeline gives an in-depth look at the events, situations and people who helped to shape the issues of the cold war from 1940's through the 1990's.
>
> The physical collection, which is looking for permanent home in the Washington area, includes, among other things, the U-2 helmet worn by Francis Gary Powers and other Powers memorabilia; nuclear attack survival kits; flags from East Germany and the Soviet Union.

- Metrorail Red, Yellow and Green Lines (Gallery Place/Chinatown and National Archives).
- Café, full-service restaurant and museum store.
- Recommended for ages 11 and up.
- Wheelchair Accessible.
- No strollers.

spy museum

Islamic Center

2551 Massachusetts Avenue, NW, Washington, DC (202-332-8343).

This mosque is one of the largest and most ornate in the United States. Guides explain the religious service and point out the rich decorations of the building - the rugs, mosaics, and art objects are outstanding examples of Islamic design and craftsmanship. Prayers are held five times daily.

- Open Saturday through Thursday 10-5, Friday 10-noon and 3-5. Female visitors must cover themselves except for face, hands and feet. Shoes must be removed.
- Call for information about guided tours and group reservations.
- Metrorail Red line (Dupont Circle).

John F. Kennedy Center

*2700 F Street, NW, Washington, DC (202-467-4600 general information, 202-416-8441) - **www.kennedy-center.org**. Take the Washington Beltway (I-495) to I-66 east across the Roosevelt Bridge. Bear right to exit to Independence Avenue. Go under Roosevelt Bridge and Kennedy Center is the second entrance on the right. Parking garage on site.*

Performances of music, opera, dance, theater, and film from the United States and abroad are presented on the stages of the Kennedy Center. There are five main theaters: the Concert Hall, Opera House, Eisenhower Theater, Terrace Theater, and Theater Lab. The first three of these theaters is separated by two great parallel halls, one decorated with the flags of the 50 states, and the other with the flags of the nations of the world. Children enjoy these impressive displays. The center has been decorated with a dazzling array of gifts from many nations.

Take Note...

Don't miss seeing the renowned bronze sculpture of President John F. Kennedy in the Grand Foyer and the view from the rooftop terrace; these are worth a trip even if you don't see a show. Also free performances are offered most evenings at 6 on the Millenium Stage.

- Building open daily. Business hours are 10 a.m. -6 p.m., open to the public from 10 a.m.-midnight.

- Metrorail Orange and Blue lines (Foggy Bottom) about a seven-minute walk. Shuttle service provided from Foggy Bottom.

- Tourmobile stop.

- Free tours by Friends of the Kennedy Center, Monday-Friday, 10-5 and Saturday-Sunday 10-2 every 15-20 minutes. Tours start in the lobby or Parking Level A.

- Tours in Spanish, German, French, and Japanese upon request. Print and online tour guides are available in eleven languages. For special tour arrangements, call 202-416-8341.

- Call 202-416-8340 to arrange for a wheelchair. Free listening system for the hearing-impaired in theaters.

- Restaurant/Snack Bar.

Special activities include performances for children and families throughout the year and an annual open house. See John F. Kennedy Center for the Performing Arts on page 174 for more information.

The Kreeger Museum

*2401 Foxhall Road, NW, Washington, DC (202-338-3552 for reservations, 202-337-3050, office) - **www.kreegermuseum.org**. Free limited parking.*

The Kreeger Museum, located at the former residence of Carmen and the late David Kreeger, contains an impressive collection of 19th and 20th century paintings and sculptures by such artists as Picasso, Van Gogh, Monet, Kandinsky, Miro, Rodin, Stella, and Moore. It also has a broad range of African art and sculpture. The setting alone is worth the visit!

- 90-minute docent-led tours available Tuesday-Friday, 10:30 and 1:30 and Saturday at 10:30. Reservations are usually required. Please call for holiday closings.
- Suggested donation, $8 per person; $5 seniors and students.
- Children over 12 years of age are welcome for weekday tours. All ages welcome during Saturday open hours. With prior arrangements, school groups (6th grade and above) are welcome.
- Wheelchair access to main floor only. Wheelchairs available. No strollers or child carriers.
- Recommended for children age ten and older.

Special activities include story time for ages 3-5, and art workshops for older elementary school children.

Marine Corps Historical Center

*Building 58, Washington Navy Yard, Washington, DC (202-433-0731) - **www.history. usmc.mil**. To Access the Navy Yard, use the 11th and O Street gate. Reservations must be make 24-hours in advance of your visit.*

The Marine Corps Historical Center consists of the Time Tunnel and the Special Exhibits Gallery that chronicle Marine Corps history from 1775 to the present. The Marine Corps History Time Tunnel guides visitors through twenty individual segments of the Marine Corps' history, from its inception in 1775 to the present day, with emphasis on its leadership.

- Monday-Friday, 10-4. Closed weekends and federal holidays.
- Guided group tours should be arranged in advance.

National Building Museum

*401 F Street, NW, Washington, DC (202-272-2448) - **www.nbm.org**.*

As soon as you step off the Metrorail escalator, you will be awed by this massive and beautiful brick structure. Adapted from palace plans of the Italian Renaissance, it was designed in 1881 to be a modern office building for the Pension Bureau. Now it serves as a museum celebrating American achievements in building. As you approach the museum, look up at the

Take Note...

The National Building Museum offers free family walk-in workshops on bridges and structures at 2:30 p.m. on weekends. Additional hands-on family programs occur two to three times per month, including model airplane flying in the Great Hall.

buff-colored terra cotta frieze. It shows six Civil War military units encircling the building on an endless march. Inside, children love the Great Hall, a space large enough to enclose a 15-story building. Exhibition galleries are in interconnecting rooms off the Great Hall and upstairs.

Make sure to go upstairs and view the permanent exhibit "Washington: Symbol and City." The touchable, large-scale models and objects of the Capitol, White House, Washington Monument, and Lincoln Memorial have hands-on appeal for families. Exhibit games ask questions that are answered by pushing a button.

Other permanent and temporary exhibits focus on the building trades, urban planning, architecture and engineering, and historic preservation. There are exciting school programs for children from elementary through high school.

- Open daily, 10-5; Sunday, 11-5. Closed Thanksgiving, Christmas, and New Year's Day.
- Suggested donation - $5.
- Metrorail Red line (Judiciary Square-F Street exit).
- Tours conducted Monday-Wednesday at 12:30 p.m.; Thursday-Saturday at 11:30 a.m., 12:30 and 1:30 p.m.; and Sunday at 12:30 and 1:30 p.m. (no reservations required). Call ahead to schedule a group tour.
- Wheelchair access, G Street entrance. Wheelchairs are available upon request at the Information Desk.
- Security Information: Security guards hand-check ALL bags, purses, etc.

■ Restaurant/Snack Bar.

Special activities include annual festivals for exploring engineering in February, origami in March/April, and building arts in September/October.

National Museum of Health and Medicine of the Armed Forces

*Walter Reed Army Medical Center, 6900 Georgia Avenue, NW, Bldg. 54, Washington, DC (202-782-2200) - **nmhm.washingtondc.juseum**. Take the Washington Beltway (I-495) to Georgia Avenue (Route 97) / Wheaton exit south; drive past the junction with East-West Highway (Route 410). Turn right onto Elder Street NW onto the Walter Reed Army Medical Center campus. Turn right at the first stop sign and follow the winding road past the hospital/garage complexes onto Dahlia Street to the museum's entrance on the right.*

Originally established during the Civil War as the Army Medical Museum, this is one of the few places where you can learn about medical history, the human body, and disease by actually seeing real specimens. Some are graphic and may not be appropriate for all ages or for those who are squeamish. The museum has four main displays: Living in a World with AIDS, Human Body/ Human Being, Civil War Medicine, and Evolution of the Microscope. For older children and teens interested in nursing or medicine as a career, this museum is worth a visit. You can see what a smoker's lung is like compared to a coal miner's lung, or touch a real brain or the inside of a stomach.

■ Open daily, 10-5:30. Closed Christmas.

■ Donations are gratefully accepted.

■ On weekdays, free parking with a pass from the museum's information desk. On weekends, parking is free, parking passes are not required.

■ The museum is a short bus ride from the Silver Spring or Takoma Park stops on the Metrorail's Red Line. Take Metrobus 70 or 71 from the Silver Spring Metro Station to the Dahlia Street bus stop. Take Metrobus 52, 53, or 54 from the Takoma Park Metro station to Butternut Street gate, or the K2 Metrobus to the Dahlia Street gate.

■ Guided tours available for grades five and up.

■ Stroller and wheelchair accessible, and there is a baby changing station. American Sign Language interpreters are available with an advance request.

■ Recommended for children age ten and older.

Special activities include the free "National Health Awareness Kickoff" program on the first Saturday of each month. Each month a new topic is highlighted. Call 202-782-2200 to make reservations.

National Museum of Women in the Arts

1250 New York Avenue, NW, Washington, DC (202-783-5000) - ***www.nmwa.org***.

This is a comfortably small museum housing art by women from the 16th century to the present day. Included are works by Mary Cassatt, photographs by Louise Dahl-Wolfe, and sculpture by Camille Claudel. Special exhibits present international women's accomplishments. The galleries in which works are displayed are not too large, so children can wander through them without feeling lost.

During the school year, the museum's Education Department offers Sunday children's programs relating to the current exhibition or aspects of the permanent collection. Special tours geared to children ages 6-12 are offered and are often followed by a related hands-on experience. Call for details.

- Open daily, 10-5; Sunday, noon-5. Closed Thanksgiving, Christmas, and New Year's Day.
- Suggested contribution for adults, $5; for senior citizens, $3; youth 18 and under, free.
- Metrorail Red, Blue, and Orange lines (Metro Center, 13th and G Streets exit).
- Walk-in tours conducted if a docent is available.
- Mezzanine Café open 11:30-2:30, Monday-Saturday.
- Wheelchair accessible - a limited number of wheelchairs are available.

Special activities include annual family festivals celebrating cultures around the world in the winter.

National Portrait Gallery

8th and F Streets, NW, Washington, DC (202-357-2700) - ***npg.si.edu***.

 The National Portrait Gallery examines American history by focusing on the individuals who have aided in the development of our nation. The collection includes paintings, sculptures, prints, drawings, and photographs of prominent American statesmen, artists, writers, scientists, Native Americans, and explorers. The Gallery is closed for renovation until 2005-06.

- Recommended for children age ten and older.
- Restaurant/Snack Bar.

National Zoo

3001 Connecticut Avenue, NW, Washington, DC (202-673-4717, 202-673-4731 zoo police, 202-673-7800- TTY) - www.natzoo.si.edu. Rock Creek Park entrance at Adams Mill Road and Beach Drive.

The 163-acre National Zoo has long been acclaimed as one of the best and most attractive facilities of its kind in the country. Particularly impressive are the baby elephant, Komodo dragons, and, of course, the giant pandas from China, best seen at the 11 a.m. and 3 p.m. feeding times. The feeding and waking times for animals vary according to the season, so refer to an Information Station for a listing of the day's events. The Wetlands Exhibit around the Birdhouse and the prairie dogs across from the outdoor giraffe yard are treats for younger children. Other favorites include the giraffes, lions and tigers, hippos, and elephants. Older children and teens will enjoy learning about intelligence in the new Think Tank exhibit, while everyone marvels at orangutans crossing overhead on the O-Line between the Great Ape House and Think Tank.

The **Amazoniana exhibit**, housed in its own building, brings the humidity of Washington summers indoors. A translucent domed roof covers the mahogany, kapok, and balsa trees from which sloths hang upside down and singing tanagers dart. Amazoniana is a good introduction to tropical rain forests and their interdependent river ecosystems. Children enjoy spotting the hidden animals and watching the water flow through the exhibit.

Take Note...

The Zoo is crowded on weekends and holidays during good weather, and the parking lots fill up fast. Try to go early in the day during the week, or go later in the day and stay for a picnic dinner. Public transportation is highly recommended, but remember, if little ones are along, it's a hike from the nearest Metrorail stop to the Connecticut Avenue entrance.

- Open May 1- September 15: grounds, 6 a.m.-8 p.m., buildings, 10-6. September 16-April 30: grounds, 6-6; buildings, 10-4:30.
- Parking fees: $5 for the first three hours, $2 for each additional hour with a cap of $11 for the entire day.
- Metrorail Red line (Woodley Park-Zoo, a 7-minute, uphill walk; or Cleveland Park, a 6-minute, level walk).

- Strollers are available for rent in the winter, 9:30-3; in the summer, 9:30-4. $7 per single stroller, $10 per double stroller.

- Schedule group tours on-line, or call 202-673-4989 or send e-mail to grouptours@fonz.org.

- **How Do You Zoo?** Is an interactive exhibit for K through grade 5 focused on careers at the zoo.

- Restaurants and snack bars are scattered throughout the grounds; picnicking is permitted.

- A limited number of wheelchairs are available. Handicapped parking is available in Lot A, near Connecticut Ave. entrance, in Lot B near the Elephant House, and in Lot D near the lower duck ponds.

Special activities include lectures, Sunset Serenades concert series in the summer (see page 55 for more information on the National Zoo), Seal Days in March, African-American Family Celebration in April, Panda Anniversary Celebration, Guppy Gala in May, and Fiesta Musical in September.

Navy Art Gallery

*805 Kidder Breese, SE, Washington Navy Yard, Washington, DC (202-433-4882) - **www.history.navy.mil**.*

Spend an intriguing afternoon at the Navy Art Gallery and view many of its over 13,000 paintings, prints, drawings, and sculpture. The Navy Art collection contains depictions of ships, personnel, and action from all eras of the U.S. naval history, with World War II, the Korean War, the Vietnam War, and Desert Shield/Storm particularly well represented.

- Open Wednesday-Friday, 9-4. Closed federal holidays.

The Navy Museum

*805 Kidder Breese SE, Washington Navy Yard, Building 76, Washington, DC (202-433-4882) – **www.history.navy.mil**/.*

Permanent exhibits are devoted to the U.S. Navy from the underdog naval forces of the young United States in the Revolutionary War, through the polar explorations of Admiral Richard Byrd and Finn Ronne, to the Navy's role in the Korean War. Check out the simulated submarine combat center where visitors learn about the fundamentals of submarine technology through interactive displays. The submarine room also traces the development and history of the American submarine from Turtle to the Los Angeles class.

- Visitors must call at least 24 hours in advance for reservations.
- Open Monday–Friday, 9–4. Closed weekends and federal holidays.

Special activities include performances by Navy bands and ensembles. All events are free and open to the public. Please call 202-433-6897 for reservations and additional information.

Newseum

*Pennsylvania Avenue and 6th Street, NW, Washington, DC (703-284-3544, 888-639-7386) - **www.newseum.org**. The Newseum's new site is under development and will open in 2006.*

Updates and progress reports are available on the Newseum web site. The web site continues to offer an excellent look at the ways that photographic, print, and electronic journalism inform us about our world.

The Octagon

*1799 New York Avenue, NW, Washington, DC (202-638-3105, 202-638-1538 TTY) - **www.archfoundation.org/octagon**. Located at 18th Street.*

The Octagon was built by Colonel John Tayloe III in 1800 to serve as his winter townhouse. During the War of 1812, the building served as the temporary White House for President and Mrs. Madison, and the Treaty of Ghent was signed here on February 17, 1815, ending that war.

The Octagon served as the headquarters for the American Institute of Architects between 1889 and 1949 and is currently owned by the American Architectural Foundation. Trained docents discuss the early history of Washington, DC, the Tayloe family, the architecture of the house, and its decorative arts furnishings, and regale visitors with ghost stories. There are changing architectural exhibitions in the second floor galleries.

- Open Tuesday-Sunday, 10-4. Closed Monday, New Year's Day, Thanksgiving, and Christmas
- Adults, $5; senior citizens and students, $1.50; children, free. Call 202-626-7387 for reservations for groups of ten or more.
- Metrorail Blue & Orange lines (Farragut West-18th and I Streets exit); Red line (Farragut North-K Street exit).
- Wheelchair access at garden entrance. Strollers are not permitted.

Old Post Office Pavillion

*1100 Pennsylvania Avenue, NW, Washington, DC (202-289-4224-Pavilion, 202-606-8691-Tower, 202-606-8694-TTD) - **www.oldpostofficedc.com**, **www.nps.gov/opot**. Take the Washington Beltway (I-495) to I-395 toward DC to 12th street exit.*

The entertainment center in downtown Washington D.C. offers live entertainment daily, shopping, and dinning. The Old Post Office was restored and rededicated in 1983. Its large interior courtyard houses a wide and lively variety of shops and specialty kiosks and is the setting for concerts and other arts programs. Take a free tour of the 315-foot tall clock tower, which offers a breathtaking view of Washington from the 270 foot observation deck, and is home to the bells of the U.S. Congress.

- Pavilion open daily; spring and fall hours vary.
- Metrorail Blue and Orange lines (Federal Triangle).
- Tours to Congress Bells and the Old Post Office Tower are available daily.
- Strollers should be left outside or in the lobby.
- Security Information: All visitors must pass through security including metal detectors.
- Restaurant/Snack Bar.

Special activities include live entertainment daily, international cuisine, shopping and seasonal special events such as Family Fun Days. Bell ringing demonstrations are occasionally held for the public.

Old Stone House

3051 M Street, NW, Washington, DC (202-426-6851, 202-426-0125-TTY).

The Old Stone House is the oldest and only surviving pre-Revolutionary building in Washington. This was the modest home and shop of a Colonial cabinet-maker and is representative of a middle-class dwelling of the period. Its small size makes it seem cozy and comfortable to children. Older children may be intrigued by the rumors of a resident ghost (see page 101 for more information on Rock Creek Park). This is a good place to stop for a picnic lunch.

- Open Wednesday-Sunday, noon- 5. Closed New Years Day, July 4, Thanksgiving Day and December 25.
- Metrorail Orange or Blue line (Foggy Bottom).
- Ranger-led talks and group programs upon request

- Wheelchair access limited to ground floor. Strollers permitted in the garden, but not in the house.

Special activities include numerous historical programs and demonstrations of period crafts. There is also a Christmas candlelight program in December.

The Phillips Collection

1600 21st Street, NW, Washington, DC (202-387-2151)
*-**www.phillipscollection.org**.*

The Phillips Collection, America's first museum of modern art, is a lovely and comfortable place to introduce children to art. This outstanding collec-tion of mainly 19th- and 20th-century European and American painting and sculpture, with a sprinkling of old masters, is tastefully displayed in the former home of the Phillips family. Youngsters like the small rooms and connecting passageways that create a less formal atmosphere than a big museum, and with chairs in each room, children have a place to rest. Try to plan your visit around one of the family tours sometimes available for special exhibits. Don't miss Renoir's "Luncheon of the Boating Party" or other fine paintings by such artists as Bonnard, Braque, Daumier, Cezanne, or Klee.

"**Family Fun Packs**," designed to facilitate visits with children to the permanent collection and special exhibitions, are available upon request. (Please call in advance.) Saturday morning teacher programs provide teachers with approaches for helping students interpret art forms.

- Open Tuesday-Saturday, 10-5; Sunday, noon-7; Thursday, 10 a.m.-8:30 p.m. Closed Monday and all major holidays.
- Admission on weekends: adults, $7.50; senior citizens and full-time students, $4; children under 18 and members, free. Suggested contributions on weekdays are the same as weekend fees.
- Metrorail Red line (Dupont Circle - Q Street exit).
- Regular tours Wednesday and Saturday at 2; call to arrange special tours for children or adults.
- Recommended for children age ten and older.
- Restaurant/Snack Bar.

Special activities include a Family Free Day with many children's activities, the first Saturday of June; chamber music concerts (free with museum admission) performed in the gallery on Sundays (fall, winter, and spring) at 5 p.m.; and occasional family workshops.

Renwick Gallery

*Pennsylvania Avenue and 17th Street, NW, Washington, DC (202-357-2531, 202-786-2424 TTY) - **americanart.si.edu**.*

Designed in 1859 by architect James Renwick, Jr. to house the collection of William Corcoran, this building was Washington's first private art museum. Due to the growth in his collection, Corcoran moved his paintings and sculpture to the Corcoran Gallery of Art, and the Renwick became a showcase for contemporary American crafts. The Highlight Tour gives a general overview of the whole gallery, including the history of its two period rooms, the Grand Salon and the Octagon Room, and a quick showing of the current exhibits.

- Open daily, 10-5:30. Closed Christmas.
- Metrorail Red line at Farragut North; Blue and Orange lines (Farragut West - Farragut Square exit).
- Walk-in tours are offered Monday-Friday from January through April (except for Federal Holidays).
- Call 202-275-1693 to arrange group tours. Please give a three-week notice. Group tours are held Monday through Friday at 10, 11, and 1.
- Wheelchair access, corner of Pennsylvania Avenue and 17th Street. Wheelchairs are available.
- Recommended for children age ten and older.

Smithsonian Art Museum

*8th and G Streets, NW, Washington, DC (202-357-2700) - **www.americanart.si.edu**.*

Formerly the National Museum of American Art, the Smithsonian Art Museum is dedicated to American crafts from the nineteenth century to the present. Approximately 7,000 American artists are represented in the collection, including John Singer Sargent, Winslow Homer, Mary Cassatt, Georgia O'Keeffe, and Jacob Lawrence. The museum is closed for renovation until 2005. Until then, a full program of exhibitions and events is being held at the Renwick Gallery.

Take Note...

Visit the website for "Bottlecaps to Brushes," an interactive art room for children; "1001 Days and Nights of American Art," a daily glimpse of our nation's art heritage; and "Ask Joan of Art," a fascinating on-line reference service.

- Metrorail Red, Green, and Yellow lines (Gallery Place - 9th Street exit).
- Restaurant/Snack Bar.

Textile Museum

2320 S Street, NW, Washington, DC (202-667-0441)
- www.textilemuseum.org.

The Textile Museum is devoted exclusively to the handmade textile arts with a collection of over 17,000 rugs and textiles. The Museum presents several changing exhibitions each year which range from Oriental carpets to contemporary fiber art, giving visitors a unique sampling of the richness and diversity of the textile arts. Of special interest to children is the "Textile Learning Center", comprised of two galleries: The Activity Gallery and the Collections Gallery. The Activity Gallery is a hands-on exhibition where visitors can learn about spinning, dyeing, weaving, and other textiles. The Collections Gallery is devoted to three rotating themes: How are Textiles Made?, Who Makes Textiles?, and Why are Textiles Important?

- Open Monday-Saturday, 10-5; and Sunday, 1-5. Closed Federal holidays and Christmas Eve.
- Suggested donation, $5.
- Metrorail Red line (Dupont Circle, Q Street exit).
- Garden area available for picnics; no seating provided.
- Stroller and wheelchair accessible. Please call in advance for accessibility information.

Special activities include Celebrations of Textile Day, held the first Saturday in June and features hands-on textile art activities and demonstrations. Family programs focused on specific exhibitions are held throughout the year.

Tudor Place

1644 31st Street, NW, Washington, DC (202-965-0400, tour information, 202-965-0166, curator) - www.tudorplace.org. From the Washington Beltway (I-495) take Wisconsin Avenue, Route 355 South for 6-7 miles past the National Cathedral. Turn left onto Q Street. Stay on Q Street for two blocks and make a left onto 31st Street. Look for the large gate and tour entrance on the left.

History buffs from third grade up find Tudor Place with its many relics from George Washington's home a logical and interesting complement to a visit to **Mount Vernon**, (see page118). Located in the heart of Georgetown on five fragrant landscaped acres, Tudor Place was built for Martha Custis Peter, granddaughter of Martha and George Washington. Purchased for $8,000 and designed by Dr. William Thornton, architect of the U.S. Capitol, Tudor Place remained in the Peter family for 180 years. The household objects, sculpture, manuscripts, etc. provide insight into America's history and culture in a setting once frequented by Henry Clay, Daniel

Webster, John C. Calhoun, and General Robert E. Lee. A children's "look and find" pamphlet helps focus young visitors' attention.

- Open Tuesday-Friday with docent-led tours at 10, 11:30, 1, and 2:30. Saturday tours are every hour on the hour from 10-3.
- Gardens are open Monday-Saturday, 10-4.
- Admission for the house tour is: adults, $6; seniors, $5; students, $3; children under 12, $2.
- Admission for the self-guided garden tour is $2.
- Partially wheelchair accessible. Strollers permitted in the gardens only.
- Recommended for children age ten and older.

Special activities include Fall Garden Day in October, a day dedicated to family-oriented activities, and candlelight tours at Christmas.

U.S. Holocaust Memorial Museum

*100 Raoul Wallenberg Place, SW, Washington, DC (202-488-0400, 202-488-0406, TDD) - **www.ushmm.org**. Located at 14th Street and Independence Avenue.*

The Holocaust Museum is one of the most popular and talked about museums in Washington. People are drawn from all over the world to learn the history of the Holocaust and to try to understand the deeper meaning of this global tragedy. From the top floor of the building, visitors guide themselves down through each of four levels and are able to track the progression of the war, from Hitler's rise to power to the liberation of the camps following the German defeat. Interspersed within the historical time line are many opportunities to read, watch, and hear personal accounts of individuals who experienced the Holocaust.

Perhaps one of the most moving parts of the museum is "Remember the Children: Daniel's Story," geared for younger children. In "Daniel's Story," children and their parents can trace the life of a young boy and his family as they struggle to survive persecution by the Nazis. As visitors move through the maze of rooms which represent the various places inhabited by Daniel's family during the War, they can see the War's impact on even the simplest level of life. At the end of the exhibit, children are encouraged to draw a picture or to write down their feelings.

- Open daily, 10:30-5:30.
- Timed tickets are required to enter the Permanent Exhibition. Reserve advance tickets (with service fee)

through ProTix, 800-400-9373, or http:// tickets.com.
A limited number of same-day tickets are available from
the 14th Street entrance beginning at 10.

- Closed on Yom Kippur and Christmas Day.

- No passes are needed for the special exhibits and the
  interactive Wexner Learning Center.

- Metrorail Blue and Orange lines (Smithsonian -
  Independence Avenue exit).

- Most museum programs are suitable for visitors
  11 years and older, and do not require tickets.

- To schedule groups larger than ten people, call
  202-488-0419 about six months in advance.

- Café, located in the Administrative Center next to the
  museum, serves snacks and sandwiches.

- The Museum Shop contains books for children
  on the Holocaust as well as audiotapes and videotapes.

U.S. Navy Memorial and Naval Heritage Center

*701 Pennsylvania Avenue, NW Suite 123, Washington, DC (202-737-2300,
extension 713 or 733) -* ***www.lonesailor.org***.

Discover a beautiful 100-foot diameter granite map of the
world, visit the Lone Sailor Statue - one of the most
photographed statues in America, participate in Navy
ceremonies, visit the U.S. Presidents Room, and enjoy evening
spring concerts by the U.S. Navy Band. A highlight is the
35-minute film explaining life at sea on an aircraft carrier.
Viewers young and old are absorbed by the demonstrations
and explanations of the way that jet pilots take off and land
safely on a ship's moving flight deck while at sea.

- Open Monday-Saturday, 9:30-5.
  Closed Mondays, November-February.

- Movie, "At Sea" and other Navy films are shown
  at noon daily. Free Admission.

- Metrorail Yellow and Green lines (Archives/Navy
  Memorial).

- For groups of 20 or more, call to schedule movie.

- Recommended for children age ten and older.

Special activities include daily military ceremonies and
outdoor concerts on the plaza with the U.S. Navy Band in the
spring and summer. Drill Team performs at 1 p.m. June to
October 1. Call 202-737-2300, extension 768, for the Special
Events Hotline.

Union Station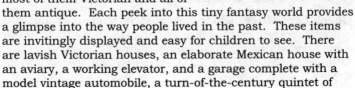

50 Massachusetts Avenue, NE, Washington, DC (202-371-9411, 202-289-1908 (shops) - www.unionstationdc.com. Massachusetts Avenue between 1st and 2nd Streets, NE. (202) 225-6832. Adjacent parking garage with entry on H Street, NE (many shops in Union Station will validate parking tickets).

Just minutes from the Capital, Union Station contains over 125 stores, an immense food court, and a nine-screen movie complex. The restored 1907 Beaux-Arts structure—once the largest train station in the world—still serves as Washington's primary train station. Its classic lines in white granite set the stage for many of the early 20th century buildings and monuments of Washington—including the Lincoln and Jefferson Memorials and the Supreme Court building.

- Union Station is open 8 a.m-9 p.m. daily.
  The shops, eateries, and movies have separate hours.
- Metrorail Red line (Union Station).

Very Special Arts ARTiculate Gallery

1100 16th Street, NW, Washington, DC (202-296-9100) - www.wvsarts.org.

This non-profit art gallery represents established and emerging artists with disabilities. The gallery's rotating, thematic exhibition schedule includes limited edition prints, paintings, textiles, contemporary folk art, and sculpture. An impressive selection of craft items, jewelry, and carvings is displayed year round.

- Open 10-5:30, Monday-Friday.
- Metrorail Red line (Dupont Circle, South).
- Wheelchair Accessible.

Washington Dolls' House and Toy Museum

5326 44th Street, NW, Washington, DC (202-244-0024, 202-363-6400) - www.dollshousemuseum.com. One block west of Wisconsin Avenue between Jennifer and Harrison Streets.

Children and adults enjoy the enchanting displays of this carefully researched collection of doll houses, dolls, toys, and games, most of them Victorian and all of them antique. Each peek into this tiny fantasy world provides a glimpse into the way people lived in the past. These items are invitingly displayed and easy for children to see. There are lavish Victorian houses, an elaborate Mexican house with an aviary, a working elevator, and a garage complete with a model vintage automobile, a turn-of-the-century quintet of

Baltimore row houses, and a 1903 New Jersey seaside hotel. Beautifully carved animals fill the cages of miniature zoos and circuses, and a Lionel train from the 1930s can be operated upon request. Arrangements can be made for birthday parties in the Edwardian tearoom. One museum shop contains a wide selection of doll's house furnishings for collectors and beginners; the other provides building and wiring supplies, kits, and books. An enlarged consignment shop has a selection of antique toys and dolls for sale.

- Open Tuesday-Saturday, 10-5; Sunday, noon-5. Closed Monday, Thanksgiving, Christmas, and New Year's Day.
- Adults, $4; children, $2; senior citizens, $3.
- Metrorail Red line (Friendship Heights-Jennifer Street exit).
- Wheelchair access for one wheelchair at a time. Strollers only permitted when the museum is not busy. There are three steps to the front door.

Special activities include an annual Christmas display highlighted by a revolving musical tree in December. Other exhibits salute baseball, Easter, Halloween, and the changing seasons.

Washington National Cathedral

Massachusetts and Wisconsin Avenues, NW, Washington, DC (202-537-6200, 202-537-6211 TTY; 202-364-6616-recorded information) - ***www.cathedral.org/cathedral****. Take the Washington Beltway (I-495) to Wisconsin Avenue South for about six miles. The Cathedral will be on the left at the corner of Wisconsin and Massachusetts.*

This splendid Episcopal 14th-century style, Gothic cathedral, started in 1907 and completed in 1990, is the sixth largest in the world. The tour of the main cathedral, small chapels, and crypts is especially interesting. The Children's Chapel impresses children with the stained glass, stonework, and other cathedral-related crafts. A visit to the Pilgrim Observation Gallery is also exciting, beginning with an elevator ride to the enclosed gallery at the roof level of the cathedral. The gallery affords an excellent view of Washington as well as the gargoyles, flying buttresses, and gardens of the cathedral. Don't miss the gardens and the herb cottage.

The Cathedral Medieval Workshop, open to the public on Saturday from 10-2, is a hands-on workshop where parents and children can work with stones to see how cathedrals are built. This workshop is appropriate for ages five and up. There is a materials fee. Please call 202-537-2934 for more information.

There are also hands-on demonstrations of the other art forms involved in the "Family Saturday", where children are introduced to the wonder and majesty of the Cathedral with storytelling, Cathedral exploration, and art projects.

Be sure to bring your binoculars and walking shoes for the "Family Gargoyle" tours. These tours feature stories about the Cathedral gargoyles, and give you a chance to see these funny and surprising creatures. A fee does apply and the tour is available by reservation between April and October by calling 202-537-2934.

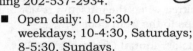

- Open daily: 10-5:30, weekdays; 10-4:30, Saturdays; 8-5:30, Sundays.

- Guided tours are adults, $3; senior citizen, $2; children, $1; and the audio tour is $5 per person.

- Metrorail red line to Tenleytown/AU station, then take any "30" series bus south for about 1 mile to the Cathedral. Obtain a bus transfer while in the Metro for discount bus fare.

- Tours last approximately 15-20 minutes and are held on Monday-Saturday, 10-11:45 a.m. and 12:45-3:15 p.m.; and Sunday, 12:45-2:30 p.m. No tours during services or special events. Maps for self-guided tours are available.

- Museum store.

- A limited number of wheelchairs are available on loan. Most of the nave and some crypt chapels are accessible with ramp entrances.

- Security Information: No strollers, bags or packages may be left unattended. Bags are subject to search at some events.

Special activities include the annual Open House, usually held the last Saturday of September. Featured are craft demonstrations, musical performances, and special activities. The "Cathedral's Flower Mart," usually held the first Friday and Saturday in May, features an antique carousel and an excellent selection of herbs and plants to purchase for your garden. For more information regarding seasonal events please call 202-537-6200.

Washington Navy Yard

Main entrance to complex at 9th and M Streets, SE, Washington, DC (202-433-2218) - www.history.navy.mil.

The Washington Navy Yard is the Navy's oldest shore establishment, home to the Naval Historical Center, which is comprised of the Navy Museum, Navy Art Gallery, and the display ship Barry, a decommissioned destroyer open to the public for self-guided tours.

- Contact the Community Projects Office to arrange visits.
- Recommended for children age ten and older.

Woodrow Wilson House

2340 S Street, NW, Washington, DC (202-387-4062) - woodrowwilsonhouse.org.

Immediately following the inauguration ceremonies for President Harding, Woodrow Wilson and his wife moved from the White House to this stately town home and lived there until his death. The only former President's house open to the public in Washington, it still reflects the presence of this scholarly and idealistic man. The drawing room and library have souvenirs from all over the world. Children might also be interested in the well-stocked kitchen of the 1920s, the 1915 elevator, and the graphoscope, an early film projector.

- Open Tuesday-Sunday, 10-4; closed major holidays.
- Adults, $5; senior citizens, $4; students, $2.50; children under seven, free. Free to National Trust Members.
- Metrorail Red line (Dupont Circle). Go West to 24th and S Street.
- Special tours and outreach programs for elementary and secondary classes are available. Call for details.
- Limited wheelchair access. Strollers should be parked downstairs.
- VA TimeTravlers Site.

Special activities include Preservation Garden party in May; Museum Walk Weekend the first weekend in June; Kalorama House and Embassy Tour the second Sunday in September; Christmas on S Street in December; and School programs, exhibitions, and other activities held throughout the year.

3. Main Sights and Museums Around the Beltway
Maryland

African Art Museum of Maryland

*5430 Vantage Point Road, Columbia, MD (410-730-7105, 301-596-0051) - **www.africanartmuseum.org**. Take Route 29 to Columbia; exit at Route 175 (Town Center) to Vantage Point Road; proceed to Historic Oakland, which houses the museum.*

This museum displays African art and offers hands-on art experiences for children. Videos and slide shows enhance the exhibits. The building was built in 1811 and is referred to as the Historic Oakland.

- Open Tuesday-Friday, 10-4; Sunday, noon-4; other times by appointment.
- Members, free; children and senior citizens, $1; adults, $2.
- Programs, by appointment, for all ages.
- Available for rental by calling the Columbia Association at 310-730-4801.
- Limited wheelchair accessibility.
- Recommended for children age ten and older.

Special activities include programs for children age 6-13.

American Indian Cultural Center/Piscataway Indian Museum

American Indian Cultural Center/Piscataway Indian Museum, Waldorf, MD (301-372-1932). Take the Washington Beltway (I-495) to Branch Avenue (Route 5) south (east towards Waldorf). Turn left onto Cedarville Road and follow for one mile. Turn right onto Country Lane; the entrance to the museum is on the left.

The **Piscataway Indian Museum** offers a vision of Native American life in Maryland before European settlers. A major exhibit of the museum is the full scale, re-constructed "longhouse," the type of home lived in by the Piscataways at the time of their first contact with the early settlers. Docents dressed in traditional clothing greet students and teach history through a presentation involving a series of hands-on, participatory activities. These activities teach students about diversity and help to break down stereotypical images associated with the term "American Indians." A learning/resource room and a Trading Post are also housed in the building.

- Hours by appointment.
- Admission, $3.
- Special tours by appointment. Open early on weekdays for schools and special trips.

Special activities include a Native American Indian Festival in June, and a fall festival in September.

Beall-Dawson House and Stonestreet Museum of 19th Century Medicine

Montgomery County Historical Society, 111 West Montgomery Avenue, Rockville, MD (301-340-2825, 301-340-6534) - www.montgomery history.org. Take the Washington Beltway (I-495) to I-270 north to Route 28 exit east toward Rockville; turn left on Montgomery Avenue (Route 28); go one block, entrance on left. Free parking behind house on Middle Lane.

This 19th-century home teaches children of all ages about the history of Montgomery County. Tour guides make the tour fascinating to young visitors by pointing out some clues about rural life in the 19th century. Children discover unusual period furniture like a candle stand, 19th century alternatives to plumbing, and subtle ways (by today's standards) that Upton Beall displayed his wealth.

The Stonestreet Museum of 19th Century Medicine is located on the grounds of the Beall-Dawson House. It is the original one-room office used by Dr. Edward Elijah Stonestreet from 1852-1903. This unique museum displays exhibits of medical, surgical, dental, and apothecary equipment. Children are delighted by the real skeleton, the Civil War amputation kit, and bleeding instruments. A hands-on reproduction of an 1850's stethoscope shows how difficult it was for a 19th century doctor to diagnose illnesses.

- Open Tuesday-Sunday, noon-4; closed major holidays.
- Adults, $3; students and senior citizens, $2. Members and children 5 and under, free.
- Metrorail Red line (Rockville).
- Call to arrange special tours.
- No wheelchair access. Strollers are permitted.
- Recommended for children age ten and older.
- Picnicking.

Special activities include "Dr. Stonestreet Holds Office Hours" the second Sunday of every month; a "Winter Pastimes Afternoon: Make old-fashioned toys" is held the first Sunday in January; "History Tour," a county-wide event with history sites throughout the county, is held during the last weekend in June; "Summer History Camp" for grades 5-7 is held in July and August; an annual "Happy Birthday, Montgomery County" community celebration is held the Sunday after Labor Day in September; "In Search of Ghosts", a Halloween ghost tour, is held the Friday before Halloween in October; an "Old-Fashioned Ornament Workshop" is held the second Sunday in December; "Holiday Decorations Tour" includes hot cider and cookies and is held during December. Groups should call ahead for all programs.

Belair Mansion

*12207 Tulip Grove Drive, Bowie, (301-809-3089) - **www.cityofbowie .org/comserv/museums.htm**. To Mansion, Stable, Genealogical Library: From the Washington Beltway (I-495) to Rt. 50 east (toward Annapolis) travel about 7 miles to Exit 11 (Rt. 197) for 1 mile and turn right on Tulip Grove Drive, and make a right at the stoplight. Proceed 1/2 mile down Tulip Grove Drive. The mansion is at the top of the hill, and the library and stable are further down the street where Tulip Grove Drive terminates at Belair Drive. Parking available.*

The Belair Mansion, a Georgian plantation house built in about 1745 by the provincial governor of Maryland, Samuel Ogle, is filled with 18th century paintings, furniture and silver.

- Hours: Thursday-Sunday, 1-4, except holidays.
- For public transportation, take Metrorail to New Carrollton Station and transfer to Metrobus B24.

Belair Stable

*2835 Belair Drive, Bowie, (301-809-3089) - **www.cityofbowie.org/comserv/museums.htm**.*

The Belair Stable was built in 1907 and produced some of the greatest American thoroughbred race-horses. A small museum, soon to undergo a substantial renovation, is on the grounds of the beautiful Belair Mansion. Groups of children can tour the estate with a docent and imagine what life might have been like on an 18th-century tobacco farm.

Bowie Train Station
and Huntington Museum ⚡️₁₆⚡️

8614 Chestnut Avenue, Old Bowie, (301-809-3089) - www.cityofbowie. org/comserv/museums.htm. From the Washington Beltway (I-495) to Rt. 50 east (toward Annapolis) travel about 7 miles to Exit 11 (Rt. 197) Collington Road/Bowie north, drive 4 miles. Left onto route 564 for 1 mile into Old Bowie. Route 564 makes a right and goes over the bridge crossing the railroad; however, continue straight on 11th Street, make a right onto Chestnut Street, and go to the end of the block alongside the tracks. Parking available.

Children will particularly enjoy the railroad museum located at the site of the junction of the old Baltimore and Potomac Railroads founded in 1872. They can climb the tower at the depot and get a bird's eye view of trains as they fly by the station. Inside, they can send an imaginary message via telegraph and get an idea of communication in the pre-e-mail era.

- Open Saturday and Sunday, 12-4, except holidays.
- Take the Metrobus B25.

Boyds Negro School House

19510 White Ground Road, Boyds, MD (301-972-0484).

This is a restored one-room schoolhouse (1896-1936) complete with furnishings and literature on the school community. Open by appointment only.

Clara Barton National Historic Site

5801 Oxford Road, Glen Echo, MD (301-492-6245) - www.nps.gov/clba. Located off MacArthur Boulevard, adjacent to Glen Echo Park. Parking

Visit the home of Clara Barton, who founded the American Red Cross in 1881. This house was not only her home from 1897-1912, but also the headquarters of the American Red Cross from 1897-1904. The Clara Barton National Historic Site, established in 1975 to commemorate both Miss Barton and the early American Red Cross, offers educational tours for children (grades K-6) stressing the role volunteers played.

- House shown by guided tour hourly on the hour, 10-4. Closed New Year's Day, Thanksgiving Day, and Christmas Day.
- Friendship Heights Montgomery County Bus #29.
- Reservations required for groups larger than ten.
- First floor is wheelchair accessible.

Special activities include spring and fall evening open house programs.

College Park Aviation Museum

*Located on the grounds of the College Park Airport, College Park, MD
(301-864-6029) - **www.pgparks.com/places/historic/cpam**. Take the
Washington Beltway (I-495) to Kenilworth Avenue south toward
Bladensburg; turn right on Paint Branch Parkway; then right at the second
traffic light on Corporal Frank Scott Drive (sign will say College Park
Airport); continue to the airport and museum. Parking on site.*

The College Park Airport was founded in 1909 by the Wright
Brothers and is the oldest continuously operating airport in
the world. It serves as the general aviation airport for small
privately-owned aircraft and is the site of many famous "first"
including the first army flying school and the first commercial
airmail service.

The College Park Aviation Museum commemorates the
historic importance of the airport. This interactive, hands-on
museum has exhibits and year-round programs including an
animatronic Wilbur Wright, vintage aircraft, and museum-
quality replicas of early airplanes. Family-oriented programs
include model-making and kite-building workshops, lectures,
film series, and children's events.

- Open daily, 10-5. Closed most major holidays.
- $4 adults; $3 seniors and groups; $2 children.
- Metrorail Green line (College Park).
- Group tours available by appointment.
- Wheelchair Accessible.

The Dennis and Philip Ratner Museum

*10001 Old Georgetown Road, Bethesda, MD (301-897-1518)
- **www.ratnermuseum.com**. From the Washington Beltway (I-495), exit
onto Old Georgetown Road. Go north toward Rockville for approximately
1/4 of a mile. Turn right on Lone Oak Drive (east) and take an immediate
left into the first driveway. Proceed to the smaller building in back.*

The Dennis and Phillip Ratner Museum was established
"to foster love of the Bible through the graphic arts." The
museum's three buildings include a Resource Center,
including library, conference space, and children's art and
literature museum. The Resource Center contains an Ark,
Eternal Light, Menorah, and Torah.

- Open Sundays, 10-4:30.
- Groups free by reservation only (Sunday-Thursday).

Glen Echo Park and Carousel

*MacArthur Boulevard at Goldsboro Road, Glen Echo, MD (301-492-6282, recording, 301-492-6229, park office) - **www.nps.gov/glec**. Take the Washington Beltway (I-495) to Exit 40 and follow signs to Glen Echo Park, about 3 miles from exit. From inner loop of Beltway (I-495), take Exit 41, Clara Barton Parkway east for 2-3 miles; then follow signs to park. From Washington, D.C., take Massachusetts Avenue until it ends at Goldsboro Road and turn left; go to MacArthur Boulevard; follow signs to park.*

Glen Echo Park was originally the site of a National Chataqua Assembly, and later a well-known amusement park. The National Park Service has converted this former amusement park into an arts center with over 500 art classes per year, covering the visual and performing arts. The park houses a number of artists-in-residence who are often available to discuss their work with the public.

The **Dentzel Carousel** is a special treat. Riding the multi-colored, hand-carved animals to the rhythm of the 1926 Wurlitzer band organ is pure joy for children. When Glen Echo Park closed and the carousel was about to be shipped to California, a group of concerned citizens raised money, bought it back, and presented it to the National Park Service. Because the carousel is covered, it operates rain or shine and is the best one in the area.

- The park is open year-round. The Dentzel carousel operates May-September, Saturday and Sunday, noon-6; Wednesday and Thursday, 10-2; 50¢ per ride.
- Two children's theaters The Puppet Company Playhouse, see page 178, and Adventure Theatre on page 169.
- Family square dances, Sunday afternoons, monthly ($5 adults, $4 children).
- Clara Barton National Historic Site is next to the park.
- Take Montgomery County Ride-On bus #29 operating daily from the Friendship Heights Metrorail station on the Red Line.
- A small playground, picnic area, and snack bar on site.
- It is a long walk from the parking lot to the carousel, theaters, and playground. Strollers are recommended for young children (although they are not allowed inside the buildings).
- Appropriate for preschool age children.

Special activities include the Washington Folk Festival (first weekend in June); Children's Chautauqua Day, a free workshop for kids (September); the Irish Feis, dance competition (May); Irish Folk Festival (September); and "Picking' in the Glen" Bluegrass Music Festival (October).

(Also see Adventure Theatre, page 169; Discovery Creek Children's Museum, page 43; and The Puppet Company, page 178.)

Good Knight Kingdom Museum

11001 Rhode Island Avenue, Beltsville, MD (301-595-8989) - www.good knight.org. Take the Washington Beltway (I-495) to Route 1 north toward Laurel; turn left at Rhode Island Avenue; proceed 1/4 mile, located on the right.

The Good Knight Kingdom features displays and activities that teach children and parents about child safety in an entertaining way. Exhibits cover basic safety tips on fire, poison, and household safety, as well as more serious topics such as drug and alcohol abuse, molestation, and abduction. Through the exhibits, children learn to face these modern "dragons" and receive a Certificate of Knighthood when they complete the sessions.

- Open daily; visits by reservation only.
- Field Trips, Birthday Parties, Picnicking, Wheelchair Accessible.

Special activities include ongoing workshops and shows.

Greenbelt Museum

Greenbelt Museum, Greenbelt, MD (301-507-6582). Take the Washington Beltway (I-495) to Kenilworth Avenue north; turn right on Crescent Road and continue to the museum on the left, just past the library parking lot.

Greenbelt is one of three "green towns" built by the U.S. government in an effort to provide jobs during the Great Depression. As one of America's earliest and most successful planned towns, Greenbelt is a National Historic Landmark. The Greenbelt Museum is located in an original home, half of a duplex building, built by the federal government. The home appears much as it did in 1937 when the first residents were selected by the government to move into the town of the future. The collection includes early photographs of the town, Art Deco pieces, and furniture.

The home is adjacent to many of the revolutionary planning features of the town: inner walkways, a pedestrian underpass, and a town center. The nearby Greenbelt Community Center is considered one of the best examples of Art Deco architecture in the area. The Museum has an exhibition room in the Greenbelt Community Center at 15 Crescent Road, next to the Greenbelt Library, open daily.

The historic section of Greenbelt has over 20 playgrounds, most of which are connected together by pedestrian paths, including the walking path around the lake.

- House open Sunday, 1-5, and by appointment. Community Center exhibit room open daily from 9 a.m.-10 p.m.
- Metrorail Green line (Greenbelt).
- Group tours available; please call for information.
- Playground and lake nearby.
- Wheelchair access to the home is limited. Strollers permitted, but the house is very small, and it is best to leave them outside.

John Poole House

19923 Fisher Avenue, Route 107, Poolesville, MD (301-972-8588). Take the Washington Beltway (I-495) to I-270 to Route 28 west. Bear left on Route 107 to Poolesville.

The oldest building in Poolesville, this log house was built in 1793 by John Poole Junior as a trading post for merchants and families of surrounding farms and plantations. It also served as a post office and was a stimulus to growth in the area. One room contains Civil War artifacts and an adjoining small arboretum displays plants native to the area before 1850.

- Open mid-April through October, Sundays, 12-5 and by appointment.
- Donations welcome.
- First floor of house and arboretum are wheelchair accessible.

Marietta House Museum

*Marietta House Museum, Glenn Dale, MD (301-464-5291, 301-277-8456 TTY) - **www.pgparks.com/palces/historic/marietta.html**. Take the Washington Beltway (I-495) to Annapolis Road east (Route 450); left on Route 193, Glenn Dale Boulevard; first left on Bell Station Road. Marietta is the first driveway on the left.*

Gabriel Duvall, a Justice of the U.S. Supreme Court, built this Federal-style country home between 1812 and 1813. The home is the current headquarters of the Prince George's County Historical Society and the Society's library. The house is furnished according to four periods of the 19th century. The land surrounding Marietta was a working farm where the Duvall family raised tobacco and grain crops. Walk around the grounds to see a root cellar, the Judge's law office, and a cemetery with family gravestones.

- Open Fridays, 11-3; Saturday and Sunday, noon-4. Closed January and February.
- Adults, $3; students (5-18 years), $1; senior citizens, $2; children four and under, free.
- No wheelchair access; no strollers.

Special activities include children-oriented events such as Mad Hatters Tea Party in March; Children's Games in June; History Days for 4th-6th graders in July; Marching Through Time-Multi Period Living History in April; a Medieval Fair in October; and Candlelight Tours in December.

Montgomery County Airpark

7940 Airpark Road, Gaithersburg, MD (301-963-7100). Take the Washington Beltway (I-495) to I-270 to the Shady Grove East Exit; follow the green airport signs for five miles to the airport.

Montgomery County Airpark is Maryland's fourth busiest airport. Visitors can see piston and jet aircraft land, eat at the on-site restaurant with a view of the runway, or take an airplane or helicopter ride. There is a grassy area for picnics. Free group tours are given by appointment.

- Open daily.
- Full-service restaurant, Airport Café, open seven days a week, 7:30-7:30.
- Free tours offered Monday-Friday, 10-5.
- Wheelchair Accessible.

NASA/Goddard Space Flight Center

*NASA/Goddard Space Flight Center, Greenbelt, MD (301-286-9041) - **www.gsfc.nasa.gov**. Take the Washington Beltway (I-495) to the Baltimore-Washington Parkway; go north and follow signs to NASA.*

Open by appointment only, NASA's Goddard Space Flight Center presents exhibits that highlight the space program's contribution to communications, navigation, and aeronautics. School children of all ages will find something to fascinate them. Real and model rockets and satellites are on exhibit both outside and inside. Dock the Manned-Maneuvering Unit Simulator with a satellite by manipulating the controls. Use the computer system to build your own satellite and rocket system. The computer will alert you to any mistakes. Sunspots and solar flares can be witnessed as they happen with the solar telescope. Watch as weather maps of the earth are transmitted here from space. View recent footage of NASA's space ventures on a giant TV.

National Capital Trolley Museum

*1313 Bonifant Road, Wheaton, MD (301-384-6088) – **www.dctrolley.org**.
Take the Washington Beltway (I-495) to Georgia Avenue north (Route 97);
turn right on Layhill Road (Route 182); after two miles, turn right on
Bonifant Road.*

The highlight of this small museum is a 20-minute ride on an
old-time trolley through the surrounding woods; the staff
relates history and anecdotes about the cars. Try to schedule
your visit for one of the occasional open houses held
throughout the year; all five trolleys run and you can choose
to ride on the German, Austrian, or DC cars. On regular
weekends, only one trolley runs at a time.

- Open Saturday-Sunday, noon-5, January-November;
  Thursday-Friday, 10-2, March-May, July-August, and
  October-November; open Memorial Day, July 4, and
  Labor Day, noon-5; Saturday-Sunday, 5-9 for Holly
  Trolley illuminations in December.

- Trolley fares for adults, $2.50; children 2-17, $2;
  children under two, free.

- Picnic area.

- Tours can be arranged for preschool, primary,
  and elementary age children.

Special activities include including Holly Trolley Feast the
second weekend in December, parade days in April when all
the trolley cars are brought out for display or use, and an
annual Open House in September.

Radio-Television Museum

*2608 Michellville Road, Bowie, MD (301-390-1020) - **www.radio
history.org**. Take the Washington Beltway (I-495) to Route 50 between
Washington, D.C. and Annapolis, MD. Take the Collington Road exit south
(Route 197) to the first traffic light just beyond the exit. Turn right on
Northview Drive and proceed for 1.3 miles to Mitchellville Road. Turn right
onto Mitchellville Road. The Museum is on the right at the first stop sign at
the intersection of Mt. Oak Road and Mitchellville Road. Located in the old
red farmhouse in the City of Bowie. On-site parking.*

Take a step back in time to the early 20th century by taking a
tour of this museum, solely devoted to the history of radio
and television. The self-guided tour features radios that date
back to the early 1900's and around the museum walls are
print advertisements of the times.

- Open weekends (except holidays) from 1-4, and by
  appointment.

- Wheelchair access on first floor only.

- Recommended for children age ten and older.

Reginald F. Lewis Museum of Maryland African American History and Culture 🔆16

*Located at the corner of President and Pratt Streets in Baltimore's Inner Harbor, Baltimore, MD - **www.africanamericanculture.org**.*

Opening to the public in 2004, this 82,000 square-foot facility will provide permanent and changing exhibits on Maryland's rich African American history and culture, along with an oral history studio and interactive learning opportunities. The museum theater hosts dance and musical performances, film festivals, and lectures.

The Sandy Spring Museum

*17901 Bentley Road, Sandy Spring, MD (301-774-0022, 301-774-5919) - **www.sandyspringmuseum.org**. Take the Washington Beltway (I-495) to New Hampshire Avenue North towards Ashton. At Route 108 turn left. Continue less than a mile past Sherwood High School to Bentley Road on the right. Turn on Bentley and into museum parking lot.*

Sandy Spring Museum is a non-profit community museum, established in 1980, whose mission is to bring local history to life by "time traveling" to the era of our founding fathers and exploring the world of the early settlers at work, play, school, and home. Their story is brought vividly to life with a rich assortment of artifacts, visual images, hands-on objects, and oral presentations. The museum's on-site and outreach programs are designed to complement classroom lessons in social studies. The museum has a collection of old-fashioned toys that children may play with during or after the tour.

- Open Monday, Wednesday, and Thursday, 9-4; Saturday and Sunday, 12-4; additional hours by appointment.
- $3 for adults; members and children, free.
- Tours are given upon request.
- Stroller and wheelchair accessible.

Special activities include a "Summer Heritage and Craft Camp" for 1st-5th grade; "Strawberry Festival," the first Saturday in June; Montgomery County History Tour; Family Fun Day, President's Day; and a Historic Homes tour. Special programs and tours for student groups are available with an appointment. Special events may include demonstrations of blacksmithing, hearth cooking, basket weaving, yarn spinning, woodcarving, rope making, and more!

Washington Temple Visitors' Center (known as the "Mormon Temple")

9900 Stoneybrook Drive, Kensington, MD (301-587-0144). Take the Washington Beltway (I-495) to Connecticut Avenue north, exit 33 toward Kensington; turn right on Beach Drive and follow to the end; turn left on Stoneybrook Drive. The Visitors Center is one-quarter of a mile on the left. Free parking available at the Visitor's Center.

The Washington D.C. Mormon Temple, dedicated in 1974, is the largest in the world. It is an extraordinary edifice covered in 173,000 feet of white marble, and situated on 57 acres in Kensington, Maryland. The International Visitors Center is open to the public, and offers films and exhibits describing the temple's construction, and programs of the church.

- Visitors Center and gardens open daily, 10-9. No access to the Temple.
- Stroller and wheelchair accessible.

Special activities include the Festival of Lights, which has a live nativity scene, 300,000 Christmas lights covering trees and bushes on the grounds, and 14 huge Christmas trees decorated by different congregations. Exhibit and holiday entertainment continue from December until the first week of January. Concerts are also offered on weekends.

White's Ferry

24801 White's Ferry Road, Dickerson, MD (301-349-5200). Take the Washington Beltway (I-495) to I-270 north; exit at Route 28 west toward Dawsonville; take Route 107 west until it becomes White's Ferry Road.

A 15-car ferry crosses the Potomac River to connect with Route 15, two miles from Leesburg on the Virginia side. The ferry is the only cable-guided fresh water ferry on the east coast, and is the last operating ferry across the Potomac River. The store sells hot and cold food, and live bait. The fishing is reputedly good in the area because a Pepco plant upstream in Dickerson warms the river. For a minimum of four people, you (and canoe) are taken to Point-of-Rocks, about ten miles upstream. Depending on weather conditions, the trip downstream will take about six hours, during which you can fish, float, or socialize. You might also plan a hike on the C&O Canal.

- Ferry operates daily, 5 a.m.-11 p.m.
- Fees per car: $5 round-trip and $3 one-way. No credit cards accepted. No charge for groups of children, such as scout troops, on foot, but advance notice is required.
- Rowboat and canoe rentals.

Virginia

Alexandria Archaeology Museum

*105 North Union Street, Studio 327, Alexandria, VA (703-838-4399) - **www.oha.ci.alexandria.va.us/archaeology**. Located in the Torpedo Factory Art Center.*

The Alexandria Archaeology Museum was formed to preserve and interpret archaeological information from the diverse city of Alexandria and to involve the public in archaeological preservation. At the museum's lab, children can observe volunteers working with artifacts, cleaning, and cataloging. Visitors also see a life-size model of an archaeologist at work. The organization encourages participation in field trips to archaeological digs when possible.

- Open Tuesday-Friday, 10-3; Saturday, 10-5; Sunday, 1-5. Closed Easter, Thanksgiving, Christmas, New Year's Day, and July 4.

- School groups can arrange to visit the lab/museum for a 45 minute hands-on Alexandria Archaeology Adventure Lesson. Programs are directed for groups with at least 20 children in grades 3-12. Reservations are required.

- Picnic in the two parks located on either side of the Torpedo Factory. There is a food court behind the Torpedo Factory.

- Recommended for children age ten and older.

- This museum is an official Virginia Time Travelers passport site. (See www.timetravelers.org.)

- Wheelchair Accessible.

Special activities include Archaeology Summer Camp in July, Public Dig Days, Art Safari, Historic Hauntings, Ornament Decorative Workshop, and seasonal site tours. Public and family events are scheduled throughout the year.

Alexandria Black History Resource Center 🔆

*638 N. Alfred Street (Old Town), Alexandria, VA (703-838-4356) - **oha.ci.alexandria .va.us/bhrc**. Take the Washington Beltway (I-495) to George Washington Parkway south into Alexandria. The parkway becomes Washington Street. Turn right on Wythe Street. The Center is on the next corner, at Wythe and N. Alfred Streets. Park on Wythe Street.*

The Center includes the Museum, the Watson Reading Room, and the Alexandria African American Heritage Park. The museum, devoted to exhibiting local and regional history, is housed in the **Robert H. Robinson Library**, originally constructed in 1940 following a peaceful sit-in at the segregated Alexandria Library.

The **Watson Reading Room** is a non-circulating research library with a focus on African-American history and culture.

The nine-acre park adjacent to the Center offers a place for celebration, a preserved one-acre 19th century African-American cemetery, and a natural wetlands habitat.

- Tuesday to Saturday: 10-4; Sunday 1-5. Closed New Year's Day, Easter, 4th of July, Thanksgiving, and Christmas.
- Take Metrorail's Yellow or Blue line to Braddock Road station. Walk across the parking lot and bear right; at the corner of West and Wythe Streets, follow Wythe five blocks east. The Center is on the corner of Wythe and Alfred Streets.
- Wheelchair accessible.

Arlington House, the Robert E. Lee Memorial

*Arlington National Cemetery, Arlington, VA (703-235-1530) - **www.nps. gov/arho**. Walk from Arlington Cemetery Visitors Center parking lot or ride the Tourmobile.*

Robert E. Lee courted and wed Mary Custis in this hilltop mansion. They lived here for 30 years, from 1831-1861, and raised seven children here. It has been restored with some of the original furnishings and similar pieces of the 1850s. Don't miss the magnificent view of the Washington skyline from the front portico, which Lafayette described as the "finest view in the world." Show the children the upstairs children's room and playroom. The house is staffed by park rangers.

- House is open daily, 9:30-4:30. Closed Christmas and New Year's Day.
- Grounds are open from 8 a.m.-7 p.m. between April 1 and September 30, and 8 a.m.-5 p.m. between October 1 and March 31.
- Metrorail Blue line (Arlington Cemetery).
- Guided group tours by appointment only.
- Tourmobile stop.
- Wheelchair lift to the first floor; tours for the visually- and hearing-impaired can be arranged by calling ahead.
- Recommended for children age ten and older.

Special activities include a special tour for African-American History Month during February; St. Patrick's Day open house in March; a candlelight open house in October; Robert E. Lee Wedding Day Open House in June; and a Christmas open house featuring mid-19th century decorations in December.

Arlington National Cemetery

*Arlington, VA (703-607-8052, 202-979-0690, group tours) - **www.arlington cemetery.org**. Located directly across the Memorial Bridge. Parking lot.*

To bring the subject of war down to a comprehensible level for both children and adults, there is no better place than the Arlington National Cemetery. The sheer expanse of the cemetery, 612 acres, with its vast number of graves spanning the time period from the American Revolution to the present, brings a sense of the finality and devastation of our wars. At the **Information Center**, one can obtain the location of the burial site for any individual buried here. In addition to soldiers' graves, sections of the cemetery are dedicated to veterans who were astronauts, chaplains, and nurses.

Children enjoy the hike up the hill to the **Kennedy gravesites**, where they can see a panoramic view of Washington with airplanes flying overhead. (Even if you plan to walk through part of the cemetery, it is advisable to buy a ticket at the Tourmobile booth at the Visitors Center so that you can board a bus at any of the Tourmobile stops.) At the **Tomb of the Unknowns**, the **Changing of the Guard** is fascinating because of the breath-taking precision of each step and maneuver made by the Tomb Guards. Across from the **Tomb of the Unknowns** is the actual mast of the U.S.S. Maine (the sinking of the Maine began the Spanish American War).

Tourmobile guides make the tours interesting by providing fascinating tidbits of information, such as when Mrs. Robert E. (Mary Custis) Lee failed to pay taxes of $92.07 on her 1100-acre property, the U.S. took over Arlington Estate and used it as headquarters for the Army of the Potomac. And when Colonel Robert E. Lee left the Union for the Confederacy, General Meigs decided to use Lee's home as a Union cemetery. Even young children can follow the history of the cemetery on a Tourmobile ride: older parts of the cemetery have various sizes of headstones, pointed headstones designate soldiers from the Confederate armies, and the more recent gravestones are arranged to look like soldiers standing at attention. (See also Arlington House on page81.)

- Open daily, October-March, 8-5; April-September, 8-7.

- Metrorail Blue line (Arlington Cemetery).
- Tourmobile stop. Stops at Kennedy gravesites, Tomb of the Unknowns, and Arlington House. Without debarking to visit the sites, the ride takes approximately 40 minutes. See Tourmobile Information in Chapter 1, "Starting Out."
- Changing of the Guard occurs April-September, every half hour; October-March, every hour on the hour. An average of 18 funerals occur per day.

Special activities include services held in the amphitheater for Easter, Memorial Day, and Veterans Day.

Carlyle House Historic Park

*121 N. Fairfax Street, Old Town, Alexandria, VA (703-549-2997) - **www.carlylehouse.org**. Located in Old Town Alexandria, across from Alexandria's City Hall.*

This English, country-style mansion was built by Scottish merchant John Carlyle in 1753. The home was a social and political center and the site of a historic governors conference at the outset of the French and Indian War. The Carlyle House is on the National Register of Historic Places and is Alexandria's only stone, 18th-century Palladian-style house.

- Open Tuesday-Saturday, 10-4:30; Sunday, noon-4:30; closed Monday.
- Adults, $4; Students 11-17, $2; 10 and younger, free.
- Metrorail Blue and Yellow lines (King Street).
- School programs and tours are offered.
- Recommended for children age ten and older.
- VA TimeTravlers Site.

Special activities include Candlelight Tours of the house decorated with Christmas decorations of the 1700s in December, and living history events throughout the year.

Christ Church

*118 North Washington Street, Alexandria, VA (703-549-1450) - **www.historicchristchurch.com**.*

This lovely colonial Georgian church, in continual use since its completion in 1773, is the oldest in Alexandria and one of the oldest on the East Coast. Visitors can sit in the boxed-in pew belonging to George Washington. Look for the little brass tablet that marks where Robert E. Lee knelt at the altar rail to be confirmed. Franklin Roosevelt and Winston Churchill attended services on the World Day of Prayer for Peace, January 1, 1942.

Children find the greatest fascination, however, in the adjacent graveyard, where searching tombstones for dates and inscriptions is an adventure in this peaceful setting.

- Open Monday-Saturday, 9-4; Sunday, 2-4. A docent greets visitors at the door. Visitors should plan for unexpected closings for weddings, funerals, and special church services, because this is an active church.
- Sunday Services at 8, 9, 11:15 a.m., and 5 p.m.
- Wheelchair access (1-step barrier; assistance is provided).

Special activities include The Blessing of the Pets in October, when people bring their pets to be blessed.

Colvin Run Mill Historic Site

10017 Colvin Run Road, Great Falls, VA (703-759-2771, 703-759-3403). Take the Washington Beltway (I-495); exit at Route 7 west (Tysons Corner); Colvin Run Mill is seven miles to west of Tysons Corner and 15 miles east of Leesburg.

Colvin Run Mill, built in the early 1800s, is a working grist-mill that produces whole grain products to sell in the on-site general store. The huge grinding stones, the wooden gears, and the outside water wheel fascinates children of all ages.

The historic site also includes the original miller's house, with hands-on exhibits such as a grain elevator that can be manipulated, the original general store, and a re-created dairy barn with typical period farming equipment of the community and a scale model of the mill.

- Open Wednesday-Monday, 11-5. except January-February, 11-4, closed Tuesdays.
- Free admission to grounds. Tours of the mill and the miller's house: adults, $4; children 5-15 and senior citizens, $2; students 16 and older with I.D., $3.
- Tours of the mill and the miller's house are given every hour on the hour.
- Picnic tables are available on the grounds. Save some breadcrumbs to feed the resident ducks.
- Conditions permitting, grinding takes place on Sundays from noon-2.
- Puppet show for preschoolers, Thursdays at 1. Admission is $3 for children; adults, free.
- Limited wheelchair access.

Special activities include Country Christmas, the third weekend in December, with Victorian decorations, Santa Claus, and family crafts. Admission is charged for this event.

Drug Enforcement Administration Museum and Visitors Center 🌟16

700 Army-Navy Drive, DEA Headquarters, Arlington, VA (202-307-3463) - **deamuseum.org**. *From the Washington Beltway (I-495) take I-395 North to Route 1 (8C). The museum is located at the end of the off-ramp.*

This provocative museum intended for teens and adults attempts to starkly show the realities of drug use in America. Drug paraphernalia and grisly photos are displayed along with a history of intoxication and drug use over the course of the last century, along with a look at the historical, global influences of drug trafficking from the ancient Silk Road to the present.

- Open Tuesday-Friday, 10-4. Call to arrange a tour for groups of 15 or more.
- Metrorail Blue and Yellow lines (Pentagon City).
- Tours are limited to groups of 30 or less, and must be arranged in advance.
- Recommended for children age ten and older.

Fort Ward Museum and Historic Site

4301 West Braddock Road, Alexandria, VA (703-838-4848) - **www.fort ward.org**. *Take I-395 to Seminary Road east; after approximately one mile, turn left onto N. Howard Street, then right onto West Braddock Road; the museum entrance in on the left. Parking on-site.*

Of special interest to Civil War buffs, this museum exhibits weapons, uniforms, musical instruments, and other memorabilia of the period. Children can learn about the everyday life of Civil War soldiers and civilians. In addition to the museum building, there is a Civil War fort, and an Officers' Hut located within the adjacent Fort Ward Park (see page 125).

- Open Tuesday-Saturday, 9-5; Sunday, noon-5. Closed Thanksgiving, Christmas, and New Year's Day.
- Call for information regarding programs and special events.
- Take DASH bus #5 from the King Street Metro Station.
- VA TimeTravlers site.
- Wheelchair Accessible.

Special activities include A Christmas in Camp Open House, the second Saturday in December; A Civil War Camp Day, the third Saturday in June; and A Ship's Company: Navy Living History in early August.

Freedom Park

*1101 Wilson Boulevard, Arlington, VA (703-285-3544) - **www.newseum.org***

Freedom Park, located adjacent to the Freedom Forum's Newseum offices, is a landscaped formal garden in tribute to the pursuit of liberty. A bronze casting of the jail-cell door from Martin Luther King Jr.'s 1963 imprisonment in Birmingham, Alabama, and a replica of the Goddess of Democracy from Tiananmen Square are among the icons to freedom in the park.

- Daily 30-minute tours at 11 a.m., 12, 1, and 2 p.m.

Friendship Firehouse

*107 S. Alfred Street, Alexandria, VA (703-838-3891, 703-838-4994) - **oha.ci.alexandria.va.us/friendship**. Located in Old Town Alexandria on South Alfred Street, between King and Prince Streets.*

The Friendship Fire Company was established in 1774 and was the first volunteer fire company in Alexandria. The company moved to this house in the 1850's. The first floor Engine Room features hand drawn fire engines, buckets, axes, hoses, and other historic fire fighting apparatus, along with reproduction equipment that children can handle.

- Open Friday-Saturday, 10-4; Sunday, 1-4.
- Metrorail Blue and Yellow lines (King Street).
- Wheelchair Accessible.

Gadsby's Tavern Museum

*134 North Royal Street, Alexandria, VA (703-838-4242) - **www.gadsbys tavern.org**. From the Washington Beltway (I-495) exit onto Route 1 North, right on King Street and then left on Royal Street. Located on the corner of North Royal and Cameron Street.*

Gadsby's Tavern Museum offers an exciting look into the operations of an eighteenth-century tavern. The Museum consists of the 1770 City Tavern and the 1792 City Hotel, named after John Gadsby, the Englishman who operated them between 1796 and 1808. The tour covers architectural highlights, a display of period objects and furnishings, and the ballroom where George Washington danced to celebrate his birthday in 1798 and 1799.

- Open November-March, Tuesday-Saturday, 11-4 and Sunday, 1-4. Open April-October, Tuesday-Saturday, 10-5 and Sunday 1-5. The Museum is closed on Thanksgiving, Christmas, New Year's Day and July 4.

- Admission is $4 for adults, $2 for children ages 11-17, and free for children age ten and under with paying adult. Group rates are available on request. $1 off for AAA membership.
- Gadsby's Tavern Restaurant is open for lunch and dinner.
- Tours start at 15 minutes before and after each hour, and last about 30 minutes.
- Limited wheelchair access. Strollers are not permitted above the first floor. A video shown in the first floor reception room offers an alternate tour of the site for persons unable to go up the steps.
- Recommended for children age ten and older.
- VA TimeTravlers site

Special activities include Time Travels, a first-person interpretive tour; Young Ladies' Tea for girls and their dolls; a summer camp program; and a variety of other children's programs.

George Washington Masonic National Memorial

101 Callahan Drive, Alexandria, VA (703-683-2007)
*- **www.gwmemorial.org**. Free parking.*

This memorial to George Washington towers over the Alexandria skyline, affording a good view of the area. Memorabilia displayed include George Washington's Bible, a clock that was stopped at the time of his death, and other Washington artifacts. Children enjoy the animatronic George Washington and the large mechanical model of a Shriner's parade, complete with platoons of brightly clad nobles marching to recorded band music.

- Open daily, 9-5. Closed Thanksgiving, Christmas, and New Year's Day. Tours daily at 9:30, 10:30, and 11:30 a.m.; 1, 2, 3, and 4 p.m.
- Metrorail Yellow and Blue lines (King Street). Amtrak and VRE - Alexandria Station.
- Call about wheelchair access. Disability accessible.
- VA TimeTravlers Site.

Gunston Hall Plantation

Gunston Road (Route 242), Mason Neck, VA (703-550-9220) -
www.gunstonhall.org*. Take the Washington Beltway (I-495) to Route 1
south from Alexandria for 14 miles; then go east on Route 242 for four miles
to Gunston Hall. Or take I-95 south, take exit 163 toward Lorton. Follow
signs to Gunston Hall.*

This Colonial plantation is one of the finest homes in the area,
with its tasteful interior and spacious grounds overlooking the
Potomac River. Gunston Hall was the home of George Mason,
an author of Virginia's Declaration of Rights. The 18th-
century furnishings and the intricately carved woodwork are
outstanding. The children's rooms and nursery contain
simple, small-scale furniture of the period. A museum
features mementos from the Mason family, and a diorama
shows how the plantation worked. Outbuildings include the
kitchen, dairy, smokehouse, schoolhouse, and laundry. The
formal gardens contain boxwood hedges.

- Open daily, 9:30-5. Closed Christmas, Thanksgiving,
  and New Year's Day.
- Adults, $7; children grades 1-12, $3; senior citizens,
  $6; children under six, free. Call in advance for group
  tours and rates.
- A marked trail wanders through the woods to the river.
- Wheelchair access can be arranged. Strollers permitted
  on the grounds, but not in the house.
- VA TimeTravlers site
- Picnicking.

Special activities include a kite festival in March; Harvest
Festival in September; and Plantation Christmas in
December.

Iwo Jima Memorial

*Located along the George Washington Memorial Parkway, McLean, VA
(703-289-2500) - **www.nps.gov/gwmp/usmc.htm**. Take the Washington
Beltway (I-495) to the George Washington Memorial Parkway south; take
Route 50 West exit; take next right (Rosslyn) then left at stop sign onto
Ft Myer Drive. Make a left onto Marshall and then a left into the park.*

The United States Marine Corps War Memorial stands as a
symbol of this grateful Nation's esteem for the honored dead
of the U.S. Marine corps. While the statue depicts one of the
most famous incidents of World War II, the raising of the
American flag on Mt. Suribachi in February 1945. The
photographer Joe Rosenthal won a Pulitzer Prize for his
photograph of the flag-raising, and sculptor Felix W.
deWeldon captured that image in the bronze sculpture at the
memorial. The memorial is dedicated to all Marines who have

given their lives in the defense of the Unites States since 1775.

At the memorial, the Marine Drum and Bugle Corps and the Marine Corps Silent Drill Platoon put on a 75-minute performance of music and marching on Tuesday evenings during the summer, a Marine Corps tradition since 1954.

- Memorial open year-round. Concerts held Tuesday nights at 7 p.m., May-September.

- Metrorail Blue and Orange lines (Arlington Cemetery or Roslyn).

- For Tuesday parades, park at Arlington Cemetery and take a free shuttle bus to the parade grounds.

- Stroller and wheelchair accessible.

Special activities include marine sunset parades, May-August.

The Lee-Fendall House Museum

*614 Oronoco Street, Alexandria, VA (703-548-1789) - **www.LeeFen dallHouse.org**. Located at the corner of N. Washington and Oronoco Streets, four blocks north of King Street. George Washington Memorial Parkway becomes N. Washington Street in Old Town. From (I-495) south take US Highway 1 traveling north. Continue north past Duke, Prince and King Streets and turn right onto Queen Street. Turn left onto Washington Street. Go two blocks and turn right onto Oronoco Street.*

Built in 1785 by Robert E. Lee's uncle, Philip Fendall, and steeped in Civil War history, this house has been restored to reflect its early Victorian period. This child-friendly house offers hands-on items and specialized educational programs. Advance reservations are recommended.

- Tuesday-Saturday, 10-4; Sunday, 1-4.

- House tour, $4; Students age 11-17, $2. Children 10 and younger, free.

- Metrorail Yellow and Blue Lines (King Street/Braddock Road) - 10 minute walk.

- Special event attendees may use the City Employee parking lot located at the corner of Oronoco Street and North Pitt Street (two blocks east of the Lee-Fendall House) on weekends, holidays, and weekdays after 5.

- VA TimeTravlers site

- Picnicking

Special activities include summer programs for children.

The Lyceum, Alexandria's History Museum

*201 South Washington Street, Alexandria, VA (703-838-4994) - **www.oha. ci.alexandria.va.us/lyceum**. Take the Washington Beltway (I-495) and exit onto Route 1 north (Alexandria); right on Prince Street, right on S. Washington Street.*

An impressive example of Greek Revival architecture, the Lyceum was built in 1839 as a cultural center. Since 1985, it has been Alexandria's History Museum.

- Open Monday-Saturday, 10-5; Sunday, 1-5. Closed Thanksgiving, Christmas, and New Year's Day.
- Metrorail Blue and Yellow lines (King Street). Approximately ten blocks from metro; DASH and Metro buses stop right out front; free parking.
- Stroller and wheelchair accessible.
- VA TimeTravlers site, Birthday Parties.

Special activities include concerts; interactive exhibitions and public programs.

Market Square/Alexandria City Hall

300 block of King Street, Alexandria, VA (703-838-4200). Parking garage.

During the original survey of Alexandria in 1749, two half-acre lots were set aside for a market place and town hall. In the course of the town's history, this site has held schools, jails, whipping posts, and a town courthouse. On Saturday mornings, it is the home of one of the oldest continuously operating markets in the country.

- Open Monday-Friday, 8-5.

Special activities include weekday lunchtime concerts in spring and summer and an annual Christmas lighting ceremony in December. For a calendar of events, call the Alexandria Convention and Visitors Bureau, 703-838-4200.

Montpelier Mansion

*9401 Montpelier Drive, Laurel, MD (301-953-1376, 301-699-2544 TDD) - **www.montpelier.org**. Take the Washington Beltway (I-495) to the Baltimore-Washington Parkway north; exit at Route 197 north toward Laurel; turn left on Muirkirk Road; entrance is immediately on the right.*

Completed in the 1780s, Montpelier is a masterpiece of Georgian architecture. The expansive grounds (75 acres) include a boxwood maze and one of the two remaining 18th-century gazebos in the nation that is still on its original site. Children enjoy seeing the Quaker classroom and secret staircase.

The Montpelier Cultural Arts Center is located in a modern barn on the property.

It is open seven days a week from 10 a.m.-5 p.m. (except holidays). The Arts Center features artists in residence, art galleries, and classes. For information on Arts Center programs, call 301-953-1993.

- Tours March-November on Sunday-Thursday, noon-4 on the hour (last tour starts at 3). Tours December-February on Sundays at 1 and 2.
- Adults, $3; children $1; senior citizens, $2.
- Group tours available.
- Wheelchair access to the first floor only - please call in advance for assistance. No strollers.

Special activities include Christmas candlelight tours in December, George Washington musicale, Herb, Bread and Tea Festival in the spring, and the Traditional American Trails Fair in the fall.

Morven Park

*17263 Southern Planter Lane, Leesburg, VA (703-777-2414) - **www.morvenpark.com**. Take the Washington Beltway (I-495) to exit at Route 7 west (Tysons Corner); continue through the town of Leesburg; then right to Morven Park Road; left to Old Waterford Road (Route 698); then right to main entrance. From Maryland, take the Beltway (I-495) to Route 192, Old Georgetown Pike; at Route 7, go west (right turn) through the town of Leesburg; then follow above directions.*

This 1,200-acre estate is operated as a memorial to Westmoreland Davis, former Governor of Virginia. Children tend to be most interested in the extensive vehicle collection. In the old carriage house and Carriage Museum, there are coaches, breaks, and gigs driven by turn-of-the-century American society members, plus everyday phaetons, surreys, carts, sleighs, a funeral hearse, and a charcoal-burning fire engine.

- The mansion and carriage house are open for tours April-November. A special children's tour is available for the mansion and carriage museum.
- Wheelchair access to the carriage museum and lower level of the mansion; some additional wheelchair access available with prior notice. Strollers are permitted in the carriage museum.
- Picnicking.

Special activities include an arts and crafts festival in June; steeplechase races in October and May; and a special Christmas tour in December.

Mount Vernon Estate and Gardens (George Washington's Home)

*South end of the George Washington Memorial Parkway, Mount Vernon, VA (703-780-2000) - **www.mountvernon.org**. Take the George Washington Memorial Parkway (becomes the Mount Vernon Memorial Highway) south; Mount Vernon is located eight miles south of Alexandria. Free parking.*

This elegant and stately plantation mansion was the home of George Washington. The 40-acre estate provides an education in the economic and social life of the South in the 18th century, which centered on the plantation.

Walk through the mansion, painted in remarkable bright and historically accurate colors and furnished with the original heirlooms. Share the same views of the Potomac River that Washington saw. More than a dozen outbuildings are meticulously restored, including a major greenhouse, stables, slave quarters, and kitchen. History abounds here with fascinating exhibits in the refurbished George Washington Museum, the Archaeology and Restoration Museum, active archaeological dig, the slave Memorial and burial ground, and the family tomb where Washington is buried.

> ## Take Note...
> To get the most from this visit, try going early in the morning on a weekday. Use the adventure map, obtained at the entrance. A fun way to see Mount Vernon is by riverboat!

At the Hands-On History tent (open Memorial Day through Labor Day, 10 a.m.-1 p.m.), children of all ages are invited to harness "Nelly," the life-size fiberglass mule, crawl into a War tent full of soldiers' gear, play colonial games, explore Martha Washington's travel trunk, and much more!

- Open daily, November-February, 9-4; September, October, and March, 9-5; April-August, 8-5. The third floor of the mansion is open to visitors from December 1-January 6.

- Adults, $9; children 6-11, $4.50; senior citizens age 62 and above, $8; children under six, free. Scouts are admitted free during winter months. Group rates for students grades 1-12, $4.50.

- Tourmobile stop.

- Picnicking is not permitted on the plantation grounds, but good riverside spots are located along the Parkway. There is a snack bar and restaurant, the Mount Vernon Inn, 703-780-0011, just outside the main gate.

- Stroller and wheelchair access to the museum and the lower level of the mansion.

- VA TimeTravlers Site

Special activities include seasonal riverboat cruises, October, "Colonial Days at Mt. Vernon," with demonstrations by blacksmiths, paper makers, and etc. A costumed actor dressed as George Washington greets guests and performs as on special occasions.

National Firearms Museum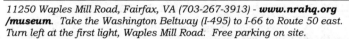

*11250 Waples Mill Road, Fairfax, VA (703-267-3913) - **www.nrahq.org /museum**. Take the Washington Beltway (I-495) to I-66 to Route 50 east. Turn left at the first light, Waples Mill Road. Free parking on site.*

Visit the National Rifle Association's collection of 3,500 historically significant firearms from 1450 to the present day. Tour a 16th-century fort and a Civil War rifle factory, visit Teddy Roosevelt's trophy room and an original Coney Island shooting gallery, and see firearms that arrived aboard the Mayflower and those owned by American presidents, generals and heroes. Learn about pivotal points in American history by viewing historical firearms and artifacts associated with the Pilgrims, the American Revolution, the Civil War, the California Gold Rush, and the taming of the West.

- Open daily, 10-4. Closed on all federal holidays.
- Schedule group tours in advance.
- Wheelchair Accessible.

Oatlands Plantation

*20850 Oatlands Plantation Lane, Leesburg, VA (703-777-3174) - **www. oatlands.org**. Take the Washington Beltway (I-495) to The Dulles Toll Road (Route 267) to the Greenway Parkway - make a right onto Route 15 South for approximately 5 miles down on left.*

This hunt-country estate dates from the early 1800s. Decorative and unusual features, such as the octagonal drawing room and a flanking pair of staircases, make for a worthwhile visit, especially for those interested in architecture. There is a terraced, four-acre, formal English garden, considered one of the finest examples of early Virginia landscape design, a tea house, and a reflecting pool.

- Open April-December, Monday-Saturday, 10-4; Sunday, 1-4.
- Grounds and Garden only $5 (12+).
- Tours: Adults, $8; students (12-18), $7; children (5-11), $1; children under five, free.
- Tours are offered Monday-Saturday every half hour, 10-4; Sunday, 1-4.

- No wheelchair access. No strollers.
- VA TimeTravlers site, Picnicking.

Special activities include point-to-point races in April;
Sheep Dog Trials in May; Summer Theatre; November Art
Show. During November and December, the mansion is
decorated with traditional greenery and ornaments.

Stabler-Leadbeater
Apothecary Shop and Museum

*105 and 107 South Fairfax Street, Alexandria, VA (703-836-3713)
- **apothecary.org**. Take the Washington Beltway (I-495) and exit onto
Route 1 north. Go 6 blocks, turn right on King Street and proceed for
seven blocks. Turn right on S. Fairfax.*

George Washington, Robert E. Lee, Daniel Webster, and other
historical figures used this actual drugstore. Original pre-
scription books and a sampling of pharmaceutical equipment
are on display. A recording relates the shop's history.

- Open Monday-Saturday, 10-4; Sunday, 1-5. Closed
  Thanksgiving, Christmas, and New Year's Day.
- Adults, $1; children under 12, free.
- Metrorail Blue and Yellow lines (King Street and
  Braddock).
- VA TimeTravlers site.

Sully Historic Site

*3601 Sully Road (Route 28), Chantilly, VA (703-437-1794) - **www.fairfax
county.gov/parks**. Take the Washington Beltway (I-495) to I-66 west; then
take Route 50 west to right turn on Route 28 north, Sully Road, turn right at
the next stop light. Sully is 1/4 mile from the intersection of Route 50 and
Route 28.*

Programs at the Sully Historic Site emphasize the enslaved
African American community, and show what life was like
throughout the 18th and 19th centuries. One of several
restored Lee family houses in Virginia, Sully Historic Site was
built in 1794 for Richard B. Lee, first Congressman of
Northern Virginia and uncle of General Robert E. Lee.

For school groups, there are special programs on textiles, food
preparation, school life, and slavery. Students learn spinning
and weaving, make beaten biscuits from an old Lee recipe,
and try old-fashioned slates and quill pens. Reservations
must be made in advance.

- Open Wednesday-Monday, 11-4; closed Tuesday and
  some holidays-call for hours.
- Adults, $5; students,$4; senior citizens and
  children 5-15, $3.

- Paved lot, handicap access.
- Limited wheelchair access. Strollers are not permitted in the house, but they can be stored at the door.
- Recommended for children age ten and older.
- VA TimeTravlers site, Field Trips, Picnicking.

Special activities include Civil War life encampment in July; Antique car show in June; Quilt Show with hands-on activities in September; Lantern Tours in October; candlelight tours and holiday concerts in December; and rotating spring programs. Weekend programs feature living history activities.

Surratt House Museum

9118 Brandywine Road, Clinton, MD (301-868-1121, 301-868-1020) - www.surratt.org. Take the Washington Beltway (I-495) to Branch Avenue/Route 5 exit; go south for three and a half miles to right exit on Woodard Road (Route 223 west); continue one mile to left turn on Brandywine Road; house is on the left, immediately after the turn. Ample free parking at visitors center.

This two-story frame house was a tavern, post office, polling place, and the home of the first woman executed by the U.S. government, Mary Surratt. In July 1865, she was hung for her alleged role in the assassination of President Abraham Lincoln. John Wilkes Booth stopped briefly at the house the evening of April 14, 1865, as he tried to escape after shooting the President. Today, costumed docents give visitors tours of the home and discuss the question of whether or not Mary Surratt was a co-conspirator in the assassination plot.

The home is a typical middle class home of the Victorian period. The displays include Victorian furniture, rugs, lace curtains, clothing, and kitchen implements.

- Open mid-January to mid-December, Thursday and Friday, 11-3; Saturday and Sunday, noon-4.
- Adults, $3; senior citizens, $2; children 5-18, $1.
- Tours every half hour, with last tour 30 minutes before closing. Group tours Wednesday, by appointment.
- John Wilkes Booth Escape Route Tour, a 12-hour bus tour, is available by reservation.
- Visitors Center with exhibits and electric map display.
- Wheelchair access on first floor only. No strollers.

Special activities include an exhibit which focuses on 19th century life, the Victorian Yuletide in December, and an exhibit of 19th century valentines and crafts in February. Spring and Fall Open House, with free tours and special activities.

Torpedo Factory Art Center

*105 North Union Street, Alexandria, VA (703-838-4565, 703-683-0693-tour information) - **www.torpedofactory.org**. Take the Washington Beltway (I-495) and exit onto Route 1 north. Go six blocks, turn right on King Street to the river, and turn left on Union Street; Art Center is ½ block on the right.*

Located on the Potomac riverfront in historic Old Town Alexandria, the Torpedo Factory Art Center has 83 studios and six galleries housing more than 165 working artist and craftsmen working, exhibiting, and selling their art in this renovated World War I munitions plant. Families may explore the Factory on their own, and have lunch at one of the Old Town's many restaurants or the Food Court located behind the Art Center.

- Open daily, 10-5. Closed Easter, July 4, Thanksgiving, Christmas, and New Year's Day.

- Take Metrorail's Yellow line to King Street station, then the Alexandria DASH Bus to King and Fairfax Street, and walk two blocks east on King Street to Union Street.

- Tours available through the Friends of the Torpedo Factory. Special demonstration tours can be arranged for groups. Visitor guides available in six languages.

- Wheelchair accessible.

Special activities include Annual Alexandria Arts Safari on the first Saturday in October, provides for a family oriented day of art activities offering artists' demonstrations in clay, painting, and enamel, as well as hands on workshops for young children in clay, wire art, and bat making. The Art League will support children in painting a mural, and the Alexandria Archaeology Museum will hold an open house.

U.S. Geological Survey
National Visitors Center

12201 Sunrise Valley Drive, Reston, VA (888-275-8748) - **mac.usgs. gov/mac/visitors/html/intro.html**. *Take the Washington Beltway (I-495) to Dulles Toll Road, to Reston Parkway - south; turn right at second light on Sunrise Valley Drive. Parking in visitor area.*

Visitors to the U.S. Geological Survey will find a wealth of information and numerous activities. In addition to watching videos on a variety of subjects, groups may take guided tours and sightsee along the woodland trail. On the tour, children can place their feet in actual dinosaur footprints in quarry stone taken from a quarry in Culpeper. Another highlight of the tour is the Carbon-14 laboratory, where wood and even cloth can be dated. In the lab is a Rube Goldberg-type set-up where substances bubble and smoke, surrounded by glass tubes, flasks, wires, and Bunsen burners. Here the scientists demonstrate ways of taking ancient material and estimating the number of years ago that glaciers or avalanches occurred during the Ice Age. Upstairs, computer experts with state-of-the-art computer-mapping equipment demonstrate how the Geographic Information Systems (GIS) operate. Experts have shown students how to track the migration of a caribou herd in Alaska. A special treat is the tour of the printing plant.

- Open weekdays 9-5, except federal holidays.
- For information or to schedule a tour, call 703-648-4748.
- Earth Science Information Center is a map store *nonpareil*. The center also provides numerous free pamphlets on rock collecting, volcanoes, earthquakes, caves, and prospecting for gold, as well as posters. Children can purchase large-scale maps of their towns and neighborhoods in the Washington, DC area at relatively low cost.
- Hiking, Picnicking, Restaurant/Snack Bar.

Special activities include annual Hispanic, Asian, and Native American exhibits.

Woodlawn Plantation/
Frank Lloyd Wright's Pope-Leighey House

*9000 Richmond Highway, Alexandria, VA (703-780-4000) - **www.national trust.org/national_trust_sites/woodlawn.html**. Take the Washington Beltway (I-495) to Route 1 south; located at the junction of Route 1 and Route 235 (Mount Vernon Memorial Highway). Parking available on-site.*

George Washington gave part of his Mount Vernon estate to his granddaughter, Nelly Custis, and his nephew, Lawrence Lewis, as a wedding present. Woodlawn Mansion, designed by Dr. William Thorton, architect of the U.S. Capitol, was built here. Adults will appreciate the elegant living room, dining room, and parlor. Youngsters like the children's bedrooms and the collection of stuffed birds acquired by Nelly Custis' son. A restored garden features roses and boxwood plantings. As a plantation site, Woodlawn was also home to over 90 slaves, as well as free hired workers, black and white.

The **Pope-Leighey** house is a "Usonian" home designed by Frank Lloyd Wright. The house reflects Wright's belief that people of moderate means are entitled to well-designed homes. Originally built in Falls Church, the Pope-Leighey House was moved to the Woodlawn property in the early 1960s. Visitors can pick up a discovery packet to compare this 20th-century home to the earlier plantation home.

- Open daily, 10-5. Closed January-February, Thanksgiving, Christmas, and New Year's Day.
- Adults, $7.50; senior citizens and students, $3.50; children under five, free. Group rates (for 15 or more). Combination ticket for Woodlawn Plantation and the Pope-Leighey house: adults, $13; senior citizens and students (grades K-12), $5; under 5, free.
- Special hands-on tours and slide presentation for school groups by appointment.
- Nature trails wind through the woods.
- Wheelchair access to the first floor only.
- Security Information: Strollers, backpacks, and shopping bags must be kept in reception area.
- Field Trips, Picnicking.

Special activities include a needlework exhibit in March; monthly in-depth tour of Pope Leighey House; ghostly tours around Halloween; a holiday exhibit in December and special events through the year. A special children's needlework workshop is held in early August. (Reservations are required for some events.)

4. The Great Outdoors

Explore history by visiting battlefields and historic farms; learn about plants, animals and the night sky; get out and play: Washington has many open-air opportunities for fun, and many ways to connect with the great outdoors.

Hiking, Fishing, Biking, and Boating in DC

Anacostia Park

*1900 Anacostia Drive, SE, Washington, DC (202-426-6905) - **nps.gov/anac**. Along the Anacostia River between South Capitol Street and Benning Road, SE. The Anacostia Freeway parallels the park boundary. From (I-495) take I-395 north (Southwest Freeway) to Pennsylvania Avenue. As you cross the bridge, stay in your right lane, make a right onto Fairlawn Drive (before gas station, K Mobile), go to stop sign and make a right onto Nicholson Drive. At stop sign, make a right onto Anacostia Drive. On-site parking.*

This large area along the east bank of the Anacostia River has playing fields for football and baseball, picnic spots, playgrounds, basketball courts, an outdoor swimming pool, and an outdoor pavilion for roller-skating and community gatherings. One section of the park has been designated as a bird sanctuary, where you might see a variety of marshland birds such as herons, egrets, ducks, and geese. For a close-up view of plants and wildlife, bring your own canoe and paddle along the banks of the river and its inlets.

> **Take Note...**
>
> Kenilworth Park and Aquatic Gardens, part of Anacostia Park, is the only National Park Service site devoted to the propagation and display of aquatic plants. The 77-acre Kenilworth marsh is the nation's Capital's last tidal marsh.

Anacostia Park Learning Center is a classroom and computer lab used for classes on environmental education and basic computer literacy courses.

- Open daily except for Thanksgiving, Christmas, and New Year's Day, dawn to dusk.
- Newly renovated tennis and basketball facilities; public boat ramp.
- Langston Golf Course offers an 18-hole course and driving range.

- Supervised roller-skating, May-September. For information, times, and fees, call 202-472-3883.
- Stroller and wheelchair accessible.
- Athletic Fields, Boating, Fishing, Picnicking, Playgrounds, Skating, Swimming.

Special activities include roller skating, walking and jogging trails, basketball, and tennis. A variety of environmental education programs are available. Call 202-426-1889

Battery-Kemble Park

*On Chain Bridge Road, NW, below Loughboro Road, Washington, DC (202-282-1063) - **www.nps.gov/rocr**. The park is bounded by Chain Bridge Road, MacArthur Boulevard, 49th Street, and Nebraska Avenue.*

Without leaving the city, you can enjoy an afternoon picnic and a nature walk in this fine, hilly, woodsy park. Historically a part of the circle of Civil War Defenses of Washington D.C, Battery-Kemble is one of the best area locations for sledding and cross-country skiing, and is ideal for kite flying.

- Open daily, dawn to dusk.
- Hiking, Picnicking.

Capital Crescent Trail

*(202-234-4874) - **www.cctrail.org**.*

The Capital Crescent Trail is an approximately 11-mile long hiker biker trail running from Silver Spring to Georgetown along the former B&O Railroad line. The trail crosses four historic bridges and runs through two historic tunnels and provides a look at the Potomac River through some of the prettiest woodlands in Washington. The trail connects with both the C&O towpath and with the Rock Creek Trail. The entrance to the trail in Bethesda is at the corner of Bethesda and Woodmont Avenues, next to the public parking lot.

- Excellent maps and descriptions also available at: **bikewashington.org/trails/cct/cct**.
- Biking, Hiking.

Glover-Archibold Parkway

*Entrances to the park at New Mexico Avenue at Massachusetts Avenue, and along 42nd Street, Washington, DC (202-895-6000) - **www.nps.gov/rocr**. This section of Rock Creek Park runs from MacArthur Boulevard and Canal Road, NW, to just south of Van Ness Street and Wisconsin Avenue, between 42nd and 44th Streets.*

Leave the hustle and bustle of the city behind as you enter this serene, heavily wooded park to wander its nature trails, bird watch, or daydream. Look for community gardens, planted and tended by local residents, in the section of the park closest to Whitehaven Park.

- Open daily, dawn to dusk.
- Hiking, Picnicking.

Rock Creek Park

*3545 Williamsburg Lane, NW, Washington, DC (202-895-6000) - **www.nps.gov/rocr**. The park includes areas on both sides of Rock Creek Parkway, NW, and connects with other parkland throughout the city. Park events recording 202-895-6239.*

Rock Creek is a wooded 1,754-acre park, about four miles long and one mile wide, that runs through northwest Washington from the Potomac River into Montgomery County. Picnic groves with tables, fireplaces, and shelters are abundant. A 1½-mile exercise course begins near Calvert Street and Connecticut Avenue, NW, and another begins at 16th and Kennedy Streets, NW. The park's many resources include: The National Zoo (see page 55), **Rock Creek Nature Center and Planetarium** (see page 152), and the **Rock Creek Gallery**, site of children's activities and art exhibits. Call 202-244-2482 for information on the gallery programs.

Bikers and walkers should note that Beach Drive, between Military and Broad Branch Roads, NW, is closed to cars on weekends and holidays. A marked bike trail, much of which is paved, runs from the Lincoln Memorial to Maryland and from the Memorial Bridge to the Mount Vernon Trail in Virginia.

Hiking trails are maintained by the Potomac Appalachian Trails Club. Check at the Nature Center (202-895-6070) for information on hiking trails.

- Open daily, dawn to dusk.
- Visitors centers are at the Nature Center, 5200 Glover Road, N.W., Peirce Barn, and at the Old Stone House, 3051 M Street, N.W. (see 58).
- Maps are available at the visitor center.
- To reserve picnic areas, call the D.C. Department of Recreation, 202-673-7646.

- Tennis courts at 16th and Kennedy Streets, NW and Beach and Tilden Streets, NW (Pierce Mill) open from April to mid-November. Tennis courts at Park Road, NW, east of Pierce Mill, open May-September by reservation only. Reserve and pay fees through Washington Area Tennis Patrons at the courts.

- The 18-hole golf course at 16th and Rittenhouse Streets, NW, 202-723-9832, is open daily, dawn to dusk. Closed Christmas. Clubs and carts can be rented.

- Rock Creek Park Horse Center, Inc., Military and Glover Roads, NW, 202-362-0117, is the only riding facility in Washington, D.C. The Center offers barn tours, a summer camp, lessons for all ages, trail rides, and more.

- Hiking, biking, roller-blading, equestrian and cross-country skiing trails, and sledding.

- Rent bikes, canoes, kayaks, rowing shells and rowboats at Thompson's Boat House, 202-333-9543, opposite the entrance to Rock Creek Parkway at Virginia Avenue, NW (near the Watergate), www.guestservices.com/tbc.

- Peirce Barn (Tilden and Beach Drive): Weekends noon - 4 p.m. Public nature and historical programs.

- Biking, Boating, Hiking, Picnicking, Tennis.

Special activities include Rock Creek Park Day in late September.

Hiking, Fishing, Biking, and Boating in Maryland

Black Hill Regional Park

*20930 Lake Ridge Drive, Boyds, MD (301-916-0220, 301-972-3476, Visitor Center) - **mc.mncppc.org**. Take the Washington Beltway (I-495) to I-270 north to Father Hurley Blvd, exit left on Route 355 to West Old Baltimore Road; continue for one mile to park entrance on the left. Parking available.*

This park is located on 1,854 acres, including Little Seneca Lake with 16 miles of shoreline. The two challenging playgrounds are favorites of younger children. There is also a picnic area (call to reserve shelters, 301-495-2480), a Visitor Center, a paved hiker/biker trail, ten miles of hiking and equestrian trails, horseshoe pits, volleyball courts, boat launching, canoe and rowboat rentals, and fishing.

- Open March-October, 6 a.m.-sunset; November-February, 7 a.m.-sunset.
- Security Information: Check Nutshell News for a schedule of events.
- Biking, Boating, Fishing, Hiking, Picnicking, Wheelchair Accessible.

Special activities include a variety of nature programs (star search, hawk watch, family hikes, cornhusk basketry) and other special events that take place throughout the year at the Visitor Center.

Calvert Cliffs State Park

*Point Lookout State Park, P.O. Box 48, Scotland, MD (301-872-5688) - **www.dnr.state.md.us/publiclands/southern/calvertcliffs** Located in Lusby, MD. Take the Washington Beltway (I-495), take Route 4 south to Lusby. Calvert Cliffs State Park is on the left about 14 miles south of Prince Frederick.*

On the western side of the Chesapeake Bay, the Cliffs of Calvert dominate the shoreline for thirty miles along the shores of Calvert County. They are as impressive a sight today as they were when Captain John Smith came upon them in his exploration of the Bay in 1608. The cliffs were formed over 15 million years ago when all of southern Maryland was covered by a warm shallow sea. These ancient sea floors can now be seen carved into the cliffs.

The park offers 13 miles of marked foot trails for hiking, including a 1.8 mile hike to a 100-yard stretch of the beach where you can go fossil hunting and search for shark's teeth and shells. Visitors may keep what they find. However, because of the constant erosion of the cliffs, access to the cliffs is no longer permitted. The trail to the beach winds through forest and marshland - great for bird watching. There is a one-acre fishing pond containing bass, bluegill, and catfish (a MD freshwater fishing license is required for persons 16 years and older), and fishing from the beach is also permitted (a sport fishing license is required to fish in the Chesapeake Bay).

- Open daily, sunrise-sunset.
- Admission: $3 per vehicle; school/charter buses, $20; small buses, $10.
- Swimming is allowed, but at your own risk.
- Pets are not allowed in the park.
- Camping is available for youth groups only.
- Recommend sturdy shoes for the hike and sandals for the beach area.
- Cliff area and beach are not wheelchair or stroller accessible.
- Field Trips, Fishing, Hiking, Picnicking, Playgrounds, Swimming.

Catoctin Mountain Park

6602 Foxville Road, Thurmont, MD (301-663-9330, 301-663-9388) - ***www.nps.gov/cato***. *Take the Washington Beltway (I-495) to I-270 north to Frederick; take Route 15 north to second Thurmont exit (Route 77 west); continue for three miles to park entrance on right.*

This park offers campsites, hiking trails, picnic tables and grills, and fishing streams (fly fishing allowed, catch and release only). In winter, when there may be up to 12 inches of snow, there is ample cross-country skiing, snow shoeing, and sledding. A variety of special events for children and adults, including campfire programs and nature walks, make this park a memorable retreat for the whole family. Group camps are also available.

- Open daily, dawn to dusk from mid-April to mid-November.
- Visitor center open all year 10-4:30. Closed federal holidays.
- Family camping is $14 per night per site.
- Wheelchair access to some areas. Call for specific information.
- Field Trips, Camping, Fishing, Hiking, Picnicking.

Cedarville State Forest

Rural Route 4, Box 106-A, Brandywine, MD (301-888-1410, 800-784-5380)
*- **www.dnr.state.md.us/publiclands/southern/cedarville** Located in*
both Prince George's and Charles Counties. Take the Washington Beltway
(I-495) to Route 5 south; go south on Route 301 to Cedarville exit; continue
east for three miles to right turn on Cedarville Road to the park.

This area was once the winter home of southern Maryland's
Piscataway Indians, who lived near Zekiah Swamp, where
wildlife was abundant and the weather was mild. There are
plenty of picnic tables, shelters, and charcoal grills (no wood
fire permitted). The park features 19.5 miles of marked trails
for hiking, biking and horseback riding, a pond for fishing,
nature walks, and campfire programs. In the summer, the
Visitors Center at Maryland's only warm water fish hatchery
is open to the public.

- Open daily, sunrise-sunset. Limited access on
  Christmas and Thanksgiving.
- See website for camping/shelter fees,
  (www.dnr.state.md.us/publiclands.oc/html).
- Family and Youth Group Camping, Hiking, Biking and
  Equestrian Trials, Horseback Riding, Birthday Parties,
  Athletic Fields, Fishing, Picnicking.

Chesapeake and Ohio (C&O) Canal
Historical Park Great Falls, MD

Canal Information Center, Great Falls Tavern, 11701 MacArthur Boulevard,
*Potomac, MD (301-299-3613, 301-767-3714) - **www.nps.gov/choh**. The*
park follows the Potomac River from Georgetown to Cumberland, MD. The
Georgetown Canal Information Center is located in the Foundry Mall
between 30th and Thomas Jefferson Streets, NW (202-653-5190).

With spectacular rock formations, the Great Falls portion of
the C&O Canal is one of the most impressive natural sights in
this area. Here the river drops more than 70 feet over
numerous falls and proceeds downstream through rapids and
river islands to its junction with the tidal estuary at Little
Falls (Chain Bridge). The park consists of 900 acres on the
Maryland side of the Potomac.

The canal towpath is a pleasant place to walk and bike ride.
Older children will enjoy the **Billy Goat Trail**, a vigorous
three-mile, three-hour, round-trip hike that provides
spectacular views of the Potomac River and Mather Gorge.
Directions for this and other less strenuous hikes are
available at the **Great Falls Visitors Center**.

Canoeing is also popular at the canal, but you should be
prepared to portage around each lock. There are various
places to enter and exit the canal and a number of picnic

sites. You will see the locks of the historic C&O Canal, through which the mule-drawn boats used to travel between Cumberland and Georgetown. Contact either visitors center for an official map and guide.

The three-room **Canal Museum** in the Great Falls Tavern features exhibits such as a lock model, artifacts from the days when the canal was operating, historic photographs, and short films explaining the story of the canal.

The **Swain's Lock** part of the canal (off River Road, north of Falls Road in Potomac, MD) is ideal for boating, fishing, hiking, and picnicking. Boat rentals, bait, and snacks are available at the lockkeeper's house.

Take Note...

Gold was mined near Great Falls in the late 1800's!

The Canal Clipper Boat, a replica of 19th-century mule-drawn boats, operates on the canal from mid-April through October. For information on trips from Great Falls Tavern, MD, call 301-299-3613, and from Georgetown, call 202-653-5190. The boat ride lasts about one hour and costs $6/adult, $5/senior citizen, and $4/child, age 3-14. The boat can be reserved by groups of ten or more for day or evening journeys.

- Open daily, dawn to dusk.
  Visitor's Center is open daily 9-4.
  Closed Thanksgiving, Christmas, and New Years.

- Entrance fee at Great Falls: $5 per vehicle for a three-day pass; $3 per person not arriving by car.

- Rent canoes, boats, and bicycles at Thompson's Boat House, 202-333-9543; Fletcher's Boathouse, 202-244-0462; or Swain's Lock, 301-299-9006.

- Snack bar at Great Falls Visitors Center is open April-October.

- **WARNING**: Do not wade in the water or climb on rocks in restricted areas. The current here is exceptionally powerful; many people who did not obey the warning signs have drowned.

- Wheelchair access to Great Falls Tavern and Georgetown boat ride.

- Field Trips, Biking, Boating, Camping, Fishing, Hiking, Picnicking, Restaurant/Snack Bar.

Special activities include Civil War Encampment during the last weekend in September; and Living History Boat Charters for school groups, April-June and September-October, for which park rangers dress in period clothing and transport students back to the 1870's.

Cosca Regional Park

*11000 Thrift Road, Clinton, MD (301-868-1397) - **www.pgpks.com**. Take the Washington Beltway (I-495) to Branch Avenue south; right on Woodyard to left on Brandywine Road; turn right on Thrift Road to the park.*

With 690 acres including rolling and wooded terrain and a 15-acre lake, Cosca Regional Park offers a variety of recreation for any outdoor enthusiast, and is home to the Clearwater Nature Center (see page 145). The park features equestrian and hiking trails, lighted athletic fields, indoor and outdoor tennis courts (for schedule and fees for indoor courts, call 301-868-6462), picnic grounds, and play areas. Campers have access to bathhouses, toilet facilities, water hook-ups, and electricity.

- Open daily, 7:30 a.m.-dusk, seven days a week; ball fields and tennis courts are open from 7 a.m.-11 p.m.
- Non-residents of Prince George's or Montgomery Counties must pay a $5 parking fee. Miniature train is $0.75 or $2 for three.
- Boating, Camping, Fishing, Hiking, Picnicking, Restaurant/Snack Bar, Tennis.

Cunningham Falls State Park

*14039 Catoctin Hollow Road, Thurmont, MD (301-271-7574, 888-432-2267, camping reservations) - **www.dnr.state.md.us/publiclands/western/cunninghamfalls** There are two areas to the park: the Manor Area and the William Houck area. Take I-270 west to Frederick; follow Route 15 north from Frederick to entrance to Manor Area, adjacent to Catoctin Mountain National Park. To reach the William Houck Area, continue north on Route 15 to second Thurmont exit (Route 77 west); continue to park entrance on Catoctin Hollow Road.*

Named for the splendid 78-foot waterfall that cascades in a rocky gorge, the 4,446-acre park offers nature walks, campfire programs, picnicking (tables, grills, and one shelter), and hiking. The 43-acre lake offers boat launching, canoe rental, fishing, and swimming. There are family campsites in both areas of the park, and a playground made from 3000 tires at the Manor area. In the winter, this is a great place for cross-country skiing and sledding.

- Admission fee year-round: $2 per person Monday through Friday; $3 per person Saturday, Sunday and holidays; seniors, age 62 and older, disabled persons, and children in car seats are free.
- Canoe rentals, Memorial Day-Labor Day.
- Family camping (171 sites), April to mid-October (reservations accepted up to nine months in advance), and winter camping (31 sites) November through firearm deer season.

- Wheelchair access includes picnic areas, campsites, fishing pier, and boardwalk to falls.
- Boating, Camping, Fishing, Hiking, Picnicking, Playgrounds, Swimming.

Dickerson Conservation Area

*20700 Martinsburg Road, Dickerson, MD (301-495-2500) - **www.mc-mncppc.org.***

This 304-acre park is located along the Potomac River and the C&O Canal just south of the boundary between Montgomery and Frederick Counties on a portion of the C&O Canal and towpath that was damaged during the flood of 1996. The park was acquired by M-NCPPC in the early 1960s. It is a fisherman's dream spot as well as a great place to picnic or stroll along the canal.

Greenbelt Park

*6565 Greenbelt Road, Greenbelt, MD (301-344-3944) - **www.nps.gov/gree**. Take the Washington Beltway (I-495) to Route 193 Greenbelt Road, turning left. Park entrance 1/2 mile.*

Greenbelt Park has 174 woodland campsites for tents, recreational vehicles, and trailers up to 30 feet long. Restrooms, picnic tables, fireplaces, showers, and water are available, but there are no utility hook-ups. There are several hiking trails and one large field for playing ball. The 1,100-acre woods have picnic areas and three nature trails. Park rangers lead campfire programs and nature walks in the summer, and offer a Junior Ranger Program for children 8-11 years old.

- Open daily, dawn to dusk; 24-hour access to the campground. Picnic areas from 8-8.
- Activity/Camping Fee - $14 per day.
- Metrorail Red line (College Park) is 2.5 miles to the campground. The F-6 bus will take you to Parkdale High School, where there is a path to the ranger station two hundred yards on the right. Alternatively, the Green Line (Greenbelt) is three miles from the park.
- Ample parking available on site.
- Family and group camping, reservations required May through October, call 1-800-365-2267. Fee is $14 per night, per site.
- Three developed picnic areas with restrooms, water, tables, and charcoal fireplaces. Call for reservations.
- Stroller and wheelchair accessible.

Lake Artemesia Park

*600 Cleveland Avenue, College Park, MD (301-927-2163) - **www.pgparks. com/places/nature/artemsia.html**. Take the Washington Beltway (I-495) to Kenilworth Avenue (Route 201) south for 0.5 mile. Turn right on Greenbelt Road (Rt.193) following it for ¾ of a mile. Turn right onto Branchville Road after Beltway Plaza (see sign for Lake Artemesia), following it for 0.7 miles. The road will bear left and left again crossing under Greenbelt Road where it changes into Ballew Avenue. Just after the stop sign at Berwyn Road, turn left into the parking lot for Lake Artemesia. The lake, not visible from the parking lot is further down Ballew Avenue. Follow bike path.*

Lake Artemesia is a 38-acre, man-made lake with over two miles of accessible hiker-biker trails. The lake is stocked with several varieties of fish (bass, bluegill, sunfish, catfish, and trout). Lake Artemesia is also part of the Anacostia Tributary Trail System that encompasses the northeast/northwest branches of the Anacostia River.

- Open year-round.
- Parking at Branchview/Ballew Avenue in Berwyn Heights. Enter the park via trails at the 5200 block of Calvert Road in College Park or at Osage Street and Swarthmore Court in Berwyn Heights.
- A stroller-accessible trail loops around the lake.
- Handicapped-accessible fishing pier.
- Biking, Fishing, Hiking.

Special activities include evening hikes, and stream conservation programs.

Lake Frank

6700 Needwood Road, Rockville, MD (301-948-5053). Take the Washington Beltway (I-495) to 270 north; exit at Shady Grove Road east; follow Shady Grove to right on Crabbs Branch Way; turn left on Redland Road; turn right onto Needwood Road; follow Needwood to entrance on the right.

Lake Frank is part of Rock Creek Regional Park. Offering shoreline hiking and fishing, this is a rustic, quiet spot to "get away from it all."

- Open sunrise-sunset.
- No swimming, no boating.
- Fishing, Hiking.

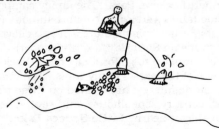

Lake Needwood Park

15700 Needwood Lake Circle, Rockville, MD (301-762-1888, 301-948-5053)
*- **www.mc-mncppc.org/parks**. Take the Washington Beltway (I-495) to*
Georgia Avenue north; turn left on Norbeck Road; turn right on Muncaster
Mill Road; turn left on Avery Road; follow signs to Visitor's Center/Boat
Rental.

Lake Needwood is a picturesque man-made lake nestled in
wooded Rock Creek Regional Park. Well used for boating and
fishing, Lake Needwood offers plenty of activities for a full day
outdoors. You can take a trip aboard the "Needwood Queen,"
a 20-passenger pontoon boat, or rent a paddleboat, rowboat,
or canoe. Lake Needwood is a good place to go fishing (you
can purchase bait and a fishing license at the boat house).
There are also hiking trails, play areas, picnic groves, a snack
bar, and bathrooms. The Meadowside Nature Center is
located here (see page 150).

- Open daily during the summer months from noon-6
  weekdays, 6:30- 6 weekends. Open weekends only
  September-May.

- Two golf courses, 18-hole and 9-hole. For schedule and
  fees, call 301-948-1075.

- Groups with advance boat reservations can ride the
  "Needwood Queen" during the week. The general public
  can ride on weekends. For boating information, call
  301-762-9500.

- Boating, Fishing, Hiking, Picnicking, Playgrounds,
  Restaurant/Snack Bar.

Little Bennett Regional Park

23701 Frederick Road, Clarksburg, MD (301-972-9222, 301-972-6581) -
***www.mc-mncpp.org/parks**. Take the Washington Beltway (I-495) to I-270*
north; exit at Boyds-Clarksburg (Exit 18); turn right on Clarksburg Road and
continue for one mile; turn left on Route 355; continue for three-quarters of a
mile to park entrance on right.

Take a short ride north of the busy Washington, D.C. area to
a pleasant and secluded camping and hiking area in Little
Bennett Regional Park. The family campground features
picnic tables and grills, comfort stations (sinks, showers, and
toilets), water spigots, horseshoes, volleyball, and activity
programs on Saturdays (April-October). This is also an
excellent place to go for a day hike. Pack a lunch and set out
on one of the park's many trails. The remains of several sites
of historic interest are located on these trails: saw mills, a
19th-century schoolhouse, and several houses. Fishing is
available at nearby **Little Seneca Lake**.

- Trails open daily, dawn to dusk.

- Family camping (91 sites) April-October; reservations accepted; fee is charged. Primitive camping areas for groups; call 301-972-9222. There is a camp store at the registration office.
- Camping, Hiking, Picnicking, Playgrounds, Snack Bar.

Patapsco Valley State Park

8020 Baltimore National Pike, Ellicott City, MD (410-461-5005) -
www.dnr.state.md.us/publiclands/central/patapscovalley.html*.
Located on the Patapsco River between Elkridge and Sykesville, MD. Take
the Washington Beltway (I-495) to Route 29 north to Route 40 east.
Entrance is located just 1/2 mile inside Howard County. From I-695 to exit
15B (I-40W), for three miles, right into park.*

In 1608, Captain John Smith discovered the river that runs through this historic park. Battles of the Revolutionary War, War of 1812, and the Civil War were fought here. Look for the old stone viaduct, the country's first train depot, and the dam that was the world's first underwater hydroelectric power plant. Patapsco offers nature walks, campfire programs, picnicking, playgrounds, hiking, mountain bike and equestrian trails, canoeing, and softball fields. Fishing is good in the river and pond. Campers have access to fireplaces, picnic tables, water, showers, and electricity.

- Open year round from 9 a.m.-sunset. Closed Thanksgiving and Christmas.
- $2 admission per person. Senior citizens and handicapped passes available by application.
- Handicap parking available; MTA #150.
- Family camping (100 sites), April-October, $18-$23/night. Youth group camping (7 sites for up to 55 persons each) by reservation; 6 cabins, $35/night.
- Wheelchair access, including a trail.
- Security Information: Rangers available 24 hours/day.
- Biking, Boating, Camping, Fishing, Hiking, Picnicking, Playgrounds, Wheelchair Accessible.

Special activities include an annual outdoor expo and Harvest Days in the fall

Patuxent River State Park, Jug Bay Natural Area

*Park is composed of several properties on the river along the eastern boundary of Prince George's Co, Upper Marlboro, MD (301-627-6074) - **www.dnr.state.md.us/publiclands/central/patuxentriver.html**. Take the Washington Beltway (I-495) to Pennsylvania Avenue, SE (Exit 11A), also known as Route 4). Go eight miles to Route 301 south. Go 1.7 miles to left on Croom Station Road; take a left on Croom Road, and then another left on Croom Airport Road. At park entrance, either go straight to group camp area or turn left and proceed 1.7 miles to Park office.*

If you are planning a visit to this scenic 2,000-acre natural area, you will need to plan ahead. Much of the parkland is open to the public, however visitors need special permits, and groups need reservations. Outdoor recreation activities include primitive camping, fishing, canoeing (canoes can be rented at Jug Bay by advance reservation), boating, and horseback riding (bring your own horse!). The park also offers the following natural attractions:

Chesapeake Bay Critical Area Driving Tour is a four-mile, self-guided, one-way drive connecting the **Pautuxent River Park** with the **Merkle Wildlife Sanctuary**. As you drive along the Patuxent River shoreline, you may see osprey, Canadian geese, bald eagles, and other wildlife. The tour includes educational displays, observation towers, and a 1,000-foot bridge across Mattaponi Creek. The drive is open for private cars on Sunday from 10 a.m.-3 p.m. and at other times in the Park's own vehicles. The drive is open for hikers and bikers on Saturday, January-September, 10 a.m.-3 p.m.

At the heart of **Jug Bay**, children will enjoy the **McCann Wetlands Study Center** with its large hands-on exhibit room. Just outside, there is an observation deck with panoramic views of the marsh and the Patuxent River and a boardwalk that winds through the marsh and leads into the forest. Children can learn about marsh ecology while exploring the area by canoe, or by using dipnets and buckets to search a pond for turtles, tadpoles, dragonflies, and aquatic insects. For young naturalists, there are excellent volunteer opportunities as well as a summer science camp.

The **Black Walnut Creek Nature Study Area** is dedicated to nature study and environmental education. You can walk out on boardwalks through the marsh and swamp and on woodland trails for an up-close view of the wetlands. Nature hikes are available by reservation for groups of eight or more.

River Ecology Boat Tours offers you a chance to board a pontoon boat and learn about wetlands, wildlife and the history of the local area. These tours are available for school programs, adult groups, and seniors, by reservation Tuesday through Saturday, and for the public on Sundays at 2 p.m. from April through October.

The **Patuxent Rural Life Museums** includes the **W.H. Duvall Tool Museum**, the Tobacco Farming Museum, a 120-year-old log cabin, and a Blacksmith shop all of which depict life along the river. Tours are available for groups by reservation.

- Open daily, 8 a.m.-dusk. Closed Thanksgiving, Christmas, and New Year's Day.

- All parklands are considered "limited use natural areas" and require a permit or reservation. Call for more information on permits.

- Activities accommodate senior citizens and handicapped visitors.

- Historic sites.

- Interpretive boat tours on Jug Bay for groups, April-October, by reservation.

- Canoeing, Cross Country Skiing, Field Trips, Boating, Camping, Fishing, Hiking.

Piscataway National Park

*3400 Bryan Point Road, Accokeek, MD (301-763-4600) - **www.nps.gov/ pisc**. Take the Washington Beltway (I-495) or the Route 295 Bypass to Indian Head Highway south (Route 210). To reach the National Colonial Farm area, continue on Indian Head Highway for ten miles to a right turn on Bryan Point Road; follow to end of the road. To reach the Marshall Hall area, continue on Indian Head Highway for four more miles; then right turn on Marshall Hall Road (Route 227) and proceed for three miles to the park entrance.*

The **Marshall Hall** area was once a thriving plantation (only the walls remain) and in later years an amusement park visited by excursion boats from Washington, DC. Today visitors can launch boats, picnic, or take a hike on a wetland trail. The **Hard Bargain Farm Environmental Center** offers educational programs for groups of school children. Students can study the wildlife found along the river, including beavers and great blue herons. The park's Visitors Center and a fishing dock are located in the **National Colonial Farm** area (see page 158 for more information on The National Colonial Farm).

- Open daily, dawn to dusk.
- Limited wheelchair access.
- Boating, Hiking, Picnicking.

Seneca Creek State Park

*11950 Clopper Road, Gaithersburg, MD (301-924-2127) - **www.dnr. state.md.us/publiclands/central/seneca.html**. Take the Washington Beltway (I-495) to Route 170 north; exit at 10, Clopper Road; continue two miles to park headquarters on the left.*

This 6500-acre stream valley park covers both sides of Great Seneca Creek for 13 miles from Route 355 north of Gaithersburg to the Potomac River. Approximately 1000 acres are developed for public day-use and self-guided tour meanders through this area. Trail maps can be found at the Visitor Center and cover the five trails and a self-guided Woodlands Trail of the old Clopper mansion ruins, and a historical mill. Also located within the park is the Schaeffer Farm area (off Schaeffer Road) with over ten miles of multi-use trails primarily suited for mountain biking. No pets, including horses, are permitted in the day-use area. For trail conditions, call 301-924-1998.

- Day-use area open year-round, 8 a.m.-sunset.
- May-September: Saturday, Sunday, and holidays, $2 per person (senior citizens and children in car seats, free); October - April: weekends $2 per car; All year: weekdays, free!
- Private picnic pavilions available for rent.
- Wheelchair access on pontoon boat tour, Visitors Center, Boat Center, picnic areas, and restrooms.
- Athletic Fields, Biking, Boating, Disk Golf, Fishing, Hiking, Playgrounds, free 18 hole Disc Golf Course, 90-Acre Lake, Open Fields.

Special activities include Gaithersburg's Winter Lights in December; the Shaker Forest Festival in September; and hay rides, bird walks, canoe tours, hay rides, pontoon tours, moonlight walks, campfires, and Junior Ranger programs in the summer.

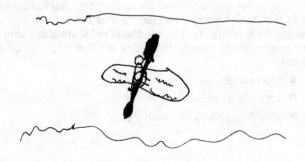

Sligo Creek Park

*Parallels Sligo Creek Parkway from University Boulevard to New Hampshire Avenue, Silver Spring, MD (301-495-2525) - **www.mc-mncppc.org.** Begin at Piney Branch Road and Sligo Creek Parkway.*

This peaceful park, which runs through Silver Spring and Takoma Park, is a pleasant place to bike, walk, or have an old-fashioned family picnic. A hiking/exercise course, playground equipment, basketball courts, and a flat bike trail paralleling the creek for ten miles, make for a delightful family outing. Follow the trail to Wheaton Regional Park.

- Open daily, dawn to dusk.
- Athletic Fields, Biking, Golf Course, Hiking, Picnicking, Playgrounds, Tennis.

Sugarloaf Mountain

*7901 Comus Road, Dickerson, MD (301-869-7846) - **www.sugarloafmd. com.** Take the Washington Beltway (I-495) to I-270 north to exit 22; turn right on Route 109 south toward Comus; go two and a half miles and turn right at Comus Road; sign at entrance. Park at the base of the mountain, or take your car part of the way up the mountain and park at overlooks.*

A visit to Sugarloaf is a pleasant way for the family to enjoy nature. This privately owned mountain is known for its lovely foliage and vistas. The auto road goes almost to the top, and there are plenty of good walking and climbing trails to match your family's hiking levels. Young children can climb to the top from the auto road. More experienced climbers may want to ascend via "Devils Kitchen." There's a great view at the top and picnic spots scattered on the mountain.

- Visitors admitted daily, 8 a.m.-one hour prior to sunset. All visitors must leave by sunset.
- Picnic tables located near the parking areas. No fires (cookouts) allowed.

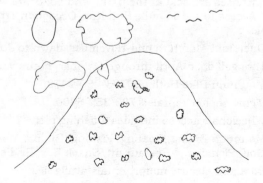

Hiking, Fishing, Biking, and Boating in Virginia

Bull Run Marina

Old Yates Ford Road, Clifton, VA (703-631-0549, 703-830-9252) - www.nvrpa.org/bullrunmarina.html. Take the Washington Beltway (I-495) to I-66 west; exit at Fairfax, Route 123 south to Clifton Road; right on Clifton Road; turn left on Henderson then take a right onto Yates Ford Road.

This heavily wooded park on Lake Occoquan is an ideal spot for teaching children the art and lore of fishing (bait and tackle for fishing can be purchased in the park). Picnic tables and grills are scattered under the trees overlooking the water. The Marina has hiking trails and a playground, and offers outdoor education courses, as well as guided canoe trips.

- Open April-October, Friday-Sunday and holidays, dawn to dusk.
- Rowboat, kayak and canoe rentals, and boat launching.
- Athletic Fields, Boating, Canoe and Kayak Rentals, Fishing, Hiking, Picnicking, Playgrounds.

Fountainhead Regional Park

10875 Hampton Road, Fairfax Station, VA (703-250-9124) - www.nvrpa. org/fountainhead.html. Take the Washington Beltway (I-495) to I-95 south to Route 123 north; go about five miles and turn left on Hampton Road; go three miles to entrance on the left.

Located at the widest point of Lake Occoquan, this scenic park is a conservation area that shelters a profusion of birds, geese, ducks, raccoons, deer, and other forest creatures. Picnic tables and grills overlook the water, and nature trails wind over hills and ravines to views of the lake and low marshlands. The park also offers miniature golf, and a five-mile mountain bike trail. It is an ideal spot to teach children to fish (licenses are sold at the park), and boats are available to rent. Access to the 17-mile Bull Run-Occoquan Trail is available.

- Open mid-March to mid-November, dawn to dusk.
- Mini golf open April through October, hours vary.
- Mountain Bike Hotline: 703-250-2473.
- Picnic shelter rentals: 703-352-5900.
- Wheelchair access includes a fishing pier.
- Mountain Biking, Boating, Fishing, Hiking, Miniature Golf, Picnicking, Restaurant/Snack Bar, Bridle Trails.
- Boat and electric motor rentals available.

Great Falls Park

9200 Old Dominion Drive, McLean, VA (703-285-2964, 703-285-2965) -
www.nps.gov/gwmp/grfa*. Take the Washington Beltway (I-495) to
Georgetown Pike (Route 193); go west four miles to right on Old Dominion
Drive (Route 738); continue one mile to park entrance.*

Great Falls is an 800-acre park overlooking the magnificent
Great Falls of the Potomac. Families come here to explore the
remains of the 18th-century Patowmack Canal, built to
bypass the falls, or to fish in the river. There are many hiking
and equestrian trails, and a snack bar (open seasonally).

- Open daily, 10-5 weekdays; 10-6 weekends; 10- 4 daily
  in winter; Visitors Center, 10-5. Closed Christmas.
- Entrance fee, $3 per individual or $5 per vehicle; the
  parking lot may be full by the middle of the day on
  weekends, so plan accordingly. Annual Park Passes
  are available for 1 year for $20.
- **WARNING**: Do not wade in the water or climb on rocks
  in restricted areas. Stay away from the river's edge and
  watch children closely at all times. The current here is
  exceptionally powerful; many people who have not
  obeyed the warning signs have drowned.
- Visitors Center is staffed by park rangers and
  volunteers. Special tours and walks are held all year.
- Handicapped parking is near the Visitor Center. The
  Patowmack Canal Interpretive Trail is accessible by
  wheelchair as far as Lock 1.
- VA TimeTravlers site, Fishing, Hiking, Picnicking,
  Restaurant/Snack Bar.

Huntley Meadows Park

3701 Lockheed Boulevard, Alexandria, VA (703-768-2525) - ***www.fairfax
county.gov/parks/huntley****. Take the Washington Beltway (I-495) to
Richmond Highway, Route 1; go south three and a half miles and turn right
at Lockheed Boulevard. Proceed three blocks to the park entrance on the
left at Harrison Lane.*

This 1,424-acre park, tucked away in the midst of suburbia,
will introduce your children to several diverse habitats -
wetlands, forest, and meadow. Dogue, Little Hunting, and
Barnyard Run Creeks flow through the park on their way to
the Potomac River. There are many species of plants and
animals. A two-thirds-mile wetland boardwalk trail with
observation platforms and tower takes you into the marsh.
Look for some of the park's residents including raccoons,
beavers, frogs, turtles, insects, and abundant bird life. Be
sure to bring your field guides, binoculars, and curiosity.

The Visitors Center includes several interactive exhibits depicting the cultural and natural history of the park and the natural habitats that are found here. Children especially enjoy the wetlands diorama and photomurals. Special programs are presented in the auditorium.

- Park open daily, dawn to dusk. Visitor's Center open Monday, Wednesday, Thursday, and Friday, 9-5, March-December. Weekend hours vary according to season. Closed Tuesday, Thanksgiving, Christmas, and New Year's Day.
- Group tours by reservation.
- Picnic at Stoneybrook or Lee District Park.
- Trails and boardwalk are wheelchair and stroller accessible. Wheelchairs are available upon request.

Mason District Park

*6621 Columbia Park, Annandale, VA (703-941-1730) - **www.co.fairfax. va.us/parks**. Take the Washington Beltway (I-495) to Little River Turnpike east; continue for two miles to left at John Marr Drive; right on Columbia Pike to park entrance on the right, just before Sleepy Hollow Road.*

Mason District Park includes 121 acres in the heart of Fairfax County. The park features tennis and basketball courts, ball fields, and jogging trails. Visitors can enjoy a wildlife pond, take a hike, or follow self-guided nature trails. There are picnic and open play areas as well as a tot lot. An amphitheater offers a full and varied schedule of day and evening programs in the summer.

- Open daily, dawn to dusk.
- Athletic Fields, Hiking, Picnicking, Playgrounds, Tennis.

Special activities include Mason Days with crafts and entertainment in September.

Mount Vernon Trail

*George Washington Memorial Parkway c/o Turkey Run Park, McLean, VA (703-285-2598, 703-285-2603) - **www.nps.gov/gwmp/mvt.html**. Parallels the Potomac River and the George Washington Memorial Parkway from Theodore Roosevelt Island to Mount Vernon.*

This 18½-mile trail is pleasurable for joggers, bikers, and walkers. There are numerous interesting places to stop for a picnic lunch or to take a rest. At Roosevelt Island, you can walk the trails; **LBJ Grove** provides a clear view of the Washington skyline; **Gravelly Point** is a favorite place to watch planes take off and land; **Daingerfield Island** has water sports and a restaurant; **Dyke Marsh** is a 240-acre wetland where you might spot some rare species of birds; and **Mount Vernon** was George Washington's home.

- Open daily, dawn to dusk.
- Parking available at Theodore Roosevelt Island, LBJ Memorial Grove, Gravelley Point, Daingerfield Island, Jones Point Lighthouse, Belle Haven, Fort Hunt Park, Riverside Park, and Mount Vernon.
- Restrooms at Theodore Roosevelt Island, LBJ Memorial Grove, Daingerfield Island, Belle Haven, Fort Hunt Park, and Mount Vernon.
- Picnicking at Daingerfield Island, Jones Point Lighthouse, Belle Haven, Fort Hunt Park, Riverside Park.
- On the route is Mount Vernon District Park and Recreation Center with its indoor ice rink and swimming pool.
- Connects to the Arlington County trail system and the Washington and Old Dominion bike trail at Theodore Roosevelt Island. Cross Memorial Bridge and connect to the C&O Canal bike trail.
- Field Trips, Athletic Fields, Biking, Boating, Fishing, Hiking, Picnicking, Playgrounds.

Potomac Overlook Regional Park

*2845 Marcey Road, Arlington, VA (703-528-5406) - **www.nvrpa.org**. Take the Washington Beltway (I-495) to George Washington Parkway East to Spout Run exit; go right on Lorcom Lane; right on Nellie Custis (becomes Military Road); right on Marcey Road to park entrance.*

Here is a welcome open area in the heart of urban Arlington! Children will enjoy visiting the nature center and participating in its many natural and human history programs, concerts, and community events. The park offers several hiking trails and picnic areas.

- Open daily, dawn to dusk. Nature Center: Tuesday-Saturday, 10-5; Sunday, 1-5.
- Schools and organized groups may arrange for special programs.
- Nature Center has wildlife and archaeological displays, and auditorium.
- Vegetable, herb, butterfly and wildflowers gardens.

Special activities include the Annual Open House and Heritage Festival on the first Sunday in May.

Prince William Forest Park

Located in Prince William County, VA., Triangle, VA (703-221-7181) -
www.nps.gov/prwi. *Take the Washington Beltway (I-495) to I-95 south for about 35 miles to Route 619 (near Quantico); follow signs.*

There are several campgrounds in this park offering a variety of camping experiences: Oak Ridge, with 80 sites for tents and trailers (no reservations); Chopawamsic, with primitive camping not accessible by cars (permits required); and Turkey Run Ridge, with group tent campsites for 25-30 people (reservations required). Ranger-guided programs are provided year-round. Groups may request special ranger-guided activities.

- Open daily, dawn to dusk. Visitor Center open daily, 8:30-5. Closed Thanksgiving, Christmas, and New Year's Day.

- Entrance fee, $4 per vehicle. Family camp sites, $10; group campsites, $30.

- 37 miles of hiking trails.

- Over 12 miles of paved and 16 miles of unpaved roads available for bicycling.

- Picnicking, Swimming.

Red Rock Wilderness Overlook Regional Park

Edwards Ferry Road, Leesburg, VA (703-779-9372) - **www.nvrpa.org/ redrock.html**. Take the Washington Beltway (I-495) to Route 7 west toward Leesburg; take Route 15 Bypass north; turn right on Edwards Ferry Road (Route 773). Drive 1.5 miles to park entrance on left. Parking on–site.

Discover a beautiful, out-of-the-way place. Hike over hills and through woods dotted with wildflowers to panoramic views of the Potomac River and the distant mountains.

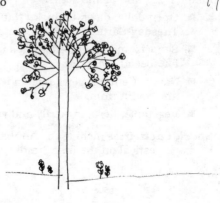

- Open year-round, dawn to dusk.

- Nature trails, scenic overlook, hiking.

- No public restrooms.

Riverbend Park

*8700 Potomac Hills Street, Great Falls, VA (703-759-9018, 703-324-8732-picnic line) - **www.co.fairfax.va.us/parks/picnics/gfallsnics**. Take the Washington Beltway (I-495) to Route 193 west; turn right on Riverbend Road; go 3 miles to right on Jeffery Road; continue 1 1/2 miles to the park.*

Riverbend Park encompasses 409 acres of Potomac shoreline and has a Visitor's Center with a wooden deck overlooking the Potomac River. The park features picnic areas with grills, a snack bar, walking trails, and fishing. The Riverbend Nature Center, 703-759-3211, has a naturalist staff, environmental exhibits, and many special programs call for details.

- Open daily, dawn to dusk. Visitor center open weekdays except Tuesday, 9-5; weekends, 12-5.

- Hiking, nature and equestrian trails, boat launches, and craft rooms.

- Wheelchair access includes a paved interpretive nature trail through upland forest.

- Field Trips, Boating, Fishing, Hiking, Picnicking, Restaurant/Snack Bar, Wheelchair Accessible.

Scotts Run Nature Preserve

7400 Georgetown Pike, McLean, VA (703-246-5700, 703-324-8702). Take the Washington Beltway (I-495) to Route 193 west; proceed on Route 193 for less than a mile to parking lot on the right.

Fairfax County naturalists refer to Scotts Run as the "Hot Spot for Wild Flowers," plus hiking, bird watching, and spectacular foliage. It is said that many of the huge trees are more than 100 years old. The scenery includes an abundance of dogwood and papaw as well as wildflowers in the spring. A three-mile trail follows a "stepping-stone stream" to a small waterfall and an awe-inspiring view of the Potomac. The trail gets more challenging as it approaches the river.

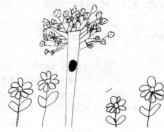

- Open daily, dawn to dusk.

- No restrooms.

- Hiking, Picnicking.

Theodore Roosevelt Island

George Washington Memorial Parkway c/o Turkey Run Park, McLean, VA (703-285-2598, 703-285-2603). Take Theodore Roosevelt Bridge to George Washington Memorial Parkway north, on the Virginia side of the Potomac River; follow signs to parking area for Roosevelt Island. Not accessible from the southbound lanes.

From the parking lot, visitors cross over a footbridge to enter this 88-acre wildlife refuge, preserved in its natural state as a tribute to conservationist President Theodore Roosevelt. The deeply wooded island includes a clearing where a 23-foot bronze statue of Roosevelt rises from a plaza that incorporates small shallow pools. It is a pleasant place to rest or have a picnic lunch. The park boasts a vast variety of plants, beasts, birds, and bugs in the swamps and forests, and is a good place to fish as well as canoe (bring your own). Sturdy low-heeled shoes are a must for exploring the two and a half miles of foot trails that meander through the varied habitats. Insect repellent is recommended, especially in the summer.

- Open daily, 7 a.m. to dusk.
- Call for information on guided tours and lectures.
- Picnicking allowed.
- Wheelchair accessible with assistance.
- Field Trips, Boating, Fishing, Hiking, Picnicking, Wheelchair Accessible.

Special activities include nature walks by appointment; ranger-led activities; Theodore Roosevelt birthday celebration in October; and Mr. Lincoln's Soldiers, featuring Civil War reenactments, in May.

Washington and Old Dominion (W&OD) Railroad Regional Park

*21293 Smiths Switch Road, Ashburn, VA (703-352-5900) - **www.nvrpa. org/wod,** also information can be found at: **wodfriends.org**. The railroad trail goes from Shirlington near I-395 to Purcellville in Loudon County.*

Called "the skinniest park in Virginia", this 45-mile strip of park follows the roadbed of the old W&OD Railroad. It is the most heavily used park in Northern Virginia. The 100-foot-wide paved path, which connects with numerous other trails and parks, serves bikers, hikers, joggers, and skate boarders from Arlington to Purcellville. The trail begins in Arlington, and there are several access points near Metro stations. Restrooms are located at several community centers along the way. Some place to access the W&OD are:

Shirlington - Take the Washington Beltway (I-495) to I-395 north to the Shirlington exit, keep to the right and turn left onto South Four Mile Run Drive (second light). The W&OD Trail will be on the right alongside the road. You can park along the side of the road. Not recommended for leaving your car overnight.

Arlington - at Manchester and 4th Street and Wilson Boulevard, west of Bon Air Rose Gardens and tennis courts, on the south side of the road.

Dunn Loring - Take the Washington Beltway (I-495) to Gallows Road north. Go past the trail and turn right on Idylwood Road and then right on Sandburg Street. There is a gravel lot on both sides of the road at the trail.

Vienna East - Take the Washington Beltway (I-495) to Route 123 into Vienna. Turn left (coming from Tysons) onto Park Street and right into the Vienna Community Center parking lot. The trail runs between the parking lot and the Community Center.

Vienna West - Take the Washington Beltway (I-495) to Route 123 into Vienna. Turn right (coming from Tysons) onto Park Street. Turn left at the four-way stop sign onto Church. Turn right onto Mill Street and then left onto Ayr Hill Road. There is parking in the gravel lot at the train station.

Reston - Take the Washington Beltway (I-495) to Route 7 west, turn left onto Reston Parkway. Make a left onto Sunset Hills Road.

Sterling - Take Route 28 several miles north of the Dulles Airport. Watch for signs. This is a good lot for horse trailers.

For additional locations in Ashburn, Leesburg and Purcellville, see the http://wodfrieds.org/parking.html.

- Open daily, dawn to dusk.
- Parking available at different places along the trail.
- Refreshment concession at Smith Switch in Ashburn (Loudon County), VA.
- Call for information on bike rentals.
- A 54-page, color Trail Guide is available for sale at all regional parks and NVRPA Headquarters.
- Dual equestrian trail west of Vienna to Purcellville.
- Biking, Hiking, Picnicking, Wheelchair Accessible.

Battlefields and Historical Sites

Antietam National Battlefield

*P.O. Box 158, Sharpsburg, MD (301-432-5124) - **www.nps.gov.anti**. Take the Washington Beltway (I-495) to I-270 north to I-70 west (in Frederick); exit at Route 65 south (Sharpsburg exit) just outside Hagerstown; follow Route 65 for 11 miles to battlefield on left.*

The Visitors Center houses a small museum with period artifacts, and shows a 26-minute film every half hour that describes the battle of Antietam. A one-hour Antietam Documentary is shown daily at noon. For a more thorough understanding of the battle, rent the self-guided tour audiotape for $4 at the bookstore and drive around the battlefield. The eight and a half mile drive, with the tape, takes about two hours and includes 11 stops.

- Open daily, 8:30-5. Summer hours are slightly longer. Closed Thanksgiving, Christmas, and New Year's Day.
- Adults 17 and above, $3; families, $5.
- Ranger programs daily during the summer. A Junior Ranger program is available for children ages 6-12.
- Restaurants in Shepherdstown, WV, five miles away.

Special activities include Living History Demonstrations (artillery, infantry, and encampment) by National Park Service volunteers, and an annual four-and-a-half mile long Memorial Illumination commemorating those lost, killed, and wounded at the Battle of Antietam in early December.

Ball's Bluff Regional Park

*NVRPA, 5400 Ox Road, Leesburg, VA (703-779-9372) - **www.nvrpa.org/ ballsbluff.html**. Take the Washington Beltway (I-495), take Route 7 west toward Leesburg. Exit on Route 15 Bypass north. Turn right on Battlefield Parkway and left on Ball's Bluff Road. The park is at the end of the street.*

Interpretive signs with Civil War-era maps and photographs lead visitors along a trail into the days of the significant Battle of Ball's Bluff. The park encompasses much of the battlefield and surrounds the Ball's Bluff National Cemetery.

- Open dawn to dusk, daily.
- Tours are offered the first Saturday in May through the last Sunday in October, at 11 and 2 on Saturday, and 1 and 3 on Sunday.
- Fishing, Hiking.

Special activities include living history lectures and walks on selected weekends.

Fort Ward Park

*4301 West Braddock Road, Alexandria, VA (703-838-4848) - **ci.alexandria
.va.us/recreation**. Take the Washington Beltway (I-495) to I-395 north to
Seminary Road east; after approximately one mile, turn left on north
Howard Street; right on West Braddock Road to entrance. Parking on-site.*

Fort Ward was the fifth largest of 68 Union forts built to
defend Washington during the Civil War. Learn more about it
at the park museum or enjoy the azalea and flower displays in
the garden area of this 40-acre park. See also Fort Ward
Museum on page 85.

- Open daily, 9 a.m.-sunset.
- Take Dash Bus #5 from King Street Metro Station.
- Park can be reserved for group picnics.
- Athletic Fields, Hiking, Picnicking, Tennis.

Special activities include self-guided tours; free twilight
concerts in the summer on Thursdays after 7; Scottish Fair
the last weekend in September.

Fort Washington Park

*13551 Ft. Washington Road, Ft. Washington, MD (301-763-4600) -
www.nps.gov/fowa. Take the Washington Beltway (I-495) to Indian Head
Highway; continue for three miles and turn right onto Fort Washington
Road; to park entrance. Parking for cars and buses on-site.*

The present Fort Washington Park is a 341-acre natural area
along the Potomac River. A large masonry Civil War Fort, it
was completed in 1824 as the only permanent fortification
built to defend the Nation's Capital. It is an outstanding
example of early 19th-century coastal defense with its 45-foot
high stone and brick walls sitting on a hillside above the
Potomac River, and offers an excellent upriver view of
Washington, D.C. After viewing the movie in the Visitor
Center and touring the Fort, you can enjoy a picnic lunch on
the grounds. Features include trails, playgrounds, picnic
areas, and other recreational and educational opportunities.

- Open daily from 9-4:30. Closed Thanksgiving,
  Christmas, and New Years Day.
- Three-day pass, $5 per vehicle; students free.
  Fee waiver for prearranged educational field trips.
- Stroller and wheelchair accessible.
- Recommended for children age ten and older.
- Fishing, Hiking, Picnicking.

Fredericksburg and Spotsylvania National Military Park

120 Chatham Lane, Fredericksburg, VA (540-310-0802, 540-373-6122) - **www.nps.gov/frsp/vc.htm**. *Take the Washington Beltway (I-495) to I-95 south to Fredericksburg, (Highway 3); follow National Park Service signs.*

This national military park represents three years of war during the height of the Confederacy as well as the beginning of the final campaign of the Civil War where commanders Robert E. Lee and Ulysses S. Grant first met on the field of battle. Two visitors centers include museum exhibits, paintings, and audio-visual programs. There are four Civil War battlefields to tour, self-guided auto tours with numerous maps, and walking trails.

- Two visitors centers open daily, 9-5.
- $4 per person, children under age 17 free. Groups should call in advance.
- Wheelchair accessibility in the Chancellorsville Visitor Center and Fredericksburg Visitor Center.
- VA TimeTravlers Site, Hiking, Picnicking.

Manassas National Battlefield Park

6511 Sudley Road, Manassas, VA (703-361-1339) - **www.nps .gov/mana**. *Take the Washington Beltway (I-495) to I-66 west to Route 234 north. The Visitor Center is 0.5 miles north of exit.*

This park commemorates one of the first battles of the Civil War in 1861. The Visitors Center features a museum with a self-activating map program and a slide show every half hour. Ranger-guided tours are given during the summer, when the stone house is also open.

- Open daily. In winter, 8:30-5. Closed Thanksgiving and Christmas.
- Adults, age 17 and older, $3; children, free. Pass is good for three days.
- Wheelchair Accessible.
- VA TimeTravlers site.

Special activities include Ranger guided tours during Summer Anniversary Living History programs (July and August).

Regional Parks and Playgrounds

Algonkian Regional Park

*47001 Fairway Drive, Sterling, VA (703-450-4655, 703-430-7683-schedule and fees, 703-450-4655-rentals) - **www.nvrpa.org /algonkian**. Take the Washington Beltway (I-495) to Route 7 west; continue about 11 miles to Cascades. Located at the Loudoun-Fairfax county line. Parkway north; drive three miles to park entrance.*

Located on the Potomac shore, this 800-acre park features a boat-launching ramp that provides public access to the wide **Seneca Lake** section of the Potomac River. Picnic tables are scattered under trees along the shoreline and covered shelters may be reserved for group picnics. There is also a snack bar on-site. **Twelve riverfront cottages** with three, four, or five bedrooms are available for rent as well as a Meeting Center/ Clubhouse. Visitors can enjoy fishing on the Potomac or playing miniature golf. In addition, there is an 18-hole, par-72 golf course. Also see, Downpour at Algonkian Regional Park, on page 206.

- Park is open daily, dawn to dusk.
- **Downpour Water Park** open daily, Memorial Day weekend-Labor Day.
- Miniature Golf open April-October. Hours vary.
- Meeting Center and Clubhouse are available for rent.
- Golf Course, Birthday Parties, Athletic Fields, Fishing, Hiking, Restaurant/Snack Bar, Swimming, Wheelchair Accessible - paved nature trails.
- Riverfront vacation cottages available for rent, 703-450-4655.
- Boat and RV storage, boat ramp.
- Picnic shelter rentals, 703-352-5900.

Allen Pond Park

3330 Northview Drive, Bowie, MD (301-262-6200, 301-809-2314) -
***www.cityofbowie.org**. Allen Pond is located off Route 197, south of Route 50. Take Route 50 eastbound to Exit 11 (Route 197 south); turn right at light at Northview Drive; go one mile to the park.*

Allen Pond Park offers a wide variety of activities guaranteed to make for a fun-filled day. Enjoy a picnic; play volleyball, softball, basketball, and horseshoes; play at Opportunity Park; go for a hike; and end the day with a sunset concert in the amphitheater (Sundays at 7 p.m., Memorial Day weekend-Labor Day weekend).

- Boat rentals, 11-7; weekends, May and September; daily, Memorial Day-Labor Day. Opportunity Park open daily, 8:30 a.m.-dusk.
- Bowie Ice Arena - open for skating July 4-April 30, (301) 809-3090.
- Allen Pond is the home of Opportunity Park, a 100% handicapped-accessible project including a tot lot, playground, fitness cluster, sensory trails, and stocked fishing pond.
- Biking, Fishing, Hiking, Picnicking, Playgrounds.

Special activities include Bowiefest the first Saturday in June, British Car Day, the fourth Sunday in June, a 4th of· July celebration in July, Antique Car Show the third Saturday in August, and an Art Expo the first Saturday in October.

Audrey Moore/Wakefield Park and Recreation Center

*8100 Braddock Road, Annandale, VA (703-329-7080) - **www.county fairfax.gov.parks**. Take the Washington Beltway (I-495) to Braddock Road west; continue to park entrance on right.*

Wakefield's 290 acres encompass both indoor and outdoor recreational facilities, including 11 lighted tennis courts, a lighted practice court, and shuffleboard. The indoor facility features a 50-meter pool, sauna and showers, weight room, gymnasium, dance and exercise rooms, game room, and courts for handball, squash, and racquetball. The 2,600 square foot mural in the pool area depicts a marvelous underwater world, including submerged towers of Atlantis. Visitors also enjoy the arts and crafts rooms as well as pottery and photography labs.

Nearby is Wakefield Chapel, which was built in 1899 as an affiliate of the Methodist church. The chapel can be rented for appropriate community activities. Call 703-321-7081 for information.

- Open Monday-Friday 5 a.m.-10 p.m.
- Pool is open Monday-Friday, 6 a.m.-9:30 p.m.; Saturdays, 7 a.m.-8 p.m.; lap lanes and classes, 9-noon; open swim, noon-6.
- Adults $5.50; youth (5-18, students, and seniors 60+) $3.75.
- Wheelchair Accessible.
- Picnicking, Swimming, Tennis.

Bluemont Park

601 North Manchester Street, Arlington, VA (703-358-6525, 703-358-4747). From Rosslyn, take Wilson Boulevard to left on North Manchester Street to park entrance.

Park facilities include basketball courts, baseball diamonds, athletic fields, lighted tennis courts (703-358-4747), and a soccer and softball area. There are also picnic areas with grills, playground equipment, and bicycle trails. The park connects to Four Mile Run bike trail. Bluemont's two best features are the nine-hole disc golf course and its stream, which is stocked for trout fishing at the end of March.

- Open daily, dawn to dusk (a half-hour before sunrise to a half-hour after sunset).
- Athletic Fields, Biking, Fishing, Hiking, Picnicking, Playgrounds, Tennis.

Brambleton Regional Park 🔆

Brambleton Regional Park Golf Course, 42180 Ryan Road, Ashburn, VA (703-327-3403) - www.nvrpa.org/brambleton.htm. Take the Washington Beltway (I-495) to Route 7 west toward Leesburg. Turn right on Belmont Ridge Road (Route 659). Drive seven miles and turn right on Ryan Road (Route 772). Continue for 1 mile to the entrance on the right.

Brambleton Regional Park features a championship 18-hole par-72 golf course, with a variety of challenging holes in the scenic woods and water holes, large bunkers, and plush putting greens. Discounted play after 2 p.m.

- Open, weather permitting, all year long.
- Green Fees for resident members.
- March-November is $23.75 (9 holes), or $37 (18 holes); Friday to Sunday and Holidays and $19.75 (9 holes), or $30 (18 holes) Monday - Thursday.
- December - February $19.75 (9 holes), or $30 (18 holes).

- Seniors (60 and older) and Juniors (15 and younger) fees are available Monday-Thursday only and are $16.75 (9 holes), and $24 (18 holes).
- Discounted play after 2 p.m. Call or check the web site for current fees.
- National Recreation and Park Association Ahrens Institute (NRPA National Headquarters).
- Tournaments can be scheduled with a minimum of 24 players Monday though Wednesday.
- Driving Range, Professional Instructions, and Pro Shop.

Special activities – see web site: www.teetimes.com.

Bull Run Regional Park

*7700 Bull Run Drive, Centreville, VA (703-631-0550, 703-631-0552, pool) - **www.nvrpa.org/bullrunpark.html**. Take the Washington Beltway (I-495) to I-66 west; exit on Route 29 west (Centreville); continue three miles to park signs.*

This park, deep in Civil War battlefield country, has 1,000 untouched acres of woods, fields, and streams. It is a sanctuary for small animals and a wide variety of birds. A half-acre outdoor fantasy pool complex is one of its chief attractions. The park offers a colorful new playground, miniature and disc golf, open play fields, tent and tent-trailer camping sites, picnic areas with grills, and some 18 miles of bridle paths. The "Blue Bell Walk" is a treat in spring when many wild flowers are in bloom. A sporting clays course, skeet and trap shooting gallery, and indoor archery range help make this a park rich in activities to please virtually all interests.

- Open daily, dawn to dusk, mid-March to Thanksgiving. Sporting clays, skeet and trap shooting, and archery open all year.
- Access to the 18-mile Bull Run Occoquan Trail.
- $4 per car; $8 per vehicle with ten or more persons.
- Snack bar is located at the pool.
- Picnic Shelter rentals, 703-352-5900.
- Appropriate for preschool age children.
- Athletic Fields, Camping, Disk Golf, Hiking, Miniature Golf, Picnicking, Playgrounds, Snack Bar, Swimming, Wheelchair Accessible.

Special activities include musical events, craft fairs, and a drive-through animated holiday lights show in December.

Burke Lake Park

*Fairfax County Park Authority, 7315 Ox Road, Fairfax Station, VA (703-323-6601) - **www.co/fairfax.va.us/parks**. Take the Washington Beltway (I-495) to Braddock Road west; continue to left on Burke Lake Road (Route 645); proceed five miles to left on Ox Road (Route 123); park is on left.*

Rent a rowboat, fish, or follow the trails around this 888-acre park. The marina rents boats and sells bait for fishing (spring-fall) in the 218-acre lake. This park has a five-mile walking trail, over 150 wooded campsites, and a camp store. For younger children, the park offers a miniature train, an old-fashioned carousel, a snack bar and ice cream parlor, and a playground. Picnic areas are plentiful in wooded spots. There is also an 18-hole, par-3 golf course (703-323-1641) and an 18-hole, disc golf course.

- Open daily, dawn to dusk.
- Admission fee per car for non-residents of county.
- Picnic areas with grills, playgrounds, and fishing pier accessible to persons with disabilities.
- Wheelchair access to fishing pier.
- Appropriate for preschool age children.
- Boating, Camping, Fishing, Hiking, Picnicking, Playgrounds, Restaurant/Snack Bar.

Cabin John Regional Park

*7400 Tuckerman Lane, Potomac, MD (301-299-0024) - **www.mncpppc.org**. Take the Washington Beltway (I-495) to Old Georgetown Road; go north to left on Tuckerman Lane; continue to the park's entrance just past Westlake Drive on the left.*

Cabin John Park is the place to go for lots of climbing, sliding, and swinging fun. The 525-acre park features **Adventure Playland**, a large play unit designed to encourage creative play on ropes, ladders, and tube slides; hiking trails through the woods; and a miniature train that offers a brief, pleasant trip through a wooded portion of the park (open daily in the summer, weekends and holidays in April and September).

Nearby, the park offers many other recreational facilities such as indoor and outdoor tennis courts (301-365-2440); ice skating (301-365-2446); handball courts; volleyball court; a lighted baseball field - Shirley Povich Field; five softball fields (three lighted); a camping area with seven sites (301-299-0034); and picnic areas with tables, grills, and shelters (301-495-2525). The park is also home to the **Locust Grove Nature Center** (see page 149).

- Open daily, dawn to dusk. Closed Thanksgiving, Christmas, and New Year's Day.
- Appropriate for preschool age children.
- Birthday Parties, Athletic Fields, Camping, Hiking, Picnicking, Playgrounds, Skating, Snack Bar, Tennis.

Special activities include Summer Twilight Concerts, June-August.

Cameron Run Regional Park and Great Waves Water Park

*4001 Eisenhower Avenue, Alexandria, VA (703-960-0767) - **www.nvrpa. org**. Take the Washington Beltway (I-495) to the Eisenhower Connector (exit 3A), turn right at traffic light onto Eisenhower Avenue and drive one-half mile to the park on the left.*

This water-oriented park is tremendous fun for both children and adults. Cameron Run features a wave pool and a 3-flume, 40-foot high water slide. The wave pool is most appropriate for strong swimmers. Children under 13 must be accompanied by a person age 16 or older. Younger children will enjoy the creative play pool featuring giant water creatures, rain jets, and a shallow body flume. There is also a very shallow wading pool for the youngest children. Cameron Run has a sand volleyball court, batting cage, miniature golf course, picnic shelter for rent (703-352-5900), and a fishing pond.

- The pool is open from Memorial Day-Labor Day, 10-8 on weekends (call for weekday hours). Miniature golf and batting cages open from March-October, weather permitting. Call for hours.
- Daily fees for the wave pool are $9 per person under age 12 and over age 60, $11 per adult. Children under age two are free. Special admission after 5 p.m. on weekdays and season passes are available. Mini golf for swimming patrons is $2.75; ages 13-59, $4.50 per round; Seniors (60 and over) and Children 12 and under $3.50; or $8.5 per person all day. Batting cages, $1 for 16 balls.
- Restaurant/Snack Bar, Wheelchair Accessible.

Candy Cane City

Located at Beach Drive at East Leland Street, Chevy Chase, MD (301-495-2525). Take the Washington Beltway (I-495) to Connecticut Avenue south; to East-West Highway; go left on East-West Highway to Beach Drive; right on Meadowbrook Lane, past stables to park entrance.

With a variety of new equipment to crawl through, slide down, climb on, and swing from, the Candy Cane City playground at Meadowbrook Park is a crowd pleaser for the very young. The name refers to the long ago time when the playground equipment was painted with red and white stripes. The elasticrete underneath helps cushion the feet and protect against injury. The adjacent recreation center, like other Montgomery County park centers, has ball fields, tennis courts, a well-equipped building, covered picnic area, and a year-round activity program. Shaded play areas and water fountain.

- Open daily, dawn to dusk.
- Parking is available in a small lot on Beach Drive, off East-West Highway at Leland Street corner. Access to park is across a small footbridge over Rock Creek.
- Athletic Fields, Picnicking, Playgrounds, Tennis.

Chinquapin Center and Park

*3210 King Street, Alexandria, VA (703-931-1127) - **ci.alexandria.va.us/ rpca**. Take the Washington Beltway (I-495) I-395 to King Street (Route 7) east exit; turn right onto Chinquapin Park Drive; entrance on left.*

Chinquapin Park is a 44-acre park in the heart of Alexandria. It has a nature area and fitness trail, picnic tables, basketball and volleyball courts, lighted tennis courts, play module (handicapped accessible), and large open fields.

The center offers a 25-meter indoor swimming pool with separate diving well, 3 racquetball courts, a fitness room, saunas, lighted outdoor tennis courts, a snack bar, and activity rooms.

- Center and Rixse Pool: Open weekdays, 6 a.m.-10 p.m.; weekends, 8-8. Call for holiday hours.
- Center and Rixse Pool: General admission fee covers use of pool, sauna, and fitness rooms. Non-residents, $8; city residents, adults age 16-59, $5, children 4-15 and senior citizens (60 plus), $3. Discount passes and group rates available.
- Tennis Reservations can be made one hour prior to schedule playing time Monday-Friday from 6 a.m.-10 p.m. and Saturday, Sunday, and holidays from 8-8.

- Volleyball - 703-931-6333.
- Three parking areas.
- Birthday Parties, Hiking, Picnicking, Snack Bar, Swimming, Tennis, Wheelchair Accessible.

Special activities include birthday parties, racquetball, fitness room, saunas for women and men, nature trail and park, garden plots, outdoor basketball and volleyball courts.

East Potomac Park

National Park Service, 1100 Ohio Drive, SW, Washington, DC (202-619-7222). Turn off Maine Avenue, SW, near the 14th Street Bridge and follow signs. Or follow Ohio Drive from the Lincoln Memorial.

East Potomac Park is a one and a half mile long finger of land between the Washington channel and the Potomac River. The path along the sea wall is fine for strolling, biking, and fishing. Kids will enjoy an unusual hands-on statue, "The Awakening," by J. Seward Johnson, which resembles a giant about to arise from the ground. A playground is nearby. Other attractions include an outdoor pool, tennis, miniature golf, a driving range, and two 18-hole golf courses. Hains Point, at the southern edge of the park, is a pleasant place to stay cool on a hot summer day. No matter how steamy the rest of the city is, there is always a breeze at Hains Point.

- Open daily, dawn to dusk.
- Outdoor tennis courts, 202-554-5962.
- Outdoor swimming pool, 202-863-1309.
- Golf and miniature golf, 202-863-9007.
- Biking, Miniature Golf, Picnicking, Playgrounds, Swimming, Tennis.

Fairland Recreational Park/
Fairland Regional Park

Fairland Recreational Park, *3928 Greencastle Road, Fairland, MD
(301-774-6625)* - ***www.mc-mncppc.org/parks***. *From the Washington
Beltway (I-495) to Route 29 North. Right on Briggs Chaney Road. Left on
Robey. Park is at the end of the road. There are multiple entrances located
behind the fields.* Fairland Regional Park, *13950 Old Gunpowder Road,
Laurel, MD (301-699-2407, 301-699-2544 TTY)* - ***www.pgparks.com/
parks/fairland.html***. *From Interstate 95, take exit 29 toward Beltsville.
At first light, make a left onto Old Gunpoweder Road. Follow Old
Gunpowder Road for approximately 1.25 miles. Fairland Regional Park is
on the left.*

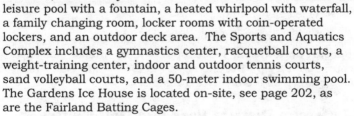

This bi-county park
includes more than 150
acres of parkland in
Prince George's County
and 322 acres in Montgomery
County, and features attractions for
a variety of recreational interests.
Trails for walking and biking run
through wooded hills and near
streams. The aquatics center
includes a heated, 50-meter, indoor
pool with a moveable floor,
a heated, indoor 25-yar
leisure pool with a fountain, a heated whirlpool with waterfall,
a family changing room, locker rooms with coin-operated
lockers, and an outdoor deck area. The Sports and Aquatics
Complex includes a gymnastics center, racquetball courts, a
weight-training center, indoor and outdoor tennis courts,
sand volleyball courts, and a 50-meter indoor swimming pool.
The Gardens Ice House is located on-site, see page 202, as
are the Fairland Batting Cages.

- Aquatic Center: 301-206-2464 (recorded information);
  301-206-2359 (general inquires); TTY 301-317-1340.

- Athletic Complex: 301-953-0030; TTY 301-490-4750.

- Tennis Bubble: 301-953-0030; TTY 301-490-4750.

- The Gardens Ice House: 301-953-0100; 410-792-4947;
  301-699-2544- TTY.

- Fairland Batting Cages (301-498-2243) offers 9 state-of-
  the-art lighted batting cages for softball, baseball, and
  fast pitch. $1 for 16 pitches. Open April-October.
  Located at 13950 Old Gunpowder Road, Laurel, MD,
  pgparks.com/places/sportsfac/specialized.html.

- Birthday Parties, Athletic Fields, Batting Cages,
  Picnicking, Playgrounds, Restaurant/Snack Bar,
  Wheelchair Accessible.

Hadley's Park

*Falls Road Park on Falls Road at the intersection of Falls Chapel Way, Potomac, MD (301-424-2112) - **www.hadleyspark.org**. Take the Washington Beltway (I-495) to I-270 north; exit at Falls Road (Potomac); park is on the right after the second traffic light.*

Hadley's Park is a one-acre, fully-accessible playground for children with disabilities. The one-acre park is designed so children of all abilities can have fun and challenge themselves on its creative play course, featuring a soft-play surface ideal for roller-skates, bikes, and wheel-chairs.

- Appropriate for preschool age children.
- Also located at Dulles Town Center, Sterling VA.

Hemlock Overlook Regional Park

*13220 Yates Ford Road, Clifton, VA (703-993-2059) - **www.nvrpa.org/ hemlock**. Take the Washington Beltway (I-495) to I-66 west to Route 123 south. Turn right on Clifton Road; go 3.7 miles and left on Yates Ford Road.*

Hemlock Overlook is an outdoor center offering a variety of outdoor and team development programs for students, teachers, businesses, teams, and churches. Activities are open to the public and special groups by reservation. Trails may be used without reservations.

- Open year-round.
- Field Trips, Camping, Ropes Course.

Special activities includes rope courses, outdoor challenge course with a zip wire, and access to the 17-mile Bull Run-Occoquan Trail (no bikes) is available.

Jefferson District Park and Golf Course

7900 Lee Highway, Falls Church, VA (703-573-0444). Take the Washington Beltway (I-495) to Route 50 west; turn right on Gallows Road; right on Route 29-211 (Lee Highway) to park entrance on left at Hyson Lane.

This 60-acre park features a 9-hole executive golf course (par 35) and an 18-hole miniature golf course.

- Open daily, dawn to dusk.
- Lighted outdoor tennis courts, April-October. Courts can be reserved for a fee.
- Miniature golf, tennis, and basketball facilities are lighted until 11 p.m., April 1-October 31.
- Picnicking, Restaurant/Snack Bar

Special activities include a hayride in October and a junior golf tournament for 8-16 year olds in June.

Lake Accotink Park

*7500 Lake Accotink Park Road, Springfield, VA (703-569-7120) - **www.co. fairfax.va.us/parks/;accotink**. Take the Washington Beltway (I-495) to Braddock Road east. Turn right on Backlick, then turn right on Highland, and follow the right fork to Lake Accotink Road. Follow signs to the park.*

The 77-acre lake is popular with fishing and boating enthusiasts. Rent a canoe, pedal boat, or rowboat, or take a ride around the lake on a tour boat. Boat launching and trout fishing are allowed from March to May and October to December. On land, children and adults enjoy miniature golf, nature walks, and biking trails. The park also features a carousel, playground, miniature golf, lovely picnic areas with tables, grills, and shelters (by reservation), a baseball field, and a basketball court.

- Open daily, dawn to dusk.
- Lucky Duck Miniature Golf, open 10 a.m.-dusk from Memorial Day to Labor Day.
- Appropriate for preschool age children.
- Birthday Parties, Hiking, Playgrounds.

Lake Fairfax Park

*1400 Lake Fairfax Drive, Reston, VA (703-471-5415) - **www.co.fairfax. a.us/parks**. Take the Washington Beltway (I-495) to Route 7 west; continue about six miles and turn left on Route 606. Turn left on Lake Fairfax Drive and follow it to the park entrance.*

This 476-acre park offers a 15-acre lake for boating (boat rentals and excursion pontoon boat rides available) and fishing, as well as a new water park, **The Water Mine Swimmin' Hole**. Plan to spend an entire day at Lake Fairfax Park, starting with a few hours at the innovative pool with its numerous water slides and rambling river, followed by a ride on the miniature train and carousel. Rent a pedal boat and enjoy some quiet time on the lake, go for a hike on a nature trail, and enjoy a family picnic near playgrounds.

- Open daily, dawn to dusk.
- Admission fee weekends and holidays.
  No fee for Fairfax County residents.
- Water Mine (admission includes carousel and tour boat), children, $9.00; adults, $11.50.
- Family camping, March-November, reservations accepted.
- Appropriate for preschool age children.
- Birthday Parties, Athletic Fields, Boating, Camping, Fishing, Hiking, Picnicking, Playgrounds, Swimming.

Lee District Park
and Robert E. Lee Recreation Center

6601 Telegraph Road, Alexandria, VA (703-922-9841). Take the Washington Beltway (I-495) to Telegraph Road south; go three miles to park entrance on left.

The recreation center boasts a 50-meter indoor swimming pool with a water slide, fitness center, gymnasium, four racquetball/handball courts, saunas, and meeting rooms. In addition to the train and carousel, the park features playing fields, tennis courts, a tot lot, softplay indoor playground, a sand volleyball court, an amphitheater, and hiking trails.

- Open daily, dawn to dusk.
- Birthday Parties, Athletic Fields, Hiking, Picnicking, Playgrounds, Swimming, Tennis.

Special activities include fireworks on the 4th of July and a Halloween Train Ride in October.

Montrose Park

Located on R Street at Avon Place, NW, in Georgetown, Washington, DC (202-895-6000). Take Wisconsin Avenue north from Georgetown to right turn on R Street. Park is on the left.

Open space provides room for games at this popular Rock Creek Park location, featuring outdoor tennis courts (no reservations needed), a boxwood maze, a playground, and picnic tables. This is a nice place to visit after a trip to Dumbarton Oaks (see page 44).

- Open daily, dawn to dusk.
- Picnicking, Playgrounds, Tennis.

Occoquan Regional Park

*9751 Ox Road, Lorton, VA (703-690-2121, 703-352-5900, picnic shelter rental) - **www.nvrpa.org/occoquan.htm**. Across the water from the Town of Occoquan, VA, on the Fairfax County shore. Take the Washington Beltway (I-495) to I-95 south to Route 123 north; follow for one and a half miles to the park's entrance on the right.*

This spacious 400-acre park is scenically located on the Occoquan River. The park offers 400 acres of recreational space, a touch of the past with its historic brick kilns and reminders of the women suffragists imprisoned here in the early 1900s. Features include: Batting cage, picnic tables, and walking trails.

- Open mid-March through November, dawn to dusk.
- Fee for batting cage and boat launching.
- Boat launching ramps are available.

- Picnic shelter and gazebo rentals: 703-352-5900.
- Soccer, Softball, and baseball fields
- Stroller and wheelchair accessible on paved trails.
- Athletic Fields, Batting Cages, Biking, Boating, Fishing, Hiking, Picnicking, Snack Bar.

Pohick Bay Regional Park and Golf Course

6501 Pohick Bay Drive, Lorton, VA (703-339-6104, 703-339-6102, pool) - **www.nvrpa.org**. *Take the Washington Beltway (I-495) to I-95 south to Lorton exit; turn left on Lorton Road; right on Armistead; right on Route 1; left on Gunston Road. Continue 1 mile to golf course on left; Go three miles to main park on the left.*

"Pohick," the Algonquin Indian word for "the water place," is an apt description of this 1000-acre waterside park. Visitors can swim, boat, canoe, kayak, and fish. Other activities include family camping (hot showers available), flying kites, miniature and disc golf, and picnicking. Golfers should find the 18-hole, par-72 course a challenge. The park also features a four-mile bridle path, hiking trails, and an observation deck that overlooks the Potomac River. Most of the area around the park is maintained as a wildlife refuge, and the recreation areas are planned to minimize the disturbance to the animals, especially the nesting area of the bald eagle.

- Open daily, dawn to dusk. Outdoor swimming pool open Memorial Day weekend to Labor Day. Mini and disc golf are open April-October. Hours vary.
- $6 per car; $10 per vehicle with ten or more persons.
- Lots throughout 1,000-acre park.
- 18-hole, par-72 golf course: 703-339-8585. Driving range, pro shop, snack bar, lessons and tournament packages.
- "Canoe the Marsh" day and evening trips available. For schedule and fees, call 703-528-5406.
- Family campsites (no reservations) and camp store. For information, call 703-339-6104.
- Boat launching, sailboat and pedal boat rentals.
- Family campground reservations available April-October: 703-339-6104.
- Group campground reservations: 703-352-5900.
- Marina building has an observation deck & snack bar.
- Nature trails and bridle paths.
- Pool is wheelchair accessible, trails are not.

- Birthday Parties, Boating, Camping, Canoe and Kayak Rentals, Disk Golf, Fishing, Hiking, Miniature Golf, Picnicking, Swimming, Wheelchair Accessible.

Special activities include spacious outdoor pool open Memorial Day weekend to Labor Day; Easter Egg Carnival.

South Germantown Recreational Park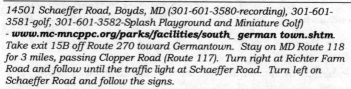

*14501 Schaeffer Road, Boyds, MD (301-601-3580-recording), 301-601-3581-golf, 301-601-3582-Splash Playground and Miniature Golf) - **www.mc-mncppc.org/parks/facilities/south_german town.shtm**. Take exit 15B off Route 270 toward Germantown. Stay on MD Route 118 for 3 miles, passing Clopper Road (Route 117). Turn right at Richter Farm Road and follow until the traffic light at Schaeffer Road. Turn left on Schaeffer Road and follow the signs.*

South Germantown Recreational Park's Central Park features two championship miniature golf courses and a splash playground with a tumbling buckets waterfall, rain tree, water tunnel, and 36' water maze. The two 18-hole putting courses provide real challenges with water features, sand traps, rough turf and natural obstacles that are part of the unique design. (The miniature golf season may extend beyond October, weather permitting.) National Youth Soccer League Championships games and some professional games are held here.

- Open end of May to early September; hours vary by season; check by phone or web for details.
- Splash Playground, $3.50; Miniature Golf-18 holes, $5 per person.
- Lockers and cubbies, showers, dressing room, restrooms, and vending area.
- Huge wooden structure playground.
- Birthday parties can be held in the indoor facility.
- Swimming, Soccer, Ball Fields.

Tuckahoe Park and Playfield

2400 Sycamore Street, Arlington, VA (703-358-3317, 703-358-4747 for reservations). From I-66, take Exit 69 at Sycamore Street/Falls Church; make a left onto Sycamore Street; follow Sycamore Street north past Lee Highway; park is on the left.

This unique, creative playground features towers, tall slides, and a maze with special interest for 7-12 year olds. This wooded, well-loved park also has softball fields, a soccer area, lighted outdoor tennis courts, and picnic tables.

- Open daily, dawn to dusk.
- Metrorail Orange line (Falls Church).
- Athletic Fields, Picnicking, Tennis.

Upton Hill Regional Park

*6060 Wilson Boulevard, Arlington, VA (703-534-3437) - **www.nvr pa.org**.
Take the Washington Beltway (I-495) to Route 50 east; at Seven Corners
take Wilson Boulevard east to the park's entrance at Patrick Henry Drive.*

This park offers visitors a woodland oasis in the heart of the
most populated area of Northern Virginia. Upton Hill has a
large swimming pool complex and woodland nature trails.
The popular miniature golf course in a garden setting features
one of the longest miniature golf holes in the world. Other
attractions feature a gazebo, picnic areas, batting cage, Bocce
ball court, horseshoe pit, and a playground.

- The park is open daily, dawn to dusk; the pool is open
  Memorial Day weekend-Labor Day, daily. Call for
  schedule and fees.

- Metrorail Orange line (East Falls Church), one mile.

- Batting Cages, Hiking, Miniature Golf, Picnicking,
  Swimming, Wheelchair Accessible.

Watkins Regional Park

*301 Watkins Park Drive, Upper Marlboro, MD (301-218-6870) - **www.pg
parks.com/places/parks/watkins.html**. Take the Washington Beltway
(I-495) to Central Avenue east (Route 214) exit; follow Route 124 through
Largo; turn right on Route 193. Park is on the right.*

This 437-acre park offers a wide variety of activities from
hiking and biking trails to a carousel and miniature golf to
camping and athletic facilities - something to please every
family member! The extensive playground has brightly
colored equipment gentle enough for toddlers and challenging
enough for 5-7 year olds. Additionally, Watkins Regional Park
is home to Watkins Nature Center and Old Maryland Farm.

Watkins Nature Center, located within Watkins Regional
Park, offers indoor and outdoor ponds, native wildlife
displays, a children's Discovery Corner, butterfly and herb
gardens, six miles of marked trails, and a puppet theater.
Open Monday-Saturday, 8:30-5; Sundays and holidays, 11-4,
this Nature Center is only a five-minute walk from picnic
areas and the playground. Call for a schedule of children's
nature programs and family special events. Wildlife birthday
parties and auditorium rentals are recent additions.

Also located in the park (behind the train station) is **Old
Maryland Farm** (301-218-6700), a great place for the whole
family. The farm features animals (from hogs to hens), herb
and vegetable gardens, antique farm equipment, educational
exhibits, and year-round volunteer opportunities.

- Open daily, 7:30 a.m.-dusk.

- Indoor and outdoor tennis courts and hitting wall. Free lighting for evening outdoor play. For fees and reservations, call 301-249-9325.
- Picnic tables, grills, group areas, and athletic fields. For fees and reservations, call 301-918-8111.
- Camping area with 34 campsites, comfort stations, and showers. For fees and permits, call 301-918-8111.
- Miniature train ride, carousel, and miniature golf open late May-Labor Day.
- Appropriate for preschool age children.
- Birthday Parties, Athletic Fields, Biking, Hiking, Playgrounds, Restaurant/Snack Bar.

Special activities include the Winter Festival of Lights from late November to January, dusk to 9:30 p.m.

Wheaton Regional Park

2000 Shorefield Road, Wheaton, MD (301-680-3803, 301-946-7035). Take the Washington Beltway (I-495) to Georgia Avenue north; right on Shorefield Road to park entrance.

This 536-acre park is a great favorite with area residents. The park abounds with child-pleasing features, including a two-mile miniature train ride, a carousel, a four-mile paved bicycle trail (also excellent for strollers and wheelchairs, and skaters), two-mile hiking trails, fishing, ice skating, ball fields, horseback riding stables, and picnic areas.

Shorefield Area: Picnic shelters for up to 40 people may be reserved by call 301-495-2525. Features include: cooking grills, picnic tables, an Adventure Playground, restrooms and drinking fountains are operational from April-October.

Also located in the Shorefield Area is Pine Lake, a five-acre lake with fishing and picnicking; the miniature train that will take you on a ten-minute tour of the park; and the restored 1915 Hershel Spillman carousel. Call 301-946-6396 or 301-942-6703 April-September.

Glenallan Area: Glenallan Area has the **Brookside Nature Center and Brookside Gardens**, a 50-acre public display garden and riding stables where you can find riding lessons for novice though advanced levels at the indoor riding arena or the outdoor facilities.

See Brookside Nature Center, page 145 and Brookside Gardens, page 165 for separate listings.

F. Frank Rubin Athletic Complex: The F. Frank Rubin Athletic Complex has four softball fields and two baseball fields for day and evening use. Permits must be obtained from the Park Permit Office to use softball and baseball fields. One outdoor basketball court and four handball courts are available on a first-come, first-served basis. For more information, call: 301-495-2525. Six outdoor tennis courts are lighted for day and evening use. There is also an indoor tennis facility with an additional six courts for year-round play. Indoor courts must be reserved. For more information, call 301-649-4049.

The athletic complex also features the Wheaton Indoor Ice Arena. Open year round with an assortment of programs offered including lessons and rental time. Sessions are available for the general public, adults only, and family time. Rental skates are available. Call 301-649-3640 for more information on fees and information about inline skating.

- Open daily, sunrise-sunset. The carousel and train ride operate weekends and school holidays only in April and September, daily May-August. Call 301-946-6396 for schedules and fees. Brookside Nature Center is open 9-5 Tuesday through Saturday and 1-5 p.m. Sunday. Closed on Monday and major holidays.

- The miniature train operates April-September (weather permitting), 301-946-6396 or 301-942-6703.

- Shorefield Area: Picnic and Playground, Pine Lake, Miniature Train, and Carousel.

- Glenallan Area: Brookside Nature Center, Brookside Gardens and horseback riding stables.

- F. Frank Rubin Athletic Complex: Outdoor sports, tennis and skating.

- Many of the facilities accommodate people with disabilities. The miniature train and Adventure Playground are designed with unique equipment to assist those with mobility challenges. Brookside Nature Center, Brookside Gardens, picnic areas, and restrooms are accessible.

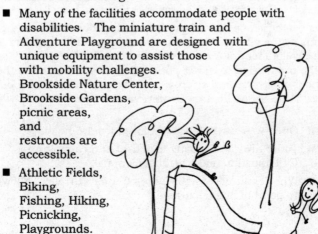

- Athletic Fields, Biking, Fishing, Hiking, Picnicking, Playgrounds.

Nature Centers, Planetariums and Sanctuaries

Arlington Public Schools Planetarium

1426 North Quincy Street, Arlington, VA (703-228-6070). Take the Washington Beltway (I-495); take I-66 east to the Glebe Road exit South. Planetarium is located on the right side before 14th street.

Used primarily for school programs during the day, this modern planetarium also offers a variety of public programs on weekends throughout the year. "Stars Tonight" is usually held on the first Monday of each month at 7:30 p.m. Call for details.

- Friday and Saturday programs, 7:30 p.m.; Sunday, 1:30 and 3 p.m.
- Adults, $2.50; senior citizens and children 12 and under, $1.50.
- Metrorail Orange line (Ballston).
- Field Trips, Birthday Parties, Scouts.

Beltsville Agricultural Research Center

U.S. Department of Agriculture, Beltsville, MD (301-504-8483). Take the Washington Beltway (I-495) to Route 1 north; go one and a half miles and turn right on Powder Mill Road; continue for two and a half miles to Center.

This center is one of the largest and most diversified research farms in the world. Work done here, for example, has led to the development of America's meaty Thanksgiving turkey and to the production of leaner pork. Visitors see first-hand the impact of agricultural science on our daily lives. After a brief orientation at the Visitors Center, visitors tour the facility by bus.

- Open weekdays, 8-4:30. Closed federal holidays.
- Tours are given mostly to school and camp groups. Call ahead to make arrangements.
- Wheelchair access at Visitors Center. Strollers allowed to point of bus departure.

Brookside Nature Center

*Wheaton Regional Park, 1400 Glenallan Avenue, Wheaton, MD (301-946-9071) - **www.mncpp.org**. Take the Washington Beltway (I-495) to Georgia Avenue north towards Wheaton. Drive three miles north on Georgia Avenue to Randolph Road and turn right. At the second traffic light turn right onto Glenallan Avenue. Continue on Glenallan Avenue to a 4-way stop sign. Go through the stop sign and make a right into the second entrance on the right after the stop sign.*

The nature center is a focus for local natural history with live and mounted specimens from the Washington region, hands-on nature discovery areas, an observation beehive, habitat demonstration garden, self-guided nature trail, and wildlife viewing areas. Call for information about Brookside's nature programs for children and an Educator's Guide to Programs.

- Open Tuesday-Saturday, 9-5; Sunday, 1-5.
  Closed Monday and federal holidays.
- Campfire and picnic shelter areas require a permit.
- Stroller and wheelchair accessible.
- Field Trips, Hiking, Picnicking.

Special activities include a Maple Sugaring Festival in February.

Clearwater Nature Center

Cosca Regional Park, 11000 Thrift Road, Clinton, MD (301-297-4575). Take the Washington Beltway (I-495) to Route 5 south; turn right onto Surrats Road; turn left on Brandywine Road (Route 381); right onto Thrift Road to the entrance.

Located in the Cosca Regional Park, this Nature Center features the "Natural Treasures of Prince George's County," exhibit which shows a view of life underground. Other highlights include a variety of live reptiles, birds of prey, a fish and indoor turtle pond, and other surprises. Herb and butterfly gardens allow you to explore the fully equipped lapidary laboratory. Five miles of hiking trails criss-cross the park where you can observe local wildlife at the lake and streams. Groups of 10 or more may reserve a guided tour or other programs. (See Cosca Regional Park, page 107.)

- Open Monday-Saturday, 8:30-5 and Sundays 11-4.
  Closed on some holidays.
- A half-mile paved loop winds through a forested area for easy wheelchair and stroller access.
- Hiking, Wheelchair Accessible.

Special activities include Birds of Prey Day, Prehistoric Party, theme hikes, scout badge programs.

Croydon Creek Nature Center

852 Avery Road, Rockville, MD (301-294-2752) - ww.ci.rockville.md.us. Locate within the Rockville Civic Center Park. Washington Beltway (I-495) to I-270 north to Route 28 east (Montgomery Avenue). Montgomery Avenue turns into Viers Mill Road after you cross Route 355 (Rockville Pike) for about 1 block. Follow Route 28 (left turn from Viers Mill Road). Right onto Baltimore Road. Go past the main entrance to Glenview Mansion and F. Scott Fitzgerald Theatre Civic Center. Turn left on Avery Road. Follow Avery Road to the nature center.

Take a walk and explore the field, forest and stream surrounding this nature center. An **Exhibit Room** and **Discovery Room** provide interactive fun and educational environmental exhibits for all ages.

The Discovery Room is geared for children in preschool through elementary school. Children learn about animals that live in and around Rockville, conduct research experiments, and make a picture from granite rubbing tiles. Puzzles abound.

The Exhibit Room has more for the middle school and older set. Here visitors can bird-watch through the binoculars, relax on the oak and hickory bent-wood benches, discover how to live with urban wildlife, learn about national, state and city symbols, and use a computer to learn more about bird songs and birds of prey.

- Monday-Saturday, 9-5:30; Sundays, 1-5:30. Closed New Year's Day, Memorial Day, July 4, Labor Day, Thanksgiving, and Christmas.
- Free admission, programs have fees. Call for details.
- Self-guided visits possible, but reservations are required.
- Stroller and wheelchair accessible.
- Field Trips, Hiking.

Special activities include Nature Parties offered on-site with themes tailored to fit almost any natural history theme, from meeting live animals, to a hike, to a theme designed around your child's favorite animal or outdoor activity. Parties can be conducted for any age group and can include meeting live reptiles and amphibians. Sign-up dates: For school year (September - middle of June): second Monday in August. For summer (middle of June - August): first Monday in April.

Gulf Branch Nature Center

3608 North Military Road, Arlington, VA (703-228-3403). Take the Washington Beltway (I-495) exit north to the George Washington Memorial Parkway. Exit onto Spout Run, turn right onto Lorcom Lane, right onto Nelly Custis and then merge with Military Road. Parking available on-site.

Located in a 38-acre wooded stream valley, this nature center features interpretive displays on Arlington and Virginia plants, animals, and natural history. Attractions include a Native-American display with a dugout canoe, a moderately strenuous 3/4-mile trail to the Potomac River, and an observation beehive. Educational programs are offered year round to organized groups and the general public. Picnicking is allowed in the adjoining **Old Glebe Park**. Points of interest include a stream, pond, and access to the Potomac River.

- Open Tuesday-Saturday, 10-5; Sunday, 1-5. Closed Monday and federal holidays.
- Free admission, some programs with fees.
- Metro bus (22's) from Ballston Metro.
- Not stroller or wheelchair accessible.
- VA TimeTravlers site, Hiking, Picnicking.

Hidden Oaks Nature Center

*Annandale Community Park, 7701 Royce Street, Annandale, VA (703-941-1065) - **www.fairfaxcounty.gov/parks/nature**. Take the Washington Beltway (I-495) to Little River Turnpike east (Route 236); turn left at first traffic light onto Hummer Road; proceed one half mile; turn left into Annandale Community Park; follow signs to Nature Center.*

The Nature Center focuses on the discovery of evidence of landscape changes caused by the forces of nature and man. There are seasonal displays and small live animals such as turtles and snakes. Many of the exhibits provide "hands-on" options. The surroundings, including an oak forest, woodland stream, and traces of a Civil War railroad, as well as timbering and farming lands, make for an interesting visit.

- Open weekdays except Tuesday, 9-5; Saturday-Sunday, noon-5. January-February, open daily, 12-5. Closed Thanksgiving, Christmas, and New Year's Day.
- Reservations are necessary for discovery programs and special events.
- Picnic area and tot lot in the park.
- Group tours for schools or other youth organizations.
- Appropriate for preschool age children.

Special activities include "Forest Fledgling," a program for children ages 3-5 years and their parents offering stories, crafts, nature activities, and outdoor exploration.

Hidden Pond Nature Center

*Hidden Pond Park, 8511 Greeley Boulevard, Springfield, VA (703-451-9588) - **www.co.fairfax.va.us/parks/hiddenpond**. Take the Washington Beltway (I-495) to I-95 south to Old Keen Mill Road (Rt. 644) west for 3.3 miles, left onto Greeley Blvd. (second left after Rolling Road) to park entrance at the end of the street. From Fairfax County Parkway, take Old Keene Mill Road east 2.9 miles to a right onto Greeley Blvd.*

Acres of undisturbed woodland, quiet trails, splashing streams, and a tranquil pond are just a few reasons to visit Hidden Pond Park and Nature Center. Situated along the Pohick Stream Valley, the park offers solitude and opportunities for exploration and discovery.

The Nature Center prepares the visitor for investigating and experiencing the ecology of ponds, streams, and wetlands. Exhibits include a live display of many of the inhabitants of the pond, a touch-table, a parent and child corner, and displays of "feature creatures" and current events in the natural world. The building also offers a lab/all-purpose meeting room for visiting school groups or special programs, and a small retail sales area with items for the nature lover.

Outside, there are self-guided trails which lead to the stream valley and surrounding woodlands. If treasure hunting is more your thing, the naturalists will gladly loan you nets, so you can go on your own to search in and around Hidden Pond. (Treasures must be returned to the pond before leaving.) Special events are offered year round.

- Open weekdays except Tuesday, 9-5; Saturday and Sunday, noon-5. January and February, open daily, noon-5, closed on Tuesdays. Open Thanksgiving, Christmas, and New Year's Day.
- Wide variety of programs for all ages. Group tours by reservation.
- Stroller and wheelchair accessible.
- Field Trips, Hiking, Picnicking, Playgrounds, Tennis, Wheelchair Accessible.

Howard B. Owens Science Center and Planetarium

9601 Greenbelt Road, Lanham-Seabrook, MD (301-918-8750) -
www.pgcps.org/~hbowens*. Take the Washington Beltway (I-495) to
Greenbelt Road; continue for three miles to entrance on right.*

This modern science center emphasizes participatory exhibits
and interactive programs. The Summer Science Enrichment
Program is open to preschool through high school students
on a first-come, first served basis. The center primarily
serves students of the Prince George's County Public Schools.

- Public Planetarium programs are held on the 2nd
  Friday of each month at 7:30 p.m. Other showings
  upon special request for scout groups, civic or fraternal
  organizations, and non-public school groups.
- Adults, $4; senior citizens and students in kindergarten
  through college, $2.
- Metrobus T15, T16, T17; The Bus Route 15.
- Stroller and Wheelchair Accessible.

Special activities include open house in November.

Locust Grove Nature Center

*Cabin John Regional Park, 7777 Democracy Boulevard, Bethesda, MD
(301-299-1990) -* ***www.mc-mncppc.org****. From the Washington Beltway
(I-495) take Old Georgetown Road exit north; turn left on Democracy
Boulevard; the Center is beyond Westlake Drive, next to the tennis courts.*

This Nature Center has a small collection of nature books,
games, puzzles, a tree exhibit, and some native snakes and
frogs on display. There are several wooded trails for moderate
hikes. A one-quarter-mile trail leads to a naturalist garden
and wildlife meadow. Another one-quarter-mile trail leaves
the nature center and follows numerous steps downhill to a
meadow that borders the Cabin John Creek.

- Open Tuesday-Saturday, 9-5. Closed Sunday, Monday,
  and holidays. Trails open, sunrise to sunset.
- Specially designed group programs for schools, camps,
  and families by reservation.
- Nature Center is wheelchair accessible.
- Appropriate for preschool age children.

Special activities include a variety of nature programs, such
as full moon hikes, campfires, story times, toddler programs,
bird walks, and much, much more. See The Nutshell News
for schedule.

Long Branch Nature Center

625 South Carlin Springs Road, Arlington, VA (703-228-6535)
*- **www.co. arlington.va.us/prcr/scripts/nature/longbranch.htm**.*
Take the Washington Beltway (I-495) to Route 50 west to South Carlin
Springs Road exit; turn left on South Carlin Springs Road; look for the Long
Branch Nature Center sign on the left side of the road. Park at the Nature
Center or in adjoining Glencarlyn Park.

This Nature Center is situated in a hardwood forest with
hiking and biking trails, swamp, meadow, and streams. The
Washington and Old Dominion Bike Path (see page 122)
passes through the area. The Nature Center offers many
things for children and adults to explore, including displays of
live reptiles and amphibians, an indoor turtle/fish pond,
seasonal displays, and a discovery corner for young
naturalists. Although most programs are free, reservations
are required and can be made by calling the Nature Center.

- Open Tuesday-Saturday, 10-5; Sunday, 1-5. Closed
  Monday and holidays.
- Picnic in nearby Glencarlyn Park.
- Field Trips, Playgrounds, Wheelchair Accessible.

Meadowside Nature Center

Rock Creek Regional Park, 5100 Meadowside Lane, Rockville, MD (301-924-
*5965) - **www.mncpp.org**. Take the Washington Beltway (I-495) to Georgia*
Avenue north; continue to left turn on Norbeck Road; turn right on Muncaster
Mill Road; left on Meadowside Lane.

This Nature Center is surrounded by 350 acres, including
seven and a half miles of nature trails, a lake, marsh, pond,
herb garden, raptor cage (with live owl, hawk, and turkey
vulture), two butterfly gardens, and a mid-1800s farmstead.
Inside the Center is a **Curiosity Corner Room** with a
microscope table and many other interactive activities. There
are live animal exhibits and a wildlife observation window as
well. **Legacy of the Land** is a diorama of Maryland habitats.
Kids love crawling into and sliding out of the cave and enjoy
looking at an underground cross-section of the earth, which
shows tree roots and a view into the bottom of a pond.
Summer Conservation Clubs, adult volunteer program, and
Junior Naturalist program are available.

- Open Tuesday-Saturday, 9-5; closed Sundays,
  Mondays, and federal holidays.
- Hiking, Picnicking, Wheelchair Accessible.

Special activities include programs for individuals and
families throughout the year. These programs are advertised
in the Nutshell News calendar that is available in any
MNCPPC nature center or on the web at www.mncppc.org.

National Wildlife Visitor Center, Patuxent Research Refuge

*U.S. Department of the Interior, 10901 Scarlet Tanager Loop, Laurel, MD (301-497-5760) - **patuxent.fws.gov**. Take the Washington Beltway (I-495) to the Baltimore-Washington Parkway (Route 295) north to the Beltsville / Powder Mill Road exit; turn right onto Powder Mill Road; go 1.9 miles; turn right into Visitor Center entrance. Parking on-site.*

The $18 million National Wildlife Visitor Center is one of the largest science and environmental education centers in the Department of the Interior. Interactive exhibits focus on global environmental issues, migratory bird studies, habitats, endangered species, creature life cycles, and the research tools and techniques used by scientists. The Visitor Center offers wildlife management demonstration areas and outdoor education sites for school classes. Additionally, there are hiking trails, interpretive programs, tram tours, wildlife observations, and films.

Take an interpretative tour around the refuge's Lake Reddington where you can see wildlife and evidence of wildlife activity. Learn about the habitats the refuge manages for the success of migratory birds, mammals, reptiles, amphibians, and more!

- Open daily, 10-5:30. Closed New Year's, Thanksgiving, and Christmas.
- Tram tickets $3 adult, $2 senior, and $1 child. Call to schedule group tram tours.
- Workshops for teachers.
- Facility and parts of trails are wheelchair and stroller accessible.
- Field Trips, Fishing, Hiking.

Special activities include children's education games throughout the year, crafts, refuge trail walks, and much more. Wildlife Tram Tours mid-March through mid-November. See the web site, patuxent.fws.gov, for updated program information.

Peace Park/Kunzang Palyul Chöling

18400 River Road, Poolesville, MD (301-428-8116).

Kunzang Palyul Chöling is one of largest communities of monks ordained in the Tibetan Buddhist tradition in North America. The beautiful temple complex is situated on 72 acres in rural Montgomery County, Maryland. It provides monastic living quarters for monks and nuns, a large wildlife refuge, peaceful walking trails, and 28 consecrated stupas.

The 65-acre Peace Park is comprised of six gardens in which the traditional peaceful meditation is a clockwise 30-minute walk. The Prayer Room, with its twenty-four-hour-a-day prayer vigil, is also open to the public for meditation and prayer.

- Of interest to older children, teens and adults

Rock Creek Nature Center and Planetarium

*5200 Glover Road, NW, Washington, DC (202-426-6829) - **www.nps/gov/rocr**. Take Connecticut Avenue; north to Military Road; turn right; make another right turn at Glover Road to the Nature Center.*

One of the best in the area, this Nature Center offers many exhibits of the flora and fauna of its surrounding woodland. Children find the live reptiles and beehive especially interesting. There are also two self-guided nature trails. The **Nature Discovery Room** contains hands-on activities, puppets, and books to help children learn about their environment.

An exciting part of your visit to the Nature Center is the planetarium show. The room darkens, stars appear, and the audience is transported outdoors on a clear night. The show for the younger children concentrates on the identification of major constellations and the movement of the heavenly bodies through the night sky. The later show, for older children, is divided into a study of the sky as it will appear that night and an in-depth astronomy presentation. Evening stargazing sessions, run in conjunction with the National Capital Astronomers, are held approximately once a month, May through October. Also see Rock Creek Park on page 101.

- Open daily, 9-5 Wednesday-Sunday. Closed Christmas, New Year's Day, and Thanksgiving. Planetarium shows on Saturday and Sunday at 1 p.m. for children age four and older (children must be accompanied by adults), and on Wednesdays at 4 p.m. for children age seven and older.
- Special programs available by reservation for groups of ten or more, Wednesday-Friday only. Call at least two weeks in advance.
- There are several picnic tables near the parking lot. No food or drink in the Nature Center.
- Strollers are permitted in the Nature Center, but not in the Planetarium.

Special activities include Ranger-led programs - please call or check the web site www.nps.gov/rocr for times and dates.

Rust Sanctuary
(Audubon Naturalist Society)🌞

*802 Children's Center Road, Leesburg, VA (703-669-0008) - **www.audubon naturalist.org**. Take the Washington Beltway (I-495) to Leesburg Pike west (Route 7) to Leesburg. Left on Catoctin Circle, right on Children's Center Road to Sanctuary drive, ignore the no outlet sign. Or from the D.C. Beltway to Dulles Toll Road Dulles Greenway, to Route 7 Leesburg Bypass. Go west on bypass, exit second exit (Leesburg Business - Caution: do not take 15 Business) and turn right at the traffic light. Turn at next right onto Catoctin Circle, right again at Children's Center Road, proceed to Sanctuary driveway. Parking available on-site.*

Located in Loudoun County Virginia, the Rust Sanctuary property includes a manor house, formally called Yoecomico, and 62 acres of land. Rust Sanctuary is committed to protecting the integrity of the natural area while providing opportunities and resources that encourage the discovery and appreciation of the natural world. The sanctuary protects six different kinds of habitats including: wildlife habitat gardens, meadows, hedge rows, mixed hardwood forest, pine plantation, and a pond. The manor house is equipped with offices, classrooms, meeting rooms, and a small nature center.

- Grounds open daily, dawn-dusk. Building open weekdays, 9-5; building closed weekends.
- The meeting rooms & classrooms are available for rent.
- There are picnic tables for family outings.
- Handicapped accessible restrooms.
- Hiking, Picnicking.

Special activities include regular bird walks, nature programs and seasonal events for children. The Sanctuary's trails and meadows are open daily for exploration and discovery.

U.S. Naval Observatory

*Massachusetts Avenue at 34th Street, NW, Washington, DC (202-762-1467, 800-821-8892) - **www.usno.navy.mil**. Parking is available just outside the South Gate on Observatory Circle across from the New Zealand Embassy.*

The work of the U.S. Naval Observatory consists primarily of determining the precise time and the measurements of star positions. Tours include a short movie on the Observatory, a look at the highly accurate electronic clocks and other exhibits, and an explanation of the workings of the 12-inch Alvan Clark refractor telescope. On clear nights, the tours include a look through the telescope.

- Half-hour public tours are offered on a limited basis on Monday evenings at 8:30 p.m. Reservations must be submitted 6-8 weeks in advance on-line or by phone, and all adult visitors must present a photo ID. Call to make a reservation, 202-762-1438. No one is admitted without a reservation.

University of Maryland Observatory

*Metzerott Road, College Park, MD (301-405-0355, recording, 301-405-3001) - **www.astro.umd.edu/openhouse**. Take the Washington Beltway (I-495) to the Route 1/College Park exit; go south on Route 1 to Route 193 (University Boulevard) west. Turn right at the first light (Metzerott Road). The observatory is past the stop light on the left. Free parking by the observatory or across the street at the University System Administration.*

Looking through telescopes at stars, planets, nebulae, and galaxies makes for a fascinating visit at the University of Maryland Observatory. After a slide-show presentation on a topic of popular interest in astronomy, ranging from archaeo-astronomy to quasars, visitors get the chance to look at the sky through the observatory's four telescopes. A program coordinator is available to answer questions and provide assistance with the telescopes.

- Open the 5th and 20th of every month, 8 p.m. EST or 9 p.m. Daylight Savings Time.

- Special programs are offered for groups of 15 or more.

- Of interest to children in 3rd grade or older.

- The lecture hall and observatory are handicap accessible, but to look through the telescopes requires ascending a ladder.

Webb Sanctuary
(Audubon Naturalist Society)

*12829 Chestnut Street, Clifton, VA (703-803-8400) - **www.audubon-naturalist.org**. Take the Washington Beltway (I-495) to I-66 west to the Fairfax County Parkway (Route 7100) south. Follow Route 7100 to the next exit and take Lee Highway (Rt. 29) south to the second stoplight. Turn left on Clifton Road. Follow Clifton Road till it ends and turn right into the town of Clifton. Turn right on Chestnut Street, 1st right after the stop sign; follow it to the sanctuary. Parking on-site.*

This 20-acre nature sanctuary has hiking and nature trails through woods and meadows on rolling terrain outside the quiet village of Clifton. Enjoy free programs or just to enjoy a walk with nature! On the weekends you can take a self-guided walk and look for resident and migrating birds, search for salamanders, discover frogs and toads, or watch for butterflies and wildflowers.

- Grounds open daily, dawn to dusk. Building open weekdays, 9-5; building closed weekends.
- The Webb Sanctuary welcomes groups for nature programs. Available dates are limited, so make reservations well in advance. Group sizes are limited due to the size of the Sanctuary and the fragility of some of the habitats.
- Field Trips, Hiking.

Special activities include beginner bird walks every third Saturday (meet in front of the sanctuary office RAIN OR SHINE) - call at 703-803-8400 by 3 p.m. the Friday before to sign-up. Scheduled walks are from 8-9 a.m. Monday Afternoon Family Programs are held on Monday holidays or early school release days.

Woodend Nature Sanctuary (Audubon Naturalist Society)

*8940 Jones Mill Road, Chevy Chase, MD (301-652-9188) - **www.audubon naturalist.org**. Take the Washington Beltway (I-495) to the Connecticut Avenue exit South for 1/2 mile. Turn left onto Manor Road, right on Jones Bridge Road, and left on Jones Mill Road. Entrance to Sanctuary is 1/3 mile on the left. Parking on-site.*

Woodend is a tranquil 40-acre wildlife sanctuary. The pond, meadows, and woods are fun to explore; a self-guided nature trail is available. Inside the main house is the Wilbur Fisk Banks Bird Collection, consisting of 594 specimens, mostly from eastern North America.

- Grounds open daily, dawn-dusk. Building open weekdays, 9-5; building closed weekends.
- Call for rentals and special programs.
- To schedule a school program at Woodend or for information on classes and events for children and families, call 301-652-9188, ext. 17.
- To hear a recording describing the location of area bird sightings, call 301-652-1088.
- Picnicking is permitted, but visitors must carry out their trash. Pets are not allowed.
- Stroller and wheelchair accessibility.

Special activities include a number of programs that center around conservation and environmental issues. After-school and summer programs are held for children; also offered are a variety of family and adult activities, including day and weekend trips, a Holiday Fair in December, and a Nature Fair in May.

Historical Farms

Carroll County Farm Museum

*500 South Center Street, Westminster, MD (800-654-4645, 410-876-2667) -
ccgov.carr.org/farm. Take the Washington Beltway (I-495) to Georgia
Avenue (route 97) north; continue about 35 miles to left turn on Route 132;
follow to left on Center Street; continue a half mile to entrance on right.
Parking on-site.*

Visitors get a look back in
history in this 1800s
farmhouse surrounded
by 140 rolling acres of
countryside. Guided
tours of the farmhouse;
self-guided tours of the
Living History Center
and exhibit buildings
including a Spring House,
Blacksmith Shop, Tinsmith Shop,
Transportation Exhibit, gardens, and more. Farm animals
stabled in the pasture area, a play area for children, and
nature trails are also available. Demonstrations are
scheduled throughout the season and may include quilting,
weaving, broom making, tinsmithing, and blacksmithing. The
General Store sells candy, souvenirs and handcrafted items
made by the resident artisans.

- Open for group tours during April, Tuesday-Friday,
  10-4; in May, facility open to general public, weekends,
  noon-5. Additional hours: July and August, Tuesday-
  Friday, 10-4. Open for tours during Christmas season.
  Call for schedule. Closed Mondays and some holidays.

- Adults, $3; children 7-18 and adults over 60, $2; six
  and under, free. Groups of 20 or more (by reservation),
  $2.50 per person.

- Wheelchair accessible. Strollers permitted outside, but
  not in Farmhouse.

- Field Trips, Hiking, Picnicking.

Special activities include Blacksmith Days and Civil War
Living History Encampment in May; Spring Muster of Antique
Fire Equipment and Fiddlers' Convention in June; an Old-
Fashioned July 4th Celebration in July; Steamshow Days in
September; Fall Harvest Days in October, and a Holiday
Theme Tour in December.

Cedarvale Farm

*2915 Coale Lane, Churchville, MD (410-734-7467) - **cedarvalefarm.com**. Take the Washington Beltway (I-495) to I-95 north past Baltimore to exit 80; turn left on Route 543; go to traffic light and then turn right on Route 136 and follow for 3 miles; turn right on Coale Lane (look for buffalo on Cedarvale Farm sign).*

This farm features a herd of 20 bison (buffalo), raised primarily to preserve the species and to educate school children about our American heritage. Bring your apples and stale bread to feed the bison!

- Open to public on Sundays, 1-5.
- Group tours by reservations.
- Picnic and recreation facilities available.

Claude Moore Colonial Farm at Turkey Run

*6310 Georgetown Pike, McLean, VA (703-442-7557) - **www.1771.org**. Take the Washington Beltway (I-495) to Georgetown Pike (Route 193) east two and a half miles; go left onto access road; farm is a half-mile on the left. Or take George Washington Memorial Parkway to Route 123 south; after one mile, turn left on Route 193; right onto access road; farm is a half-mile on the left. Public parking available.*

The Claude Moore Farm at Turkey Run is a living history museum that portrays family life on a small, low-income farm just prior to the Revolutionary War. The farm uses hands-on, interactive programs to further the public's understanding of agriculture and everyday life in 18th-century Virginia. This unique opportunity to experience colonial history first hand should not be missed!

- Open April-December, Wednesday-Sunday, 10-4:30. Closed January-March, holidays, and rainy days.
- Adults, $2; children 3-12 and Seniors, $1.
- Group visits must be scheduled in advance.
- Gravel paths with moderate inclines.
- VA TimeTravlers Site, Field Trips, Birthday Parties, Picnicking.

Special activities include an 18th-century Market Fair in May, July, and October, with merchants, crafts, and a colonial orchestra. Participate in the wheat and tobacco harvest days and the many food preservation events.
Call for a calendar of special events and a list of educational programs or visit the website. Field trip craft activities are offered to birthday groups, Wednesday-Friday.

Frying Pan Park, Kidwell Farm

*2709 West Ox Road, Herndon, VA (703-437-9101) - **www.co.fairfax. va.us/parks**. Take the Washington Beltway (I-495) to I-66 west; exit at Route 50 west; turn right on Fairfax County Parkway;left on West Ox Road; park is on the right.*

This model farm of the 1930s offers urban children a rich experience in rural living. Take a picnic lunch and spend some time looking at this subsistence farm with its blacksmith shop, historic schoolhouse, numerous farm animals, fields, farm buildings, and horse arena. The arena is generally booked on the weekends.

- Open daily, 10-6. Closed Christmas.
- 20-minute hayrides on Saturdays, mid-March through November, $2.
- Field Trips, Picnicking.

Special activities include the Fairfax County 4-H Fair in August and Saturday hayrides in the summer and fall.

The National Colonial Farm

*Piscataway National Park, 3400 Bryan Point Road, Accokeek, MD (301-283-2113) - **www.accokeek.org/ncf.htm**. Take the Washington Beltway (I-495) to Indian Head Highway (Route 210) south; proceed south on Indian Head Highway for ten miles; turn right at Bryan Point Road; follow for four miles to farm parking lot on right.*

At this beautiful site on the Potomac, opposite Mount Vernon, the Accokeek Foundation, in cooperation with the National Park Service, has recreated a working farm. It features demonstration gardens and animals of a middle-class tobacco plantation in the mid-18th century. Seasonal farm work goes on every day, as well as daily domestic activities. On the interpretive tours, children of all ages have the chance to observe the farming methods and family lifestyle characteristic of the period. Bird enthusiasts will be pleased to know that the farm is home to three pairs of bald eagles. See Piscataway Park listing on page 113.

- Open Tuesday-Sunday, 10-4. Closed Thanksgiving, Veteran's Day, Christmas, and New Year's Day.
- Group tours by reservation, Tuesday-Sunday,
- A vehicle for people with special needs is available. Call during the week to make arrangements.
- Picnicking.

Special activities include the Potomac River Heritage Festival in late September, featuring demonstrations of a variety of colonial crafts; Children's Day in the spring and fall.

Oxon Hill Farm

6411 Oxon Hill Road, Oxon Hill, MD (301-839-1176, 301-839-0211) -
www.nps.gov/oxhi*. Take the Washington Beltway (I-495) to Indian Head
Highway, exit 3A south; go right at end of ramp to Oxon Hill Road; make
immediate right into farm.*

Oxon Hill is a working farm with daily demonstrations of farm
chores, animals, crops, and equipment typical of those on
farms in the early 1900s. Children can pet the animals, and
learn about animal care and farming methods. There are
craft demonstrations, a natural spring, and a self-guided
nature walk that explains how farms utilized the surrounding
woods. An additional bonus - the spectacular view of the
Potomac River, Washington, and Virginia.

- Open daily, 8:30-4:30. Closed Thanksgiving,
  Christmas, and New Year's Day.
- Cow milking on weekdays at 10, 11:30, and 3:30 by
  reservation; on weekends, first-come, first-served basis
  at 10 and 3:30. Chicken feeding and egg gathering at
  11 weekdays, by reservation.
- Appropriate for preschool age children.
- Field Trips, Athletic Fields, Fishing, Hiking, Picnicking.

Special activities include sheep-shearing, gardening,
threshing, cider pressing, butter churning, ice cream making,
corn harvesting, and sorghum syrup cooking. Call for specific
dates.

Temple Hall Farm Regional Park

*15789 Temple Hall Lane, Leesburg, VA (703-779-9372) - **www.nvrpa.org
/templehall.html**. Take the Washington Beltway (I-495) to Route 15 north
towards Leesburg. Take 15 through Leesburg and turn right onto Limestone
School Road (Route 661). Go approximately one mile; the farm entrance is
on the left.*

This self-sustaining 286-
acre working farm
raises farm animals
(cows, goats, hogs,
peacocks, chicken,
ducks, and sheep) and
produces Orchard
grass and Alfalfa hay.
Interpretive programs designed
as outdoor classrooms are
offered to educate children about
the diverse aspects of farm life,
animals, and crops. A farm interpreter
leads tours and guides children as they participate in farm-

related activities such as feeding the animals or working in the garden. All animals are in fenced pens, this is not a petting farm.

- Open to the public on Sundays, starting with the first Sunday in April through October from 11-4.
- Groups may schedule a tour by calling 703-729-9372.
- Interpretive tours last one-two hours, depending on the age level of the group.
- Appropriate for children in pre-school-6th grade.

Special activities include a corn maize event held the last week in August through October in a nine-acre cornfield that is transformed into a giant elaborate maze. The farm also has pick-your-own-pumpkins and hayrides, and an open house by appointment twice a year during the spring and fall.

Walney Visitor Center
- Ellanor C. Lawrence Park

*5040 Walney Road, Chantilly, VA (703-631-0013) – **www.fairfaxcounty .gov/parks/ecl**. Take the Washington Beltway (I-495) to Route 66 west for eleven miles to Sully Road/Route 28 north (exit 49) north. Make an immediate right turn onto Walney Road; the entrance is one mile on the left.*

A large preserve of open space, the park's 660 acres are home to many features including: the Walney Pond, various historic ruins, Walney Visitor Center, Cabell's Mill/Middlegate complex, picnic facilities, athletic fields and hiking trails.

The Walney Visitor Center is a converted 1780 farmhouse with live animal exhibits, historical exhibits, greenhouse and classrooms. The Walney house was a home to families who farmed the Walney farm during the 18th, 19th and early 20th centuries. Outbuildings include a smokehouse, ruins of an icehouse and diary complex, and demonstration gardens.

- Open daily, dawn-dusk.
- Mostly accessible with assistance.
- Field trips, tours, self-guided studies, and summer camps offered.
- VA TimeTravlers Site, Athletic Fields, Hiking, Picnicking.

Pick Your Own

Butler's Orchard

22200 Davis Mill Road, Germantown, MD (301-972-3299, 301-428-0444). Take the Washington Beltway (I-495) to I-270 north; exit at Father Hurley Boulevard (exit 16); bear right onto Route 27; after 1.3 miles turn right onto Brink Road and look for sign on the left.

Families visiting the 300-acre Butler family farm will get an appealing and instructive view of fruits growing in the orchards and fields, and have an opportunity to pick their own produce. Kids of all ages will enjoy plucking the ripe fruit directly from the vine, tree, or  bush. And tasting in the fields is very much allowed! Crops, during an eight-month growing season, include strawberries, blackberries, blueberries, peas, pumpkins, and Christmas trees. Bring your own baskets, which will be weighed before picking, or purchase them at Butler's for a small fee. Fresh seasonal produce is also for sale at the stand.

- Open May-Christmas; call to check exact days and hours. Closed Monday, except during strawberry season, Labor Day, and Columbus Day.
- Call to hear a recorded message about the availability of your favorite crops.
- Field Trips.

Special activities include a hayride in Bunnyland in the spring, Pumpkin Festivals each weekend in October, Pumpkin Harvest Days from October-November, as well as group hayrides and Choose and Cut Christmas Trees in November-December. Fruit crops include strawberries, blueberries, tart cherries, blackberries, red raspberries, apples and pumpkins.

Cox Farms (Market and Pumpkin Patch)

*15621 Braddock Road, Centreville, VA (703-830-3710) - **www.coxfarms. com**. Take the Washington Beltway (I-495) to Braddock Road; go five miles west on Route 28 in Fairfax County. Or take the Beltway (I-495) to I-66 west; take a right onto exit 52 (Route 29 south) to the third light at Pleasant Valley Road; turn right onto Pleasant Valley Road and go four miles to Braddock Road; turn left at first driveway on the left.*

Cox Farms is set on 116 acres overlooking a lake and the Blue Ridge Mountains. Offering a seasonal farm market and greenhouse items, the farm is a child-friendly place with climbing structures and wagons for children to use. It is open every day in October with extra activities on the weekends.

The October theme is to experience harvest time at the farm. All activities center around outdoor physical activity in a rural environment such as pumpkin picking, hayrides, hay tunnels, mountain slide and swings that drop into hay pits. Weekend festivals include food, face painting, and 4 stages of live entertainment. Cowboy Jack entertains live every day.

- Open April-December (call for hours). In October, open 10-6 daily; extra festival activities on the weekends.

- Entrance fees for the Pumpkin Patch include all activities and a pumpkin. Children under age two are free. Weekends, $9, and weekdays, $7. Kids under two are free.

- Stroller and wheelchair accessible.

Special activities include a Pumpkin Patch in from the end of September till the first of November, with live entertainment, hayrides, mountain slides, rope swings, cider, apples, farm animals, tunnels and mazes.

Homestead Farm

*15600 Sugarland Road, Poolesville, MD (301-977-3761) - **www.homestead-farm.net**. Take the Washington Beltway (I-495) to I-270 north; exit at Route 28 west through Darnestown to left on Route 107 towards Poolesville. Make first left on Sugarland Road; 1 mile on right.*

Homestead Farms opens in late May when the strawberries are ripe and ready to be picked. The summer season brings blackberries, peaches, and a variety of summer vegetables including vine ripened tomatoes and sweet corn picked fresh every day. At the farm market, you will find a large selection of jams and pickles as well as honey collected from beehives located on the farm. In mid-August, the red raspberry season begins, and later in the month, Gala apples are ready to be picked. These are the first of thirteen varieties of apples grown in the orchards. During the autumn harvest, Homestead's farm market is filled with apples, pumpkins, fall squash, Indian corn, gourds, and fresh apple cider.

- Open mid-May-October 31, and weekends in December.

- Hayrides to the pumpkin patch, weekends in October.

- Educational tours for school groups are given on weekdays in September and October by reservation only. Call 301-926-6999

- Petting barnyard with pigs, chicken, sheep, and goats.

Special activities include a corn maze, July-August.

Larriland Farm

2415 Woodbine Road, Woodbine, MD (301-854-6110, 410-442-2605)
*- **www.pickyourown.com**. Located three miles south of I-70 (Exit 73) on*
Route 94, Woodbine Road. Take the Washington Beltway (I-495) to Georgia
Avenue; follow Georgia Avenue north, past Olney and Laytonsville; turn left
on Jennings Chapel Road and right on Florence Road; turn right on Route
94; farm is on the right.

This 285-acre, pick-your-own produce farm is set in the
rolling foothills of the Appalachian Mountains in Western
Howard County. Sample fresh fruits and vegetables right in
the field and take a hayride in October. With an eight acre
pond, woods, and a 125-year-old chestnut post and beam
barn which houses a farm market, this is sure to be a
delightful destination for the entire family.

- Open Tuesday-Sunday. Hours vary by season.
  Please call ahead to verify specific hours.
- Pick-your-own fruits and vegetables.
  Containers are furnished.
- Field Trips, Birthday Parties.

Phillips Farm

Located at Route 118 and Riffleford Road, Germantown, MD (301-785-8621,
*301-540-2364) - **www.phillipsfarmproduce.com**. Take the Washington*
Beltway (I-495) to I-270 north to Exit 15 Germantown - Route 118 south.
Continue on 118 for 1.5 miles to Clopper Road. Turn right on Clopper for 0.2
miles. Turn left onto Schaeffer. Entrance is 0.25 miles on the left. Parking.

All summer and fall, children will enjoy visiting Phillips Farm
to pet and feed baby animals and to climb on haystacks.
There is always fresh produce to buy. Each weekend in
October, the Harvest Festival offers a corn maze, hayrides to
the pumpkin patch, pick your own pumpkins, and other fun
activities. In the summer, head out to the farm to pick your
own flowers and string beans.

- Open early May-October 31, 10-7.
- Ride On bus comes to Clopper Road and Route 118.
- Stroller and wheelchair accessible.
- Farm animals to pet; Germantown history exhibits;
  Pumpkin Patch in October with hay rides (small fee);
  campfires in the evening, birthday parties, Scout
  campfires and activities.
- Field Trips, Birthday Parties, Wheelchair Accessible.

Special activities include the Montgomery County Farm
Tour the fourth Saturday and Sunday in July with free hay
rides and live music.

Potomac Vegetable Farms

9627 Leesburg Pike (Route 7), Vienna, VA (703-759-2119, 703-759-3844). Take the Washington Beltway (I-495) to Route 7 west; continue for four and a half miles to entrance on left.

This is a working, certified organic vegetable and berry farm with horses and chickens in a natural setting. The farm specializes in lettuce and greens, tomatoes, beans, squash, peppers, flowers, and fresh eggs. Potomac Vegetable Farms also grows pumpkins and berries for pick-it-yourselfers. The proprietors encourage informal visits to their fields, animals, and ongoing operations. In addition to tours for young children, they also have tours for groups of older children who are interested in the connection between farming and the environment, health, and ecology issues. Bring your used egg cartons (in good condition) and plastic and paper bags to recycle.

- Open July 1-October 31; call for hours.
- $4 per person for guided farm tours.
- School buses, vans, and carpooling are advised.
- Guided tours for groups of ten or more. Call to schedule school or community groups.
- Wheelchair access limited, as there are no sidewalks.
- Picnicking.

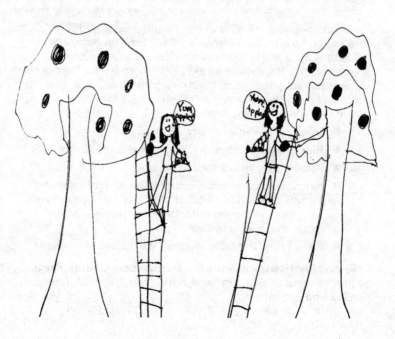

Gardens

Brookside Gardens

*1800 Glenallan Avenue, Wheaton, MD (301-946-9061) - **www.mc-mncppc.org/parks/brookside**. Take the Washington Beltway (I-495) to Georgia Avenue north to Randolph Road; right on Randolph Road for two blocks; right on Glenallan Avenue; go a half mile to entrance on right.*

This 50-acre public garden has outdoor plantings landscaped in formal and natural styles. In addition to the well-known azalea, rose, formal, and fragrance gardens, there are aquatic and Japanese gardens with a Japanese teahouse. The lake is home to water snakes and fish. Geese and ducks can be found near the aquatic gardens, and butterflies are indeed attracted to the butterfly garden. Inside the two conservatories are colorful annuals and perennials and exotic plants. In the greenhouse, a stream with stepping stones is a delight for little ones.

The garden boasts a 2,000-volume horticultural library, which contains a number of children's books (for use on site only). There are self-guided, recorded, and staff-guided interpretations of the garden. A free, self-touring cassette is available. A class schedule lists all the scheduled lectures, workshops, and programs. Seasonal displays during Christmas, Easter, and autumn.

- Gardens open sunrise to sunset.
  Conservatory open 10-5. Closed Christmas.
- Gift shop, visitors center, horticultural library.
- Partial wheelchair access.
- Recommended for children age ten and older.

Special activities include Saturday story times for ages 2-6, Groundhog Day celebration on February 2, a butterfly show in August-September, Children's Day in late September, and Garden of Light in late November-early December.

Green Spring Gardens Park

4603 Green Spring Road, Alexandria, VA (703-642-5173). Take the Washington Beltway (I-495) east on Little River Turnpike (Route 236) and travel about three miles; turn left on Green Spring Road. Or from I-395, take Duke Street west about one mile; turn right onto Green Spring Road.

This park contains demonstration gardens for the home gardener, an extensively renovated 18th-century house, and the Horticulture Center with a greenhouse and a library. The grounds include formal rose, herb, and vegetable gardens, a fruit orchard, and an iris bed. Smaller children especially enjoy the woods and two ponds with ducks and geese.

Picnicking is allowed on the grounds. Horticulture classes are offered for children of all ages.

- Grounds open daily, dawn to dusk. Horticulture Center open Monday-Saturday, 9-4:30; Sunday, noon-4:30. Manor House open Wednesday-Sunday, noon-4. Park and buildings closed Thanksgiving, Christmas, and New Year's Day; on other holidays, open noon-5.

- Field Trips, Picnicking, Wheelchair Accessible.

Kenilworth Park and Aquatic Gardens

*1550 Anacostia Avenue, NE, Washington, DC (202-426-6905) - **www.nps.gov/kepa**. From Kenilworth Avenue, take the Eastern Avenue Exit and get on the southbound service road to Douglas Street; make a right on Anacostia Avenue; located across the Anacostia from the Arboretum.*

Many varieties of flowering water plants thrive in the ponds of the Kenilworth Aquatic Gardens, a National Park Service site. Children love seeing the brightly colored flowers, watching frogs, turtles, birds, and fish in the ponds, and exploring the River Trail that borders the Anacostia River. Wildflowers begin blooming in the marsh in early spring, and the water lilies begin blooming in early summer.

- Gardens open daily, 7-4. Visitor Center open 8-4, except Thanksgiving, Christmas, and New Year's Day. Mid-morning is usually the best time to see summer flowers, earlier for wildlife.

- No fees; donations are accepted.

- Metrorail Orange line (Deanwood).

- For reservations, please call 202-426-6905.

- Stroller and wheelchair accessible.

- Picnicking.

Special activities include the Waterlily Festival the third or fourth Saturday in July.

McCrillis Gardens and Gallery

*6910 Greentree Road, Bethesda, MD (301-365-1657) - **www.mc.mncppc.org/parks/brookside/mccrilli.shtm**.*

Five acres of shaded gardens, a small art gallery, benches and a small pavilion make this a lovely place to visit. The gallery exhibits art in various styles and media by local artists.

- Open daily 10 a.m. to sunset

Meadowlark Botanical Gardens

*9750 Meadowlark Gardens Court, Vienna, VA (703-456-0916) - **www. nvrpa.org/meadowlark.html**. From I-495 take Route 7 west for five miles to Beulah Road south; go left on Beulah road for two miles and turn right into park. On-site parking.*

This scenic public garden features 95 acres of natural and landscaped areas, a butterfly garden, herb garden, three wedding gazebos, three lakes, and two miles of trails through woods, meadows, and gardens. Additionally, there are three miles of paved trails, ideal for strollers and wheelchairs.

- Open year-round, except on Thanksgiving Day, Christmas Day, New Year's Day and when snow or ice cover the trails.
- Children (7 & older) and senior citizens, $1; adults, $3.
- Groups may schedule tours for a nominal fee.
- About 80% of the garden is wheelchair and stroller accessible.
- Hiking, Picnicking, Restaurant/Snack Bar.

Special activities include gardening and biodiversity programs, tours of the gardens, plant sales and other events throughout the year.

River Farm Garden Park

*The American Horticultural Society, 7931 East Boulevard Drive, Alexandria, VA (703-768-5700, 800-777-7931) - **www.ahs.og/river_farm**. Located between Old Town and Mount Vernon. Take the George Washington Parkway through Old Town and continue south; turn left on East Boulevard Drive; follow the signs to River Farm Garden Park. On-site parking.*

The elegant **Main House** at River Farm is set amidst 25-acres of lawns, gardens, meadows, and woods, and commands a sweeping view of the Potomac. Visitors can take self-guided tours of the Main House and the vast gardens; of particular interest are the **Children's Gardens** with their unique designs - Butterfly, Dinosaur, Bat Cave, Alphabet, Boat, and Zig-Zag.

- Grounds are open year-round, Monday-Friday, 8:30-5; Saturdays, April-October, 9-1. Closed on holidays.
- Picnic grounds available.
- Wheelchair access to grounds and to house with assistance.

Special activities include Living Laboratory Tours for groups, by reservation only.

U.S. National Arboretum

3501 New York Avenue, NE, Washington, DC (202-245-2726) - ***www.us na.usda.gov***. *Take the Washington Beltway (I-495) to Route 50 west (becomes New York Avenue); at first intersection, turn left onto Bladensburg Road; go three blocks; turn left on R Street, go 300 yards to the entrance.*

Enjoy the varied shrubs and trees, gardens, overlooks, and ponds as you explore this 444-acre museum of living plants by road or footpath. It is most colorful in the spring when thousands of azaleas are in bloom, but is equally enjoyable year-round, as there is always something blooming and plenty of "stretching space" for children to expend a little excess energy. Favorite sections include the **Dwarf Conifer Collection**, about 1,500 specimens attractively planted and separated by grassy areas and walks; the **Fern Valley Trail**, a natural wooded area planted with ferns, wildflowers, and native trees and shrubs; and the Aquatic Garden, featuring tropical and local aquatic plants. The superb **Bonsai Collection**, a bicentennial gift from Japan, now includes a collection of Chinese and American bonsai. The **National Herb Garden**, approximately two acres, includes three sub-gardens: a formal "knot" garden with plants arranged in intricate patterns, resembling various kinds of knots; an **historic rose garden**; and a **specialty garden** which contains ten different "rooms" or plots, each featuring a different area of herb gardening. **Friendship Gardens** feature perennials and ornamental grasses. The **Asian Collections** include a variety of exotic oriental plants.

Twenty-two of the original 24 National Capitol Columns that once formed the east central portico of the Capitol have been relocated here. The columns were in storage for many years before private funds were raised to finance their removal and reuse. The columns are placed in a nearly-square configuration, with a water stair, fountain, and reflecting pool.

The **Washington Youth Garden** provides a first gardening experience for D.C. Children in grades 3-5.

- Open daily, 8-5; Bonsai collection and Japanese garden open daily, 10-3:30. Closed Christmas.
- Metro shuttle from Union Station on the weekends and holidays except December 25.
- Picnicking is permitted in designated areas.
- Guided tours for groups of ten or more with advance reservation. Guided, open-air tram tours offered weekends (not in winter); call for details.
- Gift shop open from March 1 until mid-December.

5. Arts and Entertainment

Whether you're a visitor to Washington or a resident, be sure to take advantage of the city's many opportunities to introduce your children to the performing arts. Check the entertainment sections of local newspapers to keep up-to-date on performances and call to confirm hours. Half-price tickets to many Washington events can be purchased on the day of the performance at TICKETplace. TICKETplace is located at the Old Post Office Pavilion, 1100 Pennsylvania Avenue NW across the street from the Federal Triangle Metro station (orange and blue lines), near to both the Metro Center (red line) and Archives (green line) metro stops. Call 202-TICKETS for information on what is available on a particular day. This chapter also lists general and specialty bookstores, as well as toy stores of particular interest.

Performing Arts

Adventure Theatre

*Glen Echo Park, 7300 MacArthur Boulevard, Glen Echo, MD (301-320-5331) - **www.adventuretheatre.org**. Located near Goldsboro Road.*

Housed in the old Penny Arcade building of the historic amusement park, this children's theater - the Washington area's longest-running children's theatre - adds vitality to Glen Echo Park every weekend. Major productions year-round provide good professional entertainment. After the matinees, children can collect autographs from the performers and then run off for a ride on the carousel (open May through September, see Glen Echo Park on page 73).

- Performances on Saturday and Sunday, 1:30 and 3:30.
- Tickets are $6 per person. Group rates available
- Birthday Parties
- Sign language available - call to make arrangements, 301-320-5331.

African Heritage Center
for African Dance and Music

4018 Minnesota Avenue, NE, Washington, DC (202-399-5252) - **www. ahdd.org**. *Located near RFK Stadium at Minnesota and Benning Road.*

The Center is a dance studio where classes and performances in African dance and music are held. The African Heritage Dancers and Drummers, one of the first African-American dance companies in the Washington area, specializes in the traditional dance of West Africa. Harvest dances, mask dances, and stick dances, many performed in colorful robes, are all fascinating to watch. The Center also offers workshops in West African dance, drumming, and instrument making.

- Weekend performances. During the first week in August, daily performances around noon.

- Admission varies. Group rates and bookings upon request.

- Metrorail Orange line (Minnesota Avenue, South).

American Film Institute;
AFI Silver Theatre and Cultural Center

8633 Colesville Road, Silver Spring, MD (301-495-6720).

This three-screen complex offers a year-round program of the best in American and international cinema, featuring an eclectic mix of festivals, premieres, retrospectives, special events, tributes, on-stage guest appearances and educational programs. The AFI was instrumental in the designation of Silver Spring as a Maryland Arts and Entertainment District.

Special activities Silver Spring Outdoor Movie Series, "Silver Screen Under the Stars," family fun and entertainment in July.

Arena Stage

1101 6th Street, SW, Washington, DC (202-554-9066) - **www.arena stage.org**. *Take the Washington Beltway (I-495) to I-395 North / US-1 North towards Washington via 14th Street. Take the I-395 N exit and then the Maine Avenue exit. Keep left at the fork in the ramp and merge onto 9th Street, SW. In less than half a mile turn left onto Maine Avenue, SW, and then left onto 6th Street, SW.*

The Arena Stage complex houses three theaters: an in-the-round (**Fichandler**) stage, a standard proscenium (**Kreeger**) stage, and a cabaret-style (**Old Vat**) room. Although most performances are intended for adult audiences, Arena offers a new subscription series of programs for children called **Kids Play**, which has been met with great response by parents.

170

This creative series for kids (and their parents) is four weeks long and meets on Saturdays. While parents attend three Saturday matinees, children are engaged with community folk artists, storytellers, Arena staff, and members of the Living Stage Theatre Company. For the fourth Saturday, the whole family will attend a play together. This is a perfect way to introduce children to the theater through education and entertainment. Programming is available for children K-5 and is $130 per child. Young Audiences offers subscriptions for regularly scheduled shows at $25 per show for students in grades K through 12. For information please call the Subscriptions Office at (202) 488-4377.

- Tours Tuesday-Thursday, 10-3. Call ahead to make arrangements. Children should be 11 years or older.
- Metrorail Green line (Waterfront-SEU). Metered parking on the street and several pay lots within easy walking distance.

Blackrock Center for the Arts

12901 Town Commons Drive, Germantown, MD (301-528-2260) - ***www.blackrockcenter.org****. 270 North to Middlebrook Road West. Cross MD Route 118. Take the next right into the Town Center Shopping area. Go two short blocks and turn left. Blackrock will be on the right. The parking lot is behind the building.*

This center provides venues for performances in dance and theatre along with film presentations, lectures and arts education. Classes in the performing, literary and visual arts are offered for children, teens and adults, including classes specifically for children with special needs.

Capitol Concerts - Armed Forces Band and National Symphony

119 D Street, NE, Washington, DC (202-224-2985, 202-554-4620) ***http://aoc.gov*** *(Armed Forces Band) and* ***www.pbs.org*** *(National Symphony). Located at the west front plaza steps and lawn of the Capitol.*

Spend a pleasant summer evening on the steps of the Capitol listening to patriotic and pops concerts presented by the Armed Forces bands. Enjoy the full majesty of the National Symphony Orchestra as it performs its holiday concerts al fresco.

- Summer performances Mondays, Tuesdays, Wednesdays, and Fridays at 8 p.m. by the Armed Forces Band, weather permitting.
- The National Symphony on July 4 and the Sundays prior to Memorial Day and Labor Day, rain or shine.
- Grounds open about 2 p.m.

- Metrorail Orange and Blue lines (Capitol South).
- Security Information: Bags and containers will be searched. No thermoses.

Children's Theater

2515 North Randloph Street, Arlington, VA (703-548-1154) - **www.arlingtonarts.org/tct/.**

Children's Theater offers fully staged and beautifully costumed musicals and dramas for children by children. Some are original, some are traditional, but all are professional and performed by talented young actors. Open auditions for ages 9-14 are held for each production. Call or visit the web site for a schedule of performances as well as classes and workshops.

- Five weekend productions per year.
- Act III Young Adult Program for high school and college students
- Students and seniors, $7; adults, $10; groups of ten or more, $5 per person.

Comedy Sportz Arena

Ballston Commons Mall, 4238 Wilson Blvd, Arlington, VA (703-486-4242) - **www.cszdc.com** *Take the Washington Beltway (I-495) to I-66 East, exit 71. Stay right onto Glebe Road. Ballston Commons Mall is on the left at Wilson Lane.*

Bring the whole family to experience this entertaining comedy sporting event. Two teams of performers compete in a battle of wits by playing a series of improvisational games, all based on suggestions from the audience. A referee governs the action on the playing field, keeping time and calling fouls for comments that make the audience groan or if a player says anything off-color or in poor taste. Audience participation encouraged. Suitable for all ages.

- Performances Thursday 8 p.m., Friday 9 p.m., Saturday 7:30 and 10 p.m.
- Ticket prices $8-$12.
- Metrorail Orange line (Ballston)
- Birthday Parties, Restaurant/Snack Bar, Wheelchair Accessible.

Fairfax Symphony Orchestra

*Packard Center, 2nd Floor; 4024 Hummer Road, Annandale, VA
(703-642-7200) -* **www.fairfaxsymphony.org**.

This concert series features a mix of folk, contemporary, and
classical music. Each summer, the Fairfax Symphony
performs 40 free concerts in area parks and historic sites.
You can pack a picnic and have a relaxing meal while you
listen to the music in a beautiful outdoor setting. About 15
concerts, called **Overture to Orchestra**, are designed to
introduce children to the different instrument sections in an
orchestra: percussion, string, brass, and woodwind. Other
concerts feature instrumental soloists or a particular style of
music, such as a Dixieland or German band. Call or visit the
web site for a calendar of the summer offerings and
information about school programs.

- "Sounds of Summer" performances from June-
  September in the late morning, early afternoon,
  and early evening at Fairfax County parks
  and historic sites.
- Wheelchair access varies by site.

Friday Night in the Park Concerts

*Potomac Overlook Regional Park, 2845 Marcey Road, Arlington, VA
(703-528-5406) -* **www.nvrpa.org/potomacoverlook**.

This concert series features a mix of folk, bluegrass,
contemporary, and classical music. Call or visit the web site
for a summer schedule. See page 119 for more information
about Potomac Overlook Regional Park.

- Performances summer through early fall, every other
  Friday evening at 7 p.m.
- Donations appreciated.

Imagination Stage - (BAPA)
Bethesda Academy of Performing Arts

*4908 Auburn Avenue, Bethesda, MD (301-881-5106, 301-229-3739, TDD) -
www.imaginationstage.org. From the Washington Beltway (I-495), take
the MD-355 exit south toward Bethesda. Turn right on Woodmont Avenue,
just past the National Library of Medicine. Turn right onto Rugby Avenue;
left onto Auburn Avenue. Public parking garage.*

The Bethesda Academy for the Performing Arts was founded
in 1979. Today BAPA's Imagination Stage is the largest and
most respected multi-disciplinary theatre arts organization for
young people in the region. The Imagination Stage season
offers professional shows for families as well as year-round

classes, performance opportunities, and school outreach programs for young people. Imagination Stage is committed to making the arts inclusive and totally accessible to all children regardless of physical, cognitive or financial abilities.

BAPA's new theatre includes a 450-seat professional theatre and a 200-seat theatre for student productions. Studios for drama, dance, music, and digital media, production rooms, birthday party rooms, a café and a boutique will be located in this theatre arts center.

- Seven days a week from 9:30-6. Performances every weekend, holidays and summer days.
- $6.50 per ticket, $5.50 per group ticket, and $4 per school ticket.
- Metrorail Red line (Bethesda).
- Stroller, wheelchair and hearing impaired accessible.
- Field Trips, Birthday Parties, Restaurant/Snack Bar, Wheelchair Accessible.

Special activities include productions and performances for preschool through young adult. Birthday parties and summer camps.

John F. Kennedy Center for the Performing Arts

*2700 F Street, NW, Washington, DC (202-467-4600, ticket information, 800-444-1324) - **www.kennedy-center.org**.*

The Kennedy Center is America's living memorial to President Kennedy and home to six theaters that host great artists and performances of music, dance, and theater from around the world. Offerings include National Symphony Orchestra concerts, plays and musicals, opera, ballet and modern dance, jazz and chamber music, performances for young people, films, and more. Times and prices vary; call ahead for schedules and reservations: 202-467-4600 or 800-444-1324. The box office is open Monday-Saturday, 10 a.m.-9 p.m., Sunday and holidays, noon-9.

The **National Symphony Orchestra** (202-416-8820, information and free schedule) has continued to reach both young people and adults with educational performances, lecture/demonstrations, and artistic training for aspiring musicians. They are held during the day for school groups, while public performances are given in the evening and on weekends. To enhance the performance experience, written performance guides for all productions are available prior to the events for teachers and families.

The **Imagination Celebration** offers performances in theater, dance, music, puppetry and opera for families and school groups.

Kennedy Center Youth and Family Programs include classics as well as commissioned works performed in the Theater Lab and Terrace Theater by groups from all over the United States. Programs are usually scheduled throughout the school year on Friday evenings and for Saturday and Sunday matinees. It is best to order tickets, although there are times when tickets are available the day of the performance.

Kennedy Center National Symphony Orchestra Family Concerts are scheduled in fall and spring on Saturday and Sunday. The December concerts usually have a holiday theme. Prior to each concert there is a hands-on activity in the grand foyer. One of the most popular of these activities is the instrument "petting zoo," where children may try out all the instruments that will be played professionally on the stage.

The Center also offers free performances every day at 6 p.m. on its Millennium Stage. The Stage was created as part of the Kennedy Center's Performing Arts for Everyone initiative to make the performing arts accessible to everyone. These free, hour-long performances include presentations of music, dance, and theater for all ages.

- Metrorail Orange and Blue lines (Foggy Bottom). Commercial parking garage.
- Tickets to all performances may be purchased at the box office, major credit cards accepted.
- Children age 18 and under can qualify for half-price tickets for most events. Check at the Friends of the Kennedy Center desk, then purchase tickets at the box office for "day of" performances.
- Call the Education Office at 202-416-8830 and ask to be put on the mailing list for children's programs and for brochures on specific events.
- The Kennedy Center sets aside certain boxes and seats for wheelchair access.
- Restaurant/Snack Bar.

Special activities include Holiday Festivals in December with holiday sing-a-longs, free performances, and concerts; an Arts Festival in the fall with free music, dance, and other entertainment for children; and multicultural children's book and author festival in November.

Marine Barracks Evening Parade

Marine Barracks, 8th and I Streets, SE, Washington, DC (202-433-6060) -
www.mbw.usmc.mil/parades.

The U.S. Marine Band concerts are followed by a one and a
half hour parade featuring the U.S. Marine Drum and Bugle
Corps, the U.S. Marine Corps Silent Drill Platoon, the U.S.
Marine Corps Color Guard, and two companies of marching
Marines. Marines, in full dress, escort each group to their
sets. It is an impressive spectacle and a wonderful way to
spend a summer evening. Parades on Friday evenings at 8:45,
May-August (arrive no later than 8 p.m.). For reservations,
write at least three weeks in advance. For group reservations,
write at least two months in advance.

- Parade parking at the Navy Yard, M and 11th Streets,
  SE. Take the free shuttle bus to & from the barracks.
- Call for information on wheelchair accessibility.
- Security Information: All guests pass through security
  checkpoints. Write to Protocol office, attn: PARADES
  at the address above; include name of party, number of
  guests, complete return address and telephone contact.

Maryland Hall for the Creative Arts

801 Chase Street, Annapolis, MD (410-263-5544, 301-261-1553) -
www.marylandhall.org. *Take Route 50 to Annapolis; exit at Rowe
Boulevard, turning right; turn right at second light (Taylor Avenue); turn
right on Spa Road; take first left on Greenfield.*

Visit this home to the arts in Anne Arundel County featuring
live theatre, hands-on art activities, gallery exhibitions and
performances.

- Open Monday-Friday, 8 a.m.-10 p.m.; Saturday, 9-5.
- Field Trips, Wheelchair Accessible.

Mount Vernon Community Children's Theatre

1900 Elkin Street, Alexandria, VA (703-360-0686) - **www.mvcct.org**.

Mount Vernon Community Children's Theater (MVCCT) has
presented more than 35 theatrical productions featuring
young actors from the Washington metropolitan community
since its incorporation in 1980. Performed by children for
children, MVCCT has consistently won awards for its
productions and programs. Workshops, classes, summer
camp, and full-scale productions of musicals and dramas
fulfill the theater's mission to provide opportunities for
children to participate in the creative process of live theater.

Netherlands Carillon Concerts

Located off Marshall Drive in, Rosslyn, VA (703-285-2603, 703-285-2600) -
www.nps.gov/gwmp/carillon.htm. *Off Route 110, near Iwo Jima
Memorial and Arlington Memorial Cemetery. From Rosslyn, VA: follow Ft.
Myer Drive, which turns into Meade Street, to Marshall Drive; go left on
Marshall Drive; then take first left into park.*

Come sit on the grass to hear the free carillon concerts of
popular, classical, and religious music. A gift from the people
of the Netherlands, the 50-bell carillon, housed in its open
steel structure, is an impressive auditory and visual
experience. Visitors may go up into the tower to watch the
carillonneur perform and to view the city of Washington.

- Performances are held Saturdays and national holidays,
  May-September. In May and September, 2-4; in June-
  August, 6-8.
- This is a good place to view the 4th of July fireworks.
- Picnicking.

Now This! Kids!

*Blair Mansion, 7711 Eastern Avenue, Silver Spring, MD (202-364-8292)
– **www.nowthisimprov.com**.*

Now This! Kids! presents a delightfully innovative and totally
improvisational show appropriate for children ages 5-12.
Every skit is an original, based on suggestions from the
audience with funny and amazing results. Party packages
and group rates are available.

- Saturdays, 1 p.m. lunch; show 1:30 p.m.
- Lunch and show, $18; dessert and show, $11.
- Metrorail Red line (Silver Spring).
- Birthday Parties, Restaurant/Snack Bar.

Olney Theater Center for the Arts

*2001 Route 108, Olney, MD (301-924-3400). Take Georgia Avenue north to
Olney; turn right on Route 108 in the center of town. Theater is a half-mile
on the left.*

The Olney Theatre Center is a professional theatre with four
performing venues, including seating for up to 500 on the
west lawn for the Theatre's Summer Shakespeare Festival.
The season includes staging of classic and contemporary
plays, some for family audiences.

- Metrorail Red line (Glenmont) and transfer to the 22
  bus, which stops directly in front of the theater.

Prince George's Publick Playhouse for the Performing Arts

*5445 Landover Road, Hyattsville, MD (301-277-1710) - **www.pgparks. com/places/artsfac/publick.html**. Located just 10 minutes from downtown Washington, D.C., just one-half mile off the Baltimore-Washington Parkway at the Cheverly exit. Free parking.*

The Playhouse, originally the 1947 art deco Cheverly Theatre, was renovated and reopened in 1975 as a theatre committed to cultural diversity in the arts. Known throughout the metropolitan area for the quality and affordability of its programs, this 462-seat theatre features nationally recognized touring companies in dance, music, and theater, and is home to many community arts groups.

- Box office hours Monday-Friday 10-4 and one hour before each performance.
- Midweek performances are offered at 10 and noon.
- Ticket prices range from $6-$12 for children.
- Wheelchair Accessible.

Puppet Company Playhouse

*Glen Echo Park, 7300 MacArthur Boulevard, Glen Echo, MD (301-320-6668) - **www.thepuppetco.org**. Located at the intersection of MacArthur Blvd. and Goldsboro Road. From the Beltway (495) take Exit 30, River Road. Go up the ramp and stay right, going East toward Washington D.C. At the 5th light turn right onto Goldsboro Road. Follow Goldsboro until it dead-ends at MacArthur Blvd. Turn right onto Mac Arthur, then take the first left onto Oxford Road. The parking lot is on the left.*

The Puppet Company performs delightful productions with clever interpretations of many children's classics. Shows are held in Glen Echo Park's historic Spanish Ballroom Building in a child-pleasing theater. Audience members sit on the carpeted floor while master puppeteers spellbind audience members. Performances Wednesday-Friday, 10 and 11:30; Saturday-Sunday, 11:30 and 1.

- $6 per ticket for everyone two and older. Reservations are strongly recommended - call the Box Office at (301) 320-6668. Group rates available with advance reservations.
- Productions change approximately every six weeks.
- Stroller and wheelchair accessible.
- Appropriate for preschool age children.
- Picnicking, Snack Bar.

Special activities include the carousel open May-October, an annual exhibit showcasing puppets from recent productions, and puppet-making demonstrations.

Round House Theatre 🔆16🔆

*(240-644-1100-box office, 240-644-1099-main office) - **www.round***
***housetheatre.org**. Bethesda: 40733 East West Highway at Waverly*
Street, Bethesda, MD 20814. Directions: take MD 355/Wisconsin Avenue
South. One block past East West Highway/MD 410 East, turn left on
Montgomery Avenue. Turn left on Waverly at the first light to the County
parking garage on Waverly; or cross East-West Highway and park in the
Round House paid attended garage on the left. Silver Spring: Colesville
Road between Georgia Avenue and Fenton Street in downtown Silver
Spring, adjacent to the historic Silver Theatre-the new home of AFI.
Directions: Take 495 to Colesville Road South. Public parking decks at
Colesville Road and Fenton Street and at Ellsworth Avenue.

Round House offers a variety of stage productions each
season, exploring different forms of theatre and the
performing arts. Limited engagements, contemporary
adaptations of the classics, world premieres, and works-in-
progress can all be found on the stages at Bethesda (seating
capacity 400) and Silver Spring (seating capacity 100-150).

Round House also provides theatre education through special
student matinees, a year-round theatre school, and an arts-
centered summer day camp program.

- Metrorail Red Line (Bethesda or Silver Spring,
  depending on which theater you are attending)

Saturday Morning at The National and Monday Night at The National

National Theater, 1321 Pennsylvania Avenue, NW, Washington, DC
*(800-447-7400 tickets, 202-628-6161 info) - **nationaltheatre.org**.*

These dynamic one-hour shows invite audience participation
and are irresistible to kids age four and older. Magicians,
dancers, mimes, and puppets are among the top performers
of local and national renown. Adult programs are also
offered on Mondays at 6 and 7:30 p.m.; some of these shows
may be appropriate for teen-age children.

- Performances throughout the school year, Saturday at
  9:30 and 11 a.m. for all ages. Monday nights at 6 and
  7:30 p.m. for teens and adults. Check the web site for
  a current schedule.
- Free admission on a first-come, first-served basis.
- Metrorail Red, Orange, and Blue lines (Metro Center).
  Parking in nearby commercial lots.
- Stroller and wheelchair accessible.

Smithsonian Discovery Theater

*Arts and Industries Building, 900 Jefferson Drive, SW, Washington, DC (202-357-1500) - **www.discovery-theater.org**.*

Thousands of children in the Washington area have had their introduction to theater at these performances. Discovery Theater offers new and diverse programming by artists of local and national reknown, including many live performances and outstanding puppet shows.

- Shows Monday-Friday 10 and 11:30 a.m.
- Performances and workshops throughout the year; call for information on shows, dates, and times.
- Admission, $5 recommended for school groups, youth organizations and families.
- Ten-admission punch card and discounts for groups available. Reservations are strongly recommended.
- Metrorail Blue and Orange lines (Smithsonian, Mall exit).
- Appropriate for preschool age children.

Strathmore Hall Arts Center

*10701 Rockville Pike, Bethesda, MD (301-530-0540) - **www.strathmore. org**. Located on Rockville Pike (Route 355) at the corner of Tuckerman Lane.*

On six Thursdays during the summer, two performances per day are presented on Strathmore's Backyard Theatre Stage. One-hour performances begin at 9:30 and 11:30 a.m. As part of Spring Break Theater, indoor programs for children are presented on four days of spring vacation at 11 a.m. and 1 p.m. The summer concert series (Tuesday and Thursday evenings, June-August), present a variety of musical styles suitable for the entire family.

- Admission for Backyard Theatre Stage and Spring Break Theater is $5 per person; $4 per person for groups of ten or more (must reserve and pay in advance). The summer concert series is free.
- There is a handicapped entrance on the side of the building with an elevator.

Special activities include the Youth Art Exhibition, a display of artwork by elementary school children; and a Presidents Day exhibit of student works showing techniques in computer graphics, music, and painting.

Sunset Serenades at the National Zoo

National Zoological Park, Washington, DC (202-673-4717). Rock Creek Park entrances at Adams Mill Road and Beach Drive, and main entrance at 3000 block of Connecticut Avenue, NW.

This summertime six-concert series features a diverse mix of ethnic and contemporary music. Past performances have included a mariachi band, classic rock and roll from the 50s and 60s, progressive reggae, and traditional Andean folk songs. Bring a picnic dinner or call 202-673-4978 a day ahead to reserve a picnic basket. Children love to dance in this relaxed outdoor environment. See page 55 for more information on the National Zoo.

- Summer performances on Thursday evenings, June 25-August 6, 6:30-8 p.m., at the Lion/Tiger Hill Stage.

- Metrorail Red line (Woodley Park-Zoo, a seven-minute, uphill walk; or Cleveland Park, a six-minute, level walk.)

- Picnicking.

Sylvan Theater

Located between 15th and 17th Streets, NW off Independence Avenue, on the Washington Monument grounds, Washington, DC (202-426-6843).

Musicals, military concerts, and July 4th celebrations under the stars are some of the attractions offered at Washington's outdoor downtown theater. Bring picnics, blankets, and insect repellent.

An impressive Torchlight Tattoo is presented by the U.S. Army Band and The Old Guard on Wednesdays at 7 p.m., mid-July to mid-August on the Ellipse. The U.S. Navy Lollipop Concert is also in August. See the Washington Monument listing on page 30.

- Spring and summer performances, weather permitting. Call 202-619-7222 or 202-619-PARK, Dial-a-Park, for information about specific events. Summer concert schedule at www.nps.gov/ncro

- Metrorail Blue and Orange lines (Smithsonian, Mall exit). Parking is very limited.

- Handicapped parking available off Independence Avenue at the rear of the theater.

Special activities include military band concerts, Memorial Day-Labor Day.

Toby's Dinner Theatre

*At South Entrance Road off Route 29, South, Columbia, MD (410-730-8311, 301-596-6161 or 800-888-6297) - **www.tobysdinnertheatre.com**.*

Since 1979, Toby's Dinner Theatre of Columbia has brought "the best of Broadway" musicals to a modern theatre-in-the-round. The only regional dinner theatre with a live orchestra, Toby's offers four family-friendly musicals each year.

Toby's Youth Theatre presents various productions throughout the year. Contact the theatre for information and group reservations.

- Field Trips.

West End Dinner Theater

*4615 Duke Street, Alexandria, VA (703-370-2500) - **www.wedt.com**. Plenty of well-lit, free parking.*

Introduce your children to the magic of live theater in an intimate setting! In addition to its regular adult programming (much of which is suitable for children as well), West End Theater offers children's shows every Saturday at 2 p.m.; suggested arrival time is 1:45 p.m. Reservations are required; snacks may be purchased. All adult evening performances and Wednesday and Sunday matinees include a full service menu. Two children's discounts are available: one for children 12 and under, and one for children 18 and under. No discounts for Saturday evening performances. West End also offers a children's summer theatre camp. Call for details and dates.

- Children's Theatre: tickets are under $15.
- Birthday Parties, Restaurant/Snack Bar, Wheelchair Accessible.

Wolf Trap Farm Park for the Performing Arts/The Barns at Wolf Trap

*1624 Trap Road, Vienna, VA (703-255-1860, box office, 703-255-1900, general information) - **www.wolftrap.org**. Take the Washington Beltway (I-495) to the Dulles Toll Road / Route 267 West; go to Wolf Trap exit (open for performances only). $4 shuttle at West Falls Church Metro for Filene Center performances.*

Wolf Trap is America's only national park for the performing arts. The **Filene Center**, surrounded by 100 acres of rolling hills, woods, and streams, combines under-the-roof and under-the-stars seating. Resident professional companies, as well as world-renowned artists, perform during the summer. During the fall and winter, performances are scheduled in the **Barns at Wolf Trap**. A wide variety of programs, from folk singing to jazz, are offered. **Theatre in Woods** presents shows for children in preschool and elementary school.

- Fielene Center is open May-September.
  Barns is open October-May.
- For information about field trips, call 703-255-1900.
- For season brochure, e-mail wolftrap@wolftrap.org or call (703) 255-1900.

Special activities include the International Children's Festival, featuring songs, dances, costumes, and crafts from around the world, held in early September; participatory theater, puppet, and dance programs for children in the summer; an Irish Festival with traditional music, dance, crafts, and more on Memorial Day weekend; and a Christmas Carol Sing-a-Long featuring a military band, local choral groups, and a candlelight procession (bring your own candle), the first Sunday in December.

Children's Books and Toys

A Likely Story Children's Bookstore

*1555 King Street, Alexandria, VA (703-836-2498) - **www.alikelystory books.com**. Take the Washington Beltway (I-495) to VA-193 exit (exit 43-44), towards George Washington Memorial Parkway/Georgetown Pike; merge into GW Parkway south, which becomes George Washington Memorial Parkway south. Turn slight right onto North Washington Street. Go about one-half mile; turn right onto King Street (VA-7).*

This child-friendly store offers the largest selection of books for children in Northern Virginia, as well as parenting and teacher professional books, audio and videotapes, puppets, puzzles, games, foreign language books and knowledgeable staff to assist in book selection. Special summer programs and book clubs are offered for all ages. Call or e-mail to be added to weekly e-mail newsletter of special events, author talks and new book reviews.

- Open Monday-Saturday, 10-6 p.m.; Sundays, 1-5 p.m.
- Story hours are held on Tuesdays at 11 and 11:30 for children under the age of two; Wednesday at 11 for children over two years old. Story times on Saturdays at 11 for ages two and up are followed by a craft.
- Metrorail Blue and Yellow lines (King Street Station).
- Appropriate for preschool age children.
- Field Trips, Wheelchair Accessible.

Special activities Monthly costume character appearances, autographing, story times, and other events.

Aladdin's Lamp Children's Books and Other Treasures

2499 Harrison Street, Suite 10, Arlington, VA (703-241-8281). Lee-Harrison Shopping Center, Lower Level (Near Harris Teetor Supermarket) - **aladlamp@speakeasy.org**. Plenty of free parking behind the store.

Aladdin's Lamp has moved to a new and much larger space. The founder and owner of this store, a former children's librarian, and the knowledgeable staff are eager to help parents and teachers choose good books to help children learn to love reading. The store stocks a wide selection of books - over 20,000 titles (from chewable infant books to folklore, nonfiction, children's classics and fantasy) for infants and toddlers to young adults, plus parenting books and teacher resources. The store carries tapes, puppets, educational toys and games, greeting cards, posters, stickers, rubber stamps, wooden puzzles, and much more.

Special services include fast special ordering for both children and adult books, wrapping and mailing, and discounts for teachers and schools. During the anniversary celebration the first week of December, special savings, giveaways and discounts are offered.

- Open Monday, Wednesday, Friday, Saturday, 10-6; Tuesday and Thursday, 10-8.

- Metrorail Orange line (East Falls Church and West Falls Church).

Special activities include programs for children ages 2½-6 on Wednesdays and Saturdays at 11, and for children six months to two years approximately once a month at 11 a.m. on Friday. Author visits are held throughout the year. Summer programs include weekly book discussion groups for grades K-2 and 3-6, an end-of-summer reading celebration, and summer reading programs for children ages 6-12.

Audubon Naturalist Woodend Bookshop

*8940 Jones Mill Road, Chevy Chase, MD (301-652-3606) - **www.audubon naturalist.org/bookshop**. Take the Washington Beltway (I-495) to the Connecticut Avenue exit south towards Chevy Chase; turn left onto Manor Road and then right on Jones Bridge Road; turn left onto Jones Mill Road to 8940 on the left.*

Located at Woodend, the home of the Audubon Naturalist Society, this shop stocks an extensive selection of books on animals and plants, nature books for children, unusual puppets and puzzles, nature games, and bird feeders. You might want to schedule your visit to coincide with the beginners' bird walk, held Saturday from 8-9 a.m. in the spring and fall. No registration is required. A visit at anytime can include a walk on the trails of Woodend's 40 acres, which border Rock Creek Park. Members of the Audubon Naturalist Society receive a 10% discount on bookshop purchases. Books maybe ordered online through the web site. See page 155 for more information on the Audubon Naturalist Society.

- Monday-Friday 10-5; Saturday 9-5 and Sunday noon-5.

Barnes and Noble

*4801 Bethesda Avenue, Bethesda, MD (301-986-1761) - **www.bn.com**. Parking one-half block west of the store on the north side of the street in a County parking garage behind Bethesda Row Shops.*

Barnes and Noble offers a broad selection of books with over 175,000 titles in stock and an extensive children's department. Children's events, such as children's author visits, story times, and children's activities, are scheduled regularly, as well as adult functions, such as book discussion groups and author appearances. This is a peaceful place to browse, have a cup of coffee, and enjoy the ambiance of fine literature all around. The Bethesda and Rockville stores have the strongest children's departments.

- Open daily, 9-11.
- Metrorail Red line (Bethesda). D.C. stores are accessible by Metrorail.
- Many additional locations.
- Restaurant/Snack Bar, Wheelchair Accessible.

Barston's Child's Play 🏵️16

*5536 Connecticut Avenue, NW, Washington, DC (202-244-3602) - **BARSTONS123@aol.com** Free parking behind store.*

This popular toy store, well known for its extremely knowledgeable and helpful staff and fine selection of toys, has greatly expanded its book section in recent years and added a children's book specialist to its staff. The store features an extensive section of board and pop-up books for young children, along with many puzzle, game, sticker and joke books, especially good for traveling families. This is a great source for book related toys, books on tape, audio and video tapes, and CDs for children. There is also a large selection of early readers, math and English workbooks, science and animal books, and "how to" books, such as children's cookbooks. The offerings for teens are primarily fantasy books.

- Open Monday-Friday, 9:30-7 (Thursdays until 8); Saturday, 9:30-6; Sunday, noon-5.

Borders Books

*White Flint Mall, 11301 Rockville Pike, Kensington, MD (301-816-1067) - **www.borders.com**. Check website for locations and directions. Parking.*

Children and their parents flock to Borders Books, not only to browse and buy, but to enjoy the delightful selection of children's entertainment, such as storytellers, musicians and children's authors, that Borders offers on a regular basis. Call or check website for schedule of events.

- Open 9 a.m.-11 p.m., Monday-Saturday; 9-9, Sunday.
- Metrorail Red line (White Flint).
- Many additional locations.
- Wheelchair and stroller accessible.
- Appropriate for preschool age children.
- Restaurant/Snack Bar.

Fairy Godmother

319 7th Street, SE, Washington, DC (202-547-5474).

This children's bookstore on Capitol Hill carries a wide range of fiction and non-fiction for infants through teens, as well as foreign language children's books and tapes. Fairy Godmother also has a large selection of creative toys and art materials, music CDs and cassettes, book-related videos and stuffed animals. The store will special order any items not in stock.

- Open Monday-Friday, 11-6; Saturday, 10-5; Sunday hours on holidays
- Metrorail Orange and Blue lines (Eastern Market).

Imagination Station

4524 Lee Highway (at Lorcum Ln), Arlington, VA (703-522-2047). Parking.

This store carries a large selection of children's books, including many *Tin Tin* books. There is a wide variety of audio and videotapes, a unique foreign language section, and a children's play area. Call to get on the mailing list for a newsletter that lists special events such as author and illustrator talks and character appearances. There is a weekly story hour for preschoolers on Fridays at 10 a.m.

- Open Monday-Friday, 10-7, Saturday, 10-6; Sunday, 10-4.

Noyes Library for Young Children

*10237 Carroll Place, Kensington, MD (301-929-5533) - **www.mont.lib. md.us**. Take the Washington Beltway (I-495) to Connecticut Avenue north exit, towards Kensington. At the sign "Welcome to Kensington," get into the right lane, so you can continue straight ahead (Connecticut Avenue bears left). Go to the stop sign, turn right onto Baltimore Street; at the next stop sign, go left to get on circle, Carroll Place. The Library is straight ahead, a small beige house at the intersection of Carroll Place and Montgomery Avenue. Limited on-street parking.*

This charming one-room library, Montgomery County's oldest, is now an historic landmark. It sits on its own triangular island surrounded by old trees and turreted Victorian homes. Once inside, children immediately sense the intimacy of this library which is just for them. There are programs for babies and toddlers, two-three year olds, preschoolers, and other special

> # Take Note...
>
> What's new at your public library?
>
> Year-round activities and summer reading programs abound at local libraries, with story time programs for young children. Books on CDs and tapes, as well as music, are also available.

events. Adults can borrow special Grandparents Kits with books, toys, and media centered on a particular theme to have on hand for visiting youngsters. For more information about children's services, contact any branch of the Montgomery County Department of Public Libraries, or visit the KidSite on the Library's website: www.montgomerylibrary.org.

- Open Tuesday, Thursday, and Saturday, 9-5.
- Appropriate for preschool age children.
- Picnicking.

Olsson's Books and Records

*106 S. Union Street, Alexandria, VA (703-684-0077) - **www.olssons.com**.*

Olsson's is the oldest independent book and music store in the Washington area. This bookstore has a good selection of children's books, as well as adult reading and music.

- Alexandria Store: Open Monday-Thursday, 10-10; Friday-Saturday, 10 a.m.-midnight; Sunday, 11-8.
- Many additional local stores.

Politics and Prose

*5015 Connecticut Avenue, NW, Washington, DC (202-364-1919) - **www.politics-prose.com**.*

The children's department of this independent, community-centered bookstore is an offshoot of the Cheshire Cat Children's Bookstore, which closed after 22 years in 1999. The Cheshire Cat was founded and run by former librarians and teachers and was known nationwide. Extremely knowledgeable personnel from the Cheshire Cat expanded and reinvented the Politics and Prose Children's book department to become the center of excellence and interest in children's literature that the former bookstore was noted as being. They feature frequent author talks, story hours, receptions for local children's book authors, and other regular and special events.

Events are announced on the bookstore's web site, and in e-mail and print newsletters. Members receive special sale discounts. Staff experts also write reviews of new children's books for the newsletter, and featured titles are discounted to members.

In addition to an extensive selection of paperback and hardback books for and about children and on parenting, there is also an expanded section of foreign language children books. They also stock children's CD's and tapes, T-shirts and book-related toys.

- Open 9 a.m.-10 p.m., Monday-Thursday; 9 a.m.-11 p.m., Friday and Saturday, 10 a.m.-8 p.m., Sunday.
- Homey, child-friendly coffeehouse, open during bookstore hours Monday–Saturday, 11-7 on Sunday.

Second Story Books

*4836 Bethesda Avenue, Bethesda, MD (301-656-0170) - **www.secondstory books.com**. Limited on-street parking; public lots nearby.*

Second Story Books has three locations (Rockville, Bethesda, and Dupont Circle). The Bethesda branch of this second-hand bookstore includes the largest selection of children's books, although all stores have some books for children and teens. Records, audiotapes, and videotapes are also available. Stock varies greatly but there are always gems to be found if you don't mind digging through the sometimes-disorganized inventory characteristic of used bookstores. Many wonderful children's books are out of print and only available at used bookstores or on Internet search services. Second Story Books can help you obtain titles that are out of print.

- Open daily, 10-10. Rockville store open 10-8, Sunday-Thursday; 10-9, Friday and Saturday.
- Metrorail Red line (Bethesda).
- Wheelchair access, but aisles are small.

Sullivan's Toy Store

3412 Wisconsin Avenue, NW, Washington, DC (202-362-1343).

This store has packed a lot of toys in a small space. There are toy, book, and art sections as well as party items. The book section is aimed primarily at very young children and features boards, pictures, books, activity and travel books and math and reading workbooks. Children will enjoy playing with the Brio train table while their parents shop. Family-owned (by the same family since it was founded), Sullivan's was the first store to carry the first edition of Going Places With Children in Washington, DC in 1958!

- Open Monday, Tuesday and Saturday, 10-6, Wednesday, Thursday and Friday, 10-7; Sunday, 12-5.
- Strollers are permitted, but the aisles are quite narrow.

189

Toys... Etc.

11325 Seven Locks Road, Potomac, MD (301-299-8300). Free parking.

A large assortment of toys and an excellent selection of books can be found at this shop in Cabin John Mall. Knowledgeable sales personnel are able and willing to make appropriate suggestions for any age child.

- Open Monday-Friday, 10-8; Saturday, 10-6; Sunday 12-5.
- Call to be added to the mailing list that announces special events, such as author talks.

Treetop Toys and Books

*Foxhall Square Mall, 3301 New Mexico Avenue, NW, Washington, DC (202-244-3500) - **www.treetopkids.com**. From the Capital Beltway, (I-495), take the River Road exit East towards Washington D.C.. Turn right onto Nebraska Avenue, NW. Turn left on to New Mexico Avenue, NW. Two and a half blocks on the right at the corner of New Mexico NW Avenue and Macomb Street NW. Free parking.*

Located near American University, this store offers high-quality toys, an excellent selection of favorite books and videos, and even children's clothing for newborns through size seven. If a book is not in stock, Tree Top will get it for you, often within two days, and will also ship items.

- Monday through Saturday, 9:30-5:30.
- Second location: Langley Shopping Center, 1382 Chain Bridge Road, McLean, VA 22101 (703-356-1400), Monday-Saturday, 9:30-6; Sunday, 10-4.
- Call to be added to the "Kidtivities" mailing list to find out about supervised art activities and new items.

Special activities include guest appearances by storybook favorites and visits from famous authors, regular visits by Turley the Magician, and a birthday club.

Whirligigs and Whimsies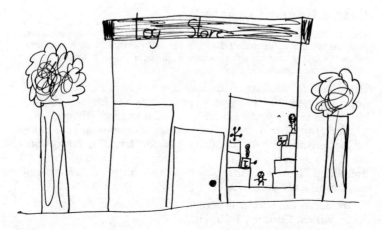

102019 Old Georgetown Road, Bethesda, MD (301-897-4940). Take the Washington Beltway (I-495) to the Old Georgetown Road exit towards Rockville; located one mile on the right in the Wildwood Shopping center. Free parking.

This charming children's toy store features toys for all ages and selection of gift books. Call the store for special events.

- Monday-Saturday 10-6, Thursdays until 7.

Zany Brainy

*1631 Rockville Pike, Rockville, MD (301-984-0112) - **www.zanybrainy. com**. Located in Congressional Shopping Center off of Rockville Pike (355) just north of Montrose Road.*

This children's toy and bookstore is a delightful place to take young children when out shopping. In addition to its outstanding selection of gifts, Zany Brainy offers a children's play area with a wooden train, and regularly scheduled story-readings, craft projects, character visits, etc. A monthly calendar of events is available on the web page or at the store, and patrons can sign up for e-mail notifications of upcoming programs.

- Open Monday-Saturday, 10-9; Sunday, 11-6.
- Additional location at the Kentlands in Gaithersburg, MD, 301-330-5160.
- Appropriate for preschool age children.

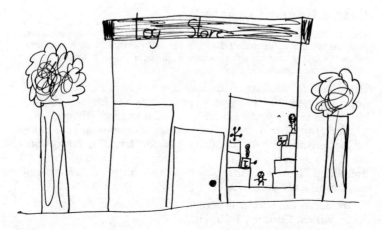

6. Sports and Recreation

Spectators

Baltimore Orioles

*Oriole Park at Camden Yards, 333 West Camden Street, Baltimore, MD (410-547-6113, 410-547-6113) - **www.theorioles.com**. Take Route I-95 north to Baltimore; follow the signs to Camden Yards. Or use I-95 north to Baltimore; take Exit 52 and follow signs.*

Glorious structure, good food, spectacular views... not to mention America's pasttime, Oriole Park at Camden Yards is nothing like the stadiums of yesteryear. A fun family outing, sure to inspire enthusiasm from the first-time or veteran fan! While you're there, visit the Babe Ruth Museum.

- Eutaw Street Corridor open, 9-3. Games Saturday and weekdays, 7:05 p.m.; Sunday, 1:35 p.m.
- Ticket prices range from $8 for standing room to $40 for club level. Most tickets cost $13-$25.
- MARC trains run from Union Station to Camden Yards, 800-325-RAIL.
- Tours during the baseball season: Monday-Friday, 11-2 every half hour; Saturday, 10:30-3 every half hour; Sunday, 12:30-3 every half hour. During off-season, two tours daily. Call for times, 410-547-6234.
- Recommended for children age ten and older.
- Security Information: No large bags or backpacks; security guards and TV monitoring of park.
- Field Trips, Picnicking.

Bowie Baysox Baseball

*4101 N.E. Crain Highway, Bowie, MD (301-805-6000) - **www.baysox.com**. Take the Washington Beltway (I-495) to Route 50 east towards Annapolis; follow Route 301 south to left at second traffic light; follow the signs to Prince George's Stadium.*

This Class AA affiliate of the Baltimore Orioles plays approximately 70 games per year. Seeing the Baysox play is a chance to watch professional baseball inexpensively and comfortably. The fireworks on special occasions are said to be "better than the 4th of July." Mascot "Louie" is always on hand to accentuate the family atmosphere created at the ballpark. There is a kids' play area for additional fun, as well as group picnic areas. Access the schedule via the website.

- Game times: April-September, Monday-Saturday, time varies; Sunday, 1:05 p.m.

- General admission: adults, $8; senior citizens, active military and children 6-14, $5; children five and under, free; and children 6-12 in their baseball uniforms Sunday through Thursday, free; reserved seats, $7.
- Full-service restaurant on-site by reservations only.
- Concessions and souvenir stands.
- Security Information: Local park police check bags at main gate.
- Birthday Parties, Restaurant/Snack Bar, Wheelchair Accessible.

Clark Griffith Collegiate Baseball League

8010 Towers Crescent Drive, 3rd Floor, Vienna, VA (703-760-1684) - www.clarkgriffithbaseball.org.

Enjoy a wooden bat baseball game at one of the area's best fields for a family summer night at the ball game. The Clark Griffith League teams present promising college players, many from our area. The ballparks feature concessions, raffles, trivia contests, special activities for children, and best of all, that great hometown feeling on game nights.

- Games in June and July — 5-7 nights each week.
- Ticket prices range from $5-10 (adults) to free for children under five or in baseball uniforms.
- **Bethesda Big Train - www.bigtrain.org** - Shirley Povich Field, 10600 Westlake Drive, Bethesda, MD - from the Washington Beltway (I-495). Take Old Georgetown exit north. Turn west (left) on Tuckerman Lane, left on Westlake Drive (½ mile). Enter at sign for Cabin John Park, stadium on right.
- **Silver Spring - Takoma Thunderbolts - www.tbolts.org** - Blair High School Stadium, 51 East University Blvd, just next to the Fire Station. From the Washington Beltway (I-495) take Colesville Road, Rt. 29 North, turn right on University Blvd. Go to the signal light at the firehouse and turn right to the field
- **Germantown Black Rox - www.blackrox.com** - Damascus Regional Park - Germantown Stadium Germantown, MD. From the Washington Beltway (I-495) take I-270 North to exit 16A, Father Hurley Blvd. Follow for 4.5 miles (at Rt. 355 it becomes Rt. 27). Turn right at the light on Kings Valley Road. Follow for 7/10th mile to field on left. Go past the two softball fields and park adjacent to Baseball Field #1.
- **Arlington Senators - www.arlingtonsenator.org** - Barcroft Field 4100 South Four Mile Run Drive,

Arlington, Virginia. From the Washington Beltway (I-495) take Arlington Boulevard/Route 50 exit towards D.C. Turn right on George Mason Drive. Take left on South Four Mile Run Drive to field.

- **Vienna Mustangs** - James Madison High School, Vienna, Virginia. From the Washington Beltway (I-495) to I-66 West. Take Nutley Street exit, turn North. Turn left at Maple Avenue (Route 123). Take immediate right on James Madison Drive to high school.

Frederick Keys Baseball

6201 New Design Road, Harry Grove Stadium, Frederick, MD (301-662-0013) - ***www.frederickkeys.com***. *Take the Washington Beltway (I-495) to I-270 north to I-70 Baltimore / Hagerstown. Take I-70 east towards Baltimore to Exit 54, then a left on Market Street.*

The Frederick Keys baseball team is the Carolina League Class A affiliate of the Baltimore Orioles. It is considered a high-quality farm team in the Carolina League. Some players become major league players! The Keys play 70 home games a season, so you have a good chance of finding a game scheduled when you are planning to visit the Frederick area.

- Open spring and summer with games scheduled evenings at 7:05 p.m. and Sunday at 1:05 p.m. Call for a schedule.
- General admission is on a first-come basis: adults, $8; children age 6-12, $5; children age five and under, free. Box seats, $11. Little Leaguers in uniform, free. Call for information on group rates, birthdays and picnics.
- Stroller and wheelchair accessible.
- Picnicking, Restaurant/Snack Bar.

Special activities include firework shows, Junior Keys Club, Funny Mascots, and much more!

Canoeing, Kayaking, and Sailing

Fletcher's Boathouse

*4940 Canal Road, NW, Washington, DC (202-244-0461) – **fletchersboat house.com**. From the Washington Beltway (I-495) take the Glen Echo exit (Clara Barton Parkway); the Clara Barton Parkway will become Canal Road at Chain Bridge; located near the intersection of Canal Road and Reservoir Road.*

Since the mid-1800s, Fletcher's Boathouse has been in operation. Situated close to Georgetown, this landmark offers the perfect embarkation point from which to rent bicycles, boats and canoes to use on the Potomac and canal. You can also purchase fishing licenses, bait, tackle, and cane poles to fish from the shoreline or from the boats. Even though summer is the best time for many of the water activities, a walk in the woods in the wintertime from this point in the C&O National Park is memorable. Hours vary with the seasons and conditions; usually open dawn to dusk March-November.

- Canoes $10/hour $20/day; Rowboats $10/hour $18/day; Bicycles $8/2 hours $12 day; fishing License $7 for DC Residents and $10 for non-residents
- Limited wheelchair access.
- Biking, Boating, Canoe and Kayak Rentals, Picnicking, Restaurant/Snack Bar.

Jack's Boats

*3500 K Street, NW, Washington, DC (202-337-9642) - **www.jacksboats. com**. Located underneath the Key Bridge in Georgetown. Street parking.*

Enjoy Washington from the water! At Jack's Boats, you can rent canoes, rowboats, and kayaks for some recreational fun in the Potomac River. View the Georgetown waterfront area, the Kennedy Center, and Watergate, and row across the river to Roosevelt Island, where you can dock your boat and do a little hiking and picnicking.

- Open 8 a.m.-sunset, April-October weather permitting.
- Rentals: one hour, $10; all day, $30. No credit cards (cash/checks only).
- K Street to end becomes Water Street. Jack's Boats has a small parking lot underneath Key Bridge.
- Life jackets available in all sizes.

Swain's Lock

10700 Swain's Lock Road, Potomac, MD (301-299-9006). Take the Washington Beltway (I-495) to River Road west, Exit 39; go five and a half miles to left onto Swain's Lock Road.

Swain's Lock is the perfect place to rent bikes for a trip along the 185-mile-long canal. Buy a hand line, bait, and tackle to fish in the Potomac, take a short bike trip of 2.3 miles to Great Falls, or rent a canoe or kayak for an idyllic outing on the canal. Picnic tables, grills, and light snacks are available.

- Open daily, 10-7, March-November.
- Handicapped portable bathroom available.
- Canoe lessons, Thursday, 6:30 p.m., April-September.
- Bike Rentals
- Field Trips, Birthday Parties, Biking, Boating, Camping, Fishing, Hiking, Picnicking.

Thompson's Boat Center

*Rock Creek Parkway and Virginia Avenue, NW, Washington, DC (202-333-9543) - **www.guestservices.com/tbc**. From the Washington Beltway (I-495) take I-395 North towards D.C. Follow the Memorial Bridge signs. Take the right lane, which passes west of the Pentagon. Cross the Memorial Bridge and bear left in as you pass the Lincoln Memorial. Turn left onto 23rd street. Continue on 23rd street for several blocks to Virginia Avenue, NW. Turn left on Virginia and get into the left lane. Thompson's parking lot is across the Parkway. (Note: You cannot turn left into Thompson's Boat Center from Rock Creek Parkway if you are headed north.).*

Enjoy a day on the Potomac River with Thompson's Boat Center. Bicycle rentals include all-terrains and cruisers. Boat rentals include: kayaks (both single and doubles); canoes (can hold up to two people); and rowing shells (single recreational, single racing, and double racing).

- Open 7-7, Monday-Saturday; 8–6, Sunday.
- Boat and bike rental rates vary. Call for specific information.
- Bicycle rentals begin at 7 a.m. Monday-Saturday, and 8 a.m. on Sunday. All rentals must be returned by 7 p.m. Monday-Saturday and 6 p.m. on Sunday.
- Boat rentals begin at 8 a.m. Monday-Saturday, and 9 a.m. on Sunday for sculls and 8:30 a.m. and 9:30 a.m. for shells. Rentals must be returned by 6:15 p.m. Monday-Saturday and 5:15 p.m. on Sunday.

Special activities include lessons and rowing programs from beginner to master for both adult and juniors. Competitive and developmental Summer Junior Programs are also available.

Washington Sailing Marina

*1 Marina Drive George Washington Memorial Parkway, Alexandria, VA (703-548-9027) - **www.guestservices.com/wsm**. Located on the George Washington Memorial Parkway one mile south of Reagan National Airport.*

This George Washington Memorial Parkway/National Park Service concession is the place to rent a Sunfish, Island Scot, or Flying Scot for a few hours for a sail around the lagoon or to see Old Town Alexandria or Haines Point from the water. The Marina is home to three sailing clubs, and offers lessons and camps for all levels.

- Sailboat rentals spring through mid-October, 11-5. Last boats out at 4. Boat rentals by reservation only and require certification from a recognized sailing school or a written test at the marina.

- Bike rentals year-round. Mount Vernon is 12 miles south along the Mount Vernon Trail.

- Restaurant; Gift Shop.

Equestrian

Meadowbrook Stables

*8200 Meadowbrook Lane, Chevy Chase, MD (301-589-9026) - **www.mc-mncppc.org**. From the Washington Beltway (I-495) take Connecticut Avenue South to East-West Highway; turn left on Meadowbrook Lane; entrance to the stables is on the right.*

Meadowbrook Stables is a horseback riding facility which offers trail rides as well as a full lesson program for ages five and older, and is home to many "A" rated horse shows.

- Open daily, 10-5. Call for schedule and fees.

Potomac Horse Center

*14211 Quince Orchard Road, Gaithersburg, MD (301-208-0200) - **www.potomachorse.com**. Take the Washington Beltway (I-495) to I-270 north; Take Exit 6B (Route 28, west); follow it for about two and a half miles; turn left on Muddy Branch Road; proceed for two miles and turn right on Quince Orchard Road.*

This nationally-known riding school has three indoor arenas, two outdoor rings, and extensive trails, and offers lessons and a therapeutic riding program for children and adults of all levels. The Center also offers horse boarding.

- Open Monday-Friday, 9-9; Saturday-Sunday, 9-5.
- Birthday Parties, Hiking, Picnicking.

Special activities include a ten-week summer camp program, horse shows, and clinics.

Rock Creek Park Horse Center

*5100 Glover Road, NW, Washington, DC (202-362-0118) - **www.rockcreekhorsecenter.com**. Located off Military Road between Connecticut Avenue and 16th Street (follow brown Park Service signs).*

See beautiful Rock Creek Park by horseback! This horse center is DC's only full-service equestrian facility. Weekend and midweek trail rides must be reserved in advance. All riders must be at least 12 years of age and must wear a helmet, which will be provided. Riding lessons for all levels, from beginners through basic dressage, as well as summer day camp, are offered for children eight years and older.

- Tuesday-Friday, noon-6; Saturday-Sunday, 9-5. Closed Mondays and Thanksgiving, Christmas, and New Year's Day.
- Call ahead for availability and reservations.
- Public stables in a beautiful park.
- Wheelchair Accessible.

Golf and Miniature Golf

Rocky Gorge 4 Seasons Golf Fairway

*Route 29 & Old Columbia Road Laurel, Maryland 20723 (301-725-0888-golf; 301-725-8947-batting cages) – **www.rockygorgegolf.com**.
From 495, take US 29 north 2½ miles past Burtonsville, to just south of MD 216; entrance on the right.*

The batting range boasts a 300-foot Home-Run Fence and sheltered cages for baseball or slow pitch softball. The 19-hole miniature golf range includes one of the world's longest miniature golf holes. The golf driving range features sheltered tees and a lighted putting green.

- Open in all weather, seven days a week, year round.
- Driving range; miniature golf; batting cages; arcade
- Batting cages 10-10.
- Golf 9 a.m.-11 p.m. $5 for 65 balls; $9 for 130 balls; miniature golf Monday-Saturday, 10-6, $4/game; $6/game Sundays, holidays and after 6 p.m.

White Flint Golf Park

*5451 Marinelli Road, Rockville, MD (301-230-7117) - **www.whiteflintgolf park.com**.*

- Open 8 a.m.-11 p.m. Tuesdays through Sundays and 11 a.m.-11 p.m. Mondays.
- $5 for ages eight and older; $3 for ages 4-7; three and younger, free.
- Birthday Parties.

Special activities include: miniature golf, driving range and golf camps for ages 7-17.

Skating, Boarding, and Blading

ARC IceSports of Rockville

50 Southlawn Court, Rockville, MD (301-294-8101, 301-315-5650) -
www.arcrockville.com. *Take Route 355 north; turn right on Route 28
(Norbeck Road); turn left on E. Gude Drive; turn right on Southlawn Lane
and then right on Southlawn Court. Parking available.*

This state-of-the-art skating facility is centrally located in
Montgomery County. In addition to two NHL-sized rinks,
there is a skate shop, Spike's Diner, an electronic game
arcade, and several party rooms for birthdays, receptions, etc.
Skating, of course, is at the heart of it all, and there are
lessons for every age and skill level in figure skating and
hockey. Children can begin group skating lessons at the age
of three years old.

For the more advanced, there is a comprehensive figure
skating training program featuring training sessions,
workshops, and clinics with National and Olympic coaches.
There is plenty of hockey played here too, with hockey
initiation programs and Montgomery Youth Hockey
Association, as well as Adult and Junior leagues.

- Hours vary daily; call or check website for schedule.
- $5.50 Weekdays; $6 Weekends; $2 Skate Rental.
  Group rates available.
- Stroller and wheelchair accessible.
- Birthday Parties, Restaurant/Snack Bar.

Bowie Skate Park

*Gallant Fox Lane at Route 197 (301-262-6200, 301-809-3001 after 5 p.m.
and on weekends) -* ***www.cityofbowie.org/leisure/skatepark.htm***

The park provides 8,000 square feet for skateboard and
rollerblade use and offers skating equipment for all skill
levels. Special safety equipment is required.

- Admission to the Skatepark is free, but all skaters are
  required to obtain a City of Bowie Skatepark User
  Identification Card in order to use the facility. This
  photo identification card must be obtained at the City
  Gymnasium located at 4300 Northview Drive.
- April–May: Wednesday-Friday, 3 p.m. – dusk;
  Saturday-Sunday, noon-dusk.
- June, July, August: Wednesday-Sunday, noon-dusk.
- September-October: Wednesday-Friday 3 p.m.–dusk;
  Saturday-Sunday, noon-dusk

- November: Saturday-Sunday, noon-dusk
- The Skate Park may be closed in the event of rain or extreme heat.
- Features: 5' Kicker Wedge; 2.5' Fun Box with grind rail; 1.5' Low wedge; 3' Medium Wedge; Kinked grind rail; Straight grind rail
- Helmet, elbow and knee pads required at all times.

Cabin John Ice Rink

10610 Westlake Drive, Rockville, MD 20852 (301-365-2246, 301-365-0585-recording) - www.mc-mncppc.org/parks/facilities/skate.shtm

Cabin John Ice Rink, completely renovated in recent years, has two large rinks for free-style skating and ice hockey games, as well as a smaller rink for lessons. This state-of-the-art facility is open year round and offers a variety of open-skating sessions, as well as private and group lessons.

- Admission ranges from $3-$6 depending on age and time of day. Skate rental is $3. Discount books are available.
- Please refer to web site for schedule of sessions.
- Pro-shop, Snack Bar, Party Room.

Fairfax Ice Arena

3779 Pickett Road, Fairfax, VA (703-323-1131, 703-323-1132) - www.fair faxicearean.com. Take the Washington Beltway (I-495) to Little River Turnpike exit, Route 236 west); at the eighth traffic light at Pickett Road, turn right; ice rink is on the right after passing three traffic lights.

Fairfax Ice Arena has year-round public skating, offering lessons for children age four and older as well as adults. Additionally, the rink offers adult hockey leagues, summer camp programs, and arcade games.

- Hours for public sessions vary season to season.
- Adults, $6; children (12 and under), $5.50; children (five and under), $4.50; skate rental, $2.50 weekdays (hockey skates, $3.50). Weekend and holiday sessions are slightly higher. Discount cards available.
- Wheelchair ramp on the side of the building.

Franconia Roller Skating Center

5508 Franconia Road, Alexandria, VA (703-971-3334). Take the Washington Beltway (I-495) to Franconia/Van Dorn Street exit; at light, bear right; go to fourth light (half a mile) and turn left on Franconia Road; go one-quarter mile; at Crown Gasoline Station, turn left to rink.

Visit this family-oriented skating center for some rollerskating fun. Special sessions are reserved for children and families, as well as adults and teens.

- Open Friday, 7-11 p.m.; Saturday, 10-12 and 1-4; Sunday, 1-7; all other evenings, 7-10.
- Admission, $3.50-$5; skate rental, $1.50.
- Restaurant/Snack Bar.
- Toe-stops must be light colored.

Gardens Ice House

*13800 Old Gunpowder Road, Laural, MD (301-953-0100) - **www.thegar densicehouse.com**. From the Washington Beltway (I-495) take I-95 North towards Baltimore. Take the first exit to Powder Mill Road East (Route 212). Turn left on Old Gunpowder Road. (first left). The rink is about 2 miles down the road on the left side.*

The Gardens is an impressive year-round skating facility for hockey, figure skating, speed skating, in-line skating, ice dancing, and even indoor soccer, ice dancing, and curling.

The facilities include an Olympic size rink and two National Hockey League size rinks with spectator seating.

- Skate rental, café, party rooms, game room, pro shop, fitness club, locker rooms; birthday parties.

Reston Ice Skating Pavilion

*1818 Discovery Lane, Reston, VA (703-709-6300) - **www.restontown center.com**. Take the Washington Beltway (I-495) to the Dulles Toll Road to Reston Parkway exit; go two blocks and turn left on Bluemont Way. NOTE: Do not get on the Dulles Access Road.*

This beautiful outdoor ice-skating rink is located in the middle of Reston Town Center, surrounded by restaurants, shops, and a movie theater. Rentals are available for children's double-bladed skates and helmets, and for adults as well. The facility is available for rent and birthday parties.

- Open daily, mid-November through mid-March: 11-7, Monday and Thursday; until 11 p.m. on Friday and Saturday; until 9 p.m. on Tuesday and Wednesday.
- Adults, $5.75; children (age 12 and under), $4.75; skate rental, $2.50.
- Restaurant/Snack Bar, Wheelchair Accessible.

Rockville Roller Skating Center

1632 E. Gude Drive, Rockville, MD (301-340-7767). Located two blocks off Norbeck Road (Route 28 east). Take the Washington Beltway (I-495) to I-270 north to Montrose Road east. Turn left onto Tower Oaks Blvd; turn right onto Wooton Parkway, which becomes 1st Street / MD 911 east, which becomes MD 28 east. MD 28 east become Norbeck road after approximately .25 miles. Turn left onto east Gude Drive.

Whether you're an in-line or traditional quad skater, you'll appreciate the real maple wood skate floor of this large family-oriented rink which has been operating for over 21 years.

- Open Saturday and Sunday, as well as Montgomery County school holidays, 1-4; evening skating on Friday-Sunday nights; Tuesday evening session for adults only, 7-10; and Saturday mornings sessions for young children, 10-noon. Private sessions available for groups or fundraisers, Monday- Wednesday.

- Afternoons, $7.50; evenings, $8.25; Saturday mornings, $6.05. Skate rental, $1.65.

- Birthday Parties, Restaurant/Snack Bar.

Rockville Skate Park at Welsh Park

355 Martin Lane (at Mannakee Street), Rockville, MD (240-876-2655). Take the Washington Beltway (I-495) to I-270 north to Route 28 (West Montgomery Avenue) towards Rockville. Take a left onto Mannakee Road. Continue around the traffic circle on Mannakee Road. Take a right onto Martins Lane. Park is on the right.

This 10,300 square foot skating arena is a great place for in-line skaters, skateboarders, and free style bikers.

Skate-N-Fun Zone

7878 Sudley Road, Manassas, VA (703-361-7465, 800-203-4605) – **skaten** **funzone.com***. Take the Washington Beltway (I-495) to I-66 west to Exit 47A (Route 234 south); go straight through four traffic lights to Skate-N-Fun on the right on Sudley Road. Approximately 30 minutes from D.C.*

Skate-N-Fun offers in-line and roller-skating, as well as "Laser Storm", a laser tag game, a soft-play area, rock climbing wall and a video arcade. Skating lessons and private parties are also available.

- Offers a wide variety of session themes and activity combinations.

- Admission for skating varies with the season; call for hours.

- Stroller and wheelchair accessible.

- Birthday Parties, Playgrounds, Wheelchair Accessible.

Snowboarding and Skiing

Liberty Mountain Resort

78 Country Club Drive, Carroll Valley, PA (717-642-8282) - **www.ski liberty.com**. Take the Washington Beltway (I-495) to I-270 north to Frederick. Take Route 15 north to Emmitsburg; exit onto South Seton Avenue. At light, turn left onto Route 140 west; follow it to Pennsylvania Route 116 east. Turn right onto Route 116 east; follow it for three miles.

Take a day trip to the slopes at Ski Liberty, a nearby (1-1½ hours from D.C.) ski resort that offers many different instructional choices for children and adults, from all day children's ski camps and childcare, to skiing, to snowboarding and snow tubing.

- Open non-holiday weekdays, 9 a.m.-10 p.m.; weekends and holidays, 8 a.m.-10 p.m.
- Rates for rentals and lift tickets vary. Call for a current brochure or visit the website for more information.
- Wheelchair Accessible.

Roundtop

925 Roundtop Road, Lewisberry, PA (717-432-9631, 717-432-7000) - **www.skiroundtop.com**. Take the Washington Beltway (I-495) to I-270 north to Frederick; take Route 15 north to Dillsburg, PA. Turn right at the first light (Harrisburg Street). At top of hill, turn right. At next light, turn left. Turn left onto Pineforest Road to Roundtop Road. Located about two hours from DC.

Roundtop is primarily a ski and snowboard resort with 16 trails and 9 chair lifts. Snow tubing is also popular. In the summer, Roundtop offers three paintball fields. Rental equipment is available for all activities.

- Open in winter for skiing and snowboarding, 9 a.m.-10 p.m.; for tubing, 10-10. In the summer, paintball is open 9-9.
- Admission varies; group rates available.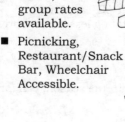
- Picnicking, Restaurant/Snack Bar, Wheelchair Accessible.

Wisp at Deep Creek Mountain Resort

P.O. Box 629, 296 Marsh Hill Road, McHenry, MD (301-387-4911) -
www.skiwisp.com. *180 miles from Washington. I-270 to Frederick, MD;*
take I-70 West to Handcock, MD to I-68 West and Cumberland. Take Exit
14A to U.S. Route 219 South to McHenry. Follow signs one mile to Wisp.

Wisp is situated near Deep Creek Lake, and offers 22 ski
trails covering 100 acres of terrain. Children's programs for
ages 3-14 are available for half- and full-days, by advance
reservations.

The resort includes an 18-hole championship golf course,
driving range, and Outdoor Adventures with a 20,000 square
foot paved and wood skate park, paintball, scenic chairlift
rides, mountain boarding and mountain biking. Sailboats are
available for rent in the summer through mid-October.

Whitetail Resort

13805 Blair Valley Road, Mercersburg, PA (717-328-9400) - ***www.ski***
whitetail.com. *Take the Washington Beltway (I-495) to I-270 north to*
I-70 west to Exit 18, Clear Spring. Turn right at the end of the exit; go
through the traffic light; at the island, turn right onto Broadfording Road.
Go one-half mile to left on Blairs Valley Road.

The Whitetail Resort features skiing, snowboarding and snow
tubing on 108 acres of terrain with 17 trails, 6 lifts and a
935-foot vertical drop. Whitetail offers a variety of ski school
programs for children as well as childcare and ski camp
packages. In the spring, summer, and fall, Whitetail offers
more than 30 miles of hiking trails, scenic chairlift rides, fly-
fishing, and outdoor skills programs. There is also a summer
Junior Adventure Camp program for children ages 12-16.

- Open daily in the winter for skiing, 8:30 a.m.-10 p.m.
  (opens at 12 noon Christmas Day),

- Snow tubing, 4-10, Monday-Thursday, and 10-10
  Friday-Sunday and holidays. There is a shuttle that
  will take you to the tubing area. Wear warm boots; ski
  boots are not allowed on the tubes.

- Note that Whitetail no longer offers mountain biking.

- Ski rental, lift ticket, and lesson prices vary.
  Call for a current brochure or visit the website

- Be sure to arrive early to reserve a snowboard.

- Free ski and snowboard checking available.

- Camping, Fishing, Hiking, Picnicking,
  Restaurant/Snack Bar.

Swimming and Splashing

Bohrer Park at Summit Hall Farm

*Activity Center at Bohrer Park, 506 South Frederick Ave., Gaithersburg, MD (301-258-6350, 301-258-6445, pool) - **www.ci.gaithersburg.md.us**. Take the Washington Beltway (I-495) to I-270 north; exit at Shady Grove Road; turn right on Shady Grove Road to left turn on Frederick Avenue (Route 355) for approximately 1.5 miles. The Farm Park is on your left on Education Boulevard.*

This park features a pool with two 250-foot water slides, a boat with water cannons, and a raindrop umbrella. For children under five, the splash pool features a frog slide, seal spray, and a floating alligator. The miniature golf course in a natural park setting has a large waterfall and garden pond, which empty into streams that flow through the course. The park also has three putting greens, a children's playground, and a skate park. The Activity Center features two gymnasiums, three multi-purpose rooms, fitness room, and offices for the Department of Parks and Recreation.

- Park offices open Monday-Friday, 8-5.
  Pool open in summer, daily, 11-8.

- Miniature golf open daily in the summer, 11-11.

- Picnicking, two pavilions available for group rental; two concession stands.

Downpour at Algonkian Regional Park

*47001 Fairway Drive, Sterling, VA (703-352-5900, 703-359-4603) - **www.nvrpa.org**. Take the Washington Beltway (I-495) take Route 7 west for 15 miles to the Cascades Parkway north exit. Continue on Cascades Parkway for three miles to the park entrance.*

Downpour, the water playground at **Algonkian Regional Park**, is brimming with buckets of summertime water fun. A huge water bucket pours 800 gallons into the play pool every three minutes, drenching everyone in range. The bucket tops an intricate interactive tower in the play pool that invites children to climb, shoot water cannons, slide down one of two slides and activate a variety of water jets. In the main pool, a 20-foot slide tower leads to two slides. Floating polyethylene-foam alligators and snakes, and a shipwreck slide add to the water fun in this free-form pool.

Algonkian Regional Park offers a popular 18-hole champion-ship golf course, a meeting and reception complex, 12 vacation cottages, group and family picnicking, boat launching, fishing, miniature golf and a nature trail. See Algonkian Regional Park, on page 127 for additional information.

- Opens the last weekend in May from 11-7, daily through the middle of August, when weekday hours may be limited.

- Daily admission: Individuals 48" or taller, $7; Individuals 48" or shorter, $6; Seniors (60+), $6; Children age two or younger, free. Fees are reduced after 4 p.m. on weekdays. Discount tickets available.

Martin Luther King, Jr. Swim Center (MLK)

1201 Jackson Road, Silver Spring, MD (301-989-1206). Take the Washington Beltway (I-495) to New Hampshire Avenue north; turn right on Jackson Road. The swim center is located on the right.

One of Montgomery County's three indoor pools, this center features an Olympic-sized indoor swimming pool (with classes for a full range of ages and abilities). Separate shallow warm water pool with easy access, hydrotherapy pool, weight and exercise room and an all purpose room

- Open daily, 7 a.m.-sundown.
- Birthday Parties, Athletic Fields, Fishing, Picnicking, Playgrounds, Tennis, Wheelchair Accessible.

Montgomery Aquatic Center

*5900 Executive Boulevard, Rockville, MD (301-468-4211) – **montgomery countymd.gov/mc/services/rec/aq.htm**. Take Rockville Pike (Route 355) north to left on Nicholson Lane; turn right on Executive Boulevard. Turn left into the pool complex at traffic light.*

This spectacular facility has a 50-meter, L-shaped indoor swimming pool. For divers there are one- and three-meter springboards and an 18-foot diving well. For an exciting thrill, children and parents will enjoy the 233-foot water slide. For younger children, there is a shallow pool with a beach-style entry featuring a waterfall.

- Open weekdays, 6 a.m.-10 p.m.; Saturday, 8 a.m-7:45 p.m..; Sunday, 10-6. Call to confirm hours.
- Montgomery County residents: adults, $4.50; children and senior citizens, $3.50. Non-residents: adults, $6; children and senior citizens, $5. Family and seasonal passes are also available.
- Metrorail Red line (White Flint).
- Racquetball court and workout room.
- Swimming lessons, and swim and diving teams.
- Appropriate for preschool age children.
- Birthday Parties, Playgrounds.

Olney Indoor Swim Center

Olney Manor Park, 16601 Georgia Avenue, Olney, MD (301-570-1210) - ***www.montgomerycounty.org/services/req/ag.html****. Take the Washington Beltway (I-495) to George Avenue north; swim center is on the right. Parking available.*

The Olney Swim Center offers many enticing features for children such as "Tumble Buckets," a waterfall mushroom, kiddy slides, and a beach-style entry. There are two hydrotherapy pools for adults, an 8-lane, 25-yard pool with separate diving areas for 1 and 3 meter boards. There is a sauna in each locker room, and a special dressing/locker room area for families or people with special needs.

- Montgomery County residents: adults, $4.25; children and seniors, $3.50. Non-residents: children and seniors, $4.50; adults, $5.50.
- Located in a park setting with outside playground and picnic tables.
- Swim lessons are offered regularly.
- Family swim sessions daily, call for scheduled recreational swim hours, 301-570-1210. Call for other swim sessions and lesson schedule.
- Stroller and wheelchair accessible.
- Appropriate for preschool age children.

Special activities children's programs include swimming lessons, swim and dive teams.

Rockville Municipal Swim Center

355 Martins Lane, Rockville, MD (301-309-3040, schedule and fees, 301-309-3045) - ***www.ci.rockville.md.us/swim/swim.html****. Take the Washington Beltway (I-495) to I-270 north to Route 28 (West Montgomery Avenue) towards Rockville. Take a left onto Mannakee Road. Continue around the traffic circle on Mannakee Road. Take a right onto Martins Lane. The swim center is on the right.*

The Rockville Swim Center has two indoor and two outdoor pools (one with a water slide), saunas, whirlpool, and exercise rooms. The pool offers a large variety of classes and has many features that will appeal to children.

- Open daily, 6 a.m.-9 p.m.; call for specific hours.
- During swim season, Rockville residents pay $4.50 for adults; $3.50 for ages 17 and younger. Nonresidents pay $1 more. Admission covers both the swim center facilities and Bankshot basketball. After Labor Day, the pools close and Bankshot is free.
- Athletic Fields, Picnicking, Playgrounds, Restaurant/Snack Bar, Tennis.

South Germantown Recreational Park - Splash Playgound and Miniatuure Golf

14501 Schaeffer Road, Boyds, MD (301-601-3580-recording, 301-601-3581-golf, 301-601-3582-splash playground). Take exit 15B off I-270 toward Germantown. Stay on MD Route 118 for 3 miles, passing Clopper Road (route 117). Turn right at Richter Farm Road, turn left at the traffic light at Schaeffer Road; follow signs.

South Germantown Recreational Park's Central Park features two championship miniature golf courses, and a splash playground with a rain tree, a water tunnel, a tumbling buckets waterfall, and a 36' water maze. The two 18-hole putting courses provide real challenges with water features, sand traps, rough turf and natural obstacles that are part of the unique design. The miniature golf season may extend beyond October, weather permitting. Call for information.

- Open end of May to early September; hours vary by season; check by phone or web for details
- Splash Playground, $3.50; Miniature Golf, 18 holes, $5 per person. Discount books available.
- Lockers, showers, dressing room, vending area.

Splash Down Water Park

7500 Ben a.m. Park Drive, Manassas, VA (703-361-4451) - **www.splash downwaterpark.com**. *Take I-66 west to Route 234; proceed on Route 234 south for one mile. Turn left on Sudley Manor Drive; after two miles, turn left into park.*

Like a day at the beach without the drive, Splash Down Water Park offers 13 acres of fun with five unique water attraction areas, a shallow-entry beach area, water slides for all ages and thrill levels, water raindrops and bubblers, a 770 foot lazy river, special children's area, and plenty more!

- Open Sunday-Thursday, 11-7; Friday-Saturday, 11-9.
- $12.25 for anyone over 48" tall; $9.25 for visitors under 48". Group rates and season passes.
- Birthday Parties, Athletic Fields, Picnicking, Playgrounds, Restaurant/Snack Bar, Tennis, Wheelchair Accessible.

7. Indoor Recreation

When it's too cold to walk in the rain or too hot for a day outside consider these possibilities for creative or athletic - or just entertaining indoor play.

Indoor Play and Arcades

Chuck E Cheese

*516 North Frederick Avenue, Gaithersburg, MD (301-869-9010, 301-948-1613) - **www.chuchecheese.com**. Five locations in the Washington Metropolitan area. The website has a restaurant locator.*

With rides appropriate for very young toddlers, sophisticated arcade games for older kids, and a climbing playstation with tunnels, slides and ball pits, this children's arcade and pizza parlor is a place for a rainy afternoon. Have a pizza lunch, enjoy the mechanical animal musical revue, and say hello to Chuck E Cheese himself... a human-size mouse who comes out to shake hands with the kids and dance with birthday celebrants.

- Open daily.
- Free admission, but tokens must be purchased for games and rides.
- Appropriate for preschool age children.
- Birthday Parties, Restaurant/Snack Bar.

Dave and Buster's

*White Flint Mall, North Bethesda, MD (301-230-5151) - **www.daveand busters.com**. Take the Washington Beltway (I-495) to I-270 north; exit at Democracy Boulevard, east. Take Democracy Boulevard to Old Georgetown Road; turn left. At Tuckerman Lane (third traffic light), turn right, to Rockville Pike (Route 355). Turn left onto Rockville Pike; White Flint Mall is on the right.*

Excitement bombards you from every direction in this 60,000 square feet new-age video arcade. Rechargeable interactive power cards may be purchased at the center kiosk for use with arcade and video games as well as for simulated theatrical thrill rides.

Dave and Buster's welcomes younger guests, but is primarily an adult establishment. Guests under the age of 21 must be accompanied by a parent or guardian; one parent or guardian can accompany up to a maximum of three underage guests who must remain with them at all times.

- Open daily at 11:30 a.m.; closes at midnight, Sunday–Tuesday; 1 a.m., Wednesday and Thursday; 2 a.m., Friday and Sunday.
- After 10 p.m., Friday and Saturday, admission $5.
- Metrorail Red line (White Flint). Plenty of parking on the third parking level of White Flint Mall.
- Recommended for children age ten and older.
- Birthday Parties, Restaurant/Snack Bar, Wheelchair Accessible.

ESPN Zone

*Corner of 11th and E Street, Washington, DC (202-783-3776) - **espn.go. com/espninc/zone**. 601 E. Pratt Avenue, Baltimore, MD (410-685-3776). From the Washington Beltway (I-495) take Connecticut Avenue towards Washington D.C. past Dupont Circle. Turn left onto K Street and then right onto 11th Street. ESPN is on the corner of 11th and E Street.*

This sports dining and entertainment complex has over 100 interactive games and attractions in the Sports Arena. The Zone is also the place to catch a live broadcast with ESPN. The video wall includes a 16-foot screen!

- Opens daily at 11:30 a.m. till 12:30 a.m. Monday through Thursday, 12:30 a.m. on Friday and Saturday, and 11 p.m. on Sunday. Last entry is one hour prior to closing time.
- Baltimore times vary - see website or call.
- Restaurant/Snack Bar.

ExploraWorld

*6570 Dobbin Road, Columbia, MD (410-772-1540) - **www.explora world.com**. Take the Washington Beltway (I-495) to Route 29 (Columbia Pike north); take Route 175 east for approximately three miles. Turn right onto Dobbin Road. Travel .7 miles and turn right into parking lot.*

ExploraWorld is Maryland's largest hands-on activity center for children, with 24,000 square feet to explore and 25 different theme exhibits appropriate for children ages 1-10. Your child might choose to sing on the karaoke stage, shop in the child-size grocery store, play on the medieval castle, explore the Chesapeake Bay room or participate in more than 35 other fun and educational activities.

- Open Monday-Thursday 9:30-5:30, Friday-Saturday 9:30-8, Sunday 11:30-6.
- Children ages 2-14, $7.95; children age one, $3.95; under age one, free; adults (age 15 and above), $2. (One adult must accompany each group of 1-6 children.)

- Café
- Birthday parties and field trips.
- Wheelchairs and strollers welcome.
- Appropriate for preschool age children.

Special activities include daily events for young children (call for an activity calendar).

Jeepers

700 Hungerford Drive, Rockville, MD (301-340-3308, 800-533-7377) - **www.jeepers.com**. *Located on Route 355, one block south of Montgomery College. 6000 Greenbelt Road, Greenbelt, MD (301-982-2444). Located in the Beltway Plaza Mall.*

This indoor playland for children age 2-12 has a large softplay area with tunnels and slides, a roller coaster, bumper cars, and a large arcade area with over 50 games to play.

- Open Monday-Thursday, 11-9; Friday-Saturday, 10-10; Sunday, 11-8.
- Visitors may pay for each ride and game, or get an unlimited all-day pass. Discounts for toddlers shorter than 36".
- Popular birthday party site.
- On-site fast food dining.
- Wheelchair Accessible.

Parenting Resource Centers

332 W. Edmonston Drive, Rm. D4, Rockville, MD (301-279-8497, 301-929-2025). Connecticut Park Center, 12518 Greenly Street, Room 10, Silver Spring, MD 20906 (301-929-2037).

The Parenting Resource Centers are a program of the Montgomery County Schools, providing opportunities for parents and children to play and learn together with the guidance of a parent educator. The centers promote school readiness, encourage language, social skills, curiosity, and cognitive development, provide resources, help with parenting problems, and opportunities to share ideas and concerns.

- Hours vary by location. Call for schedule. Centers are open on a drop-in basis to families with infants, toddlers, and preschoolers.
- Families may register in person at any center. The membership fee is $55 per family per year, plus a $5 materials fee for children over one year of age. Reduced fees, scholarships and payment plans are available.
- Appropriate for preschool age children.

Climbing and Laser Tag

Galyan's Trading Company ✦16✦

*Gaithersburg, MD - **www.gaylans.com**. Washingtonian Center, 2 Grand Corner Avenue, Gaithersburg, MD 20878 301-947-0200. From the Washington Beltway (I-495) take I-270 North to I-370 west. Take the Shelburne Terrace. Exit (first exit) and proceed to Rio Blvd (the second traffic circle). Galyan's is located on the left. Also located at 12501 Fairlakes Circle, Fairfax, VA 22033 (703) 803-0300. At the corner of Independence Boulevard and Columbus Street. From the Washington Beltway (I-495) take I-66 West to Fairfax County Parkway. Turn right onto Fair Lakes Circle. Galyan's is located on the right side.*

Sign up in the store to climb the two-story wall while being belayed by a Galyan's staff member. A parent or guardian is required to sign a waver and must be present during the climb.

- Free Admission, ages 5 and up.

Laser Quest

*14517 Potomac Mills Road, Woodbridge, VA (703-490-4180) - **www.laser quest.com**. Take the Washington Beltway (I-495) to I-95 south to Potomac Mills exit; turn right on Potomac Mills Rd; located in Potomac Festival Mall.*

- Open Tuesday-Thursday, 6-10 p.m.; Friday, 5-9 p.m.; Saturday, noon-11 p.m.; Sunday, noon-7 p.m. Call for summer hours.
- $7 per person; group rates available.
- Recommended for children age ten and older.
- Field Trips, Birthday Parties, Wheelchair Accessible.

Special activities before, during and after hours available for group functions.

Shadowland ✦16✦

*624 Quince Orchard Road, Gaithersburg, MD (301-330-5546) - **www.sha dowlandadventures.com**. Take the Washington Beltway (I-495) to I-270 North to Clopper Road (Exit 10). Go 0.5 miles to Quince Orchard Road and turn left. Continue on Quince Orchard road for 100 yards and take a right into the shopping center. Shadowland is located behind the Trak Auto. In Columbia Maryland: 9179 Red Branch Road, Columbia, Maryland, 21045 (410) 740-9100 (fax: 410-740-9704). Off of Route 20 to Route 108 East. Go to second stop light and turn left onto Red Branch Road. Park in the parking lot for Top Flight Gymnastics.*

Laser adventure with as many as 30 players in high-tech suites and handsets interact in the 6000 square 2-level arena. Special effects - lighting, astral music, and laser-enhancing fog - add to the excitement.

- Monday, 11-6 (rentals after 6 p.m.); Tuesday-Thursday, 11-10; Friday, 11 a.m.-midnight; Saturday 10 a.m.-midnight; Sunday 1-10.

- General admission is $7.25 for one adventure, $14, for two adventures, and $19.50 for Triple Play adventures.

- Birthday Parties, Snack Bar.

Sportrock Climbing Center

*14708 Southlawn Lane, Rockville, MD (301-762-5111) - **www.sportrock** .com. To Rockville location: take Route 355 North to East Gude Drive; turn right. At fourth traffic light, turn right on Southlawn Lane. Other locations: 5308 Eisenhower Avenue, Alexandria, VA (703-212-7625) and 45935 Maries Road, Sterling VA 20166 (571-434-7625).*

Sportrock Climbing Center is an indoor rock climbing facility that provides instruction for children, teens and adults. In addition to birthday parties and summer camps, it offers a variety of programs. On Friday evenings, children ages 6-13 can take part in Kid's Night, which introduces them to general principles of climbing and includes one and a half hours of climbing time (similar one-hour sessions are available on weekends). Older children can take part in a basic skills course and then join a junior climbing club on Thursday evenings which provides instruction in movement, technical skills, and ropes management. Fees vary; call for details. Participants must pre-register and pre-pay, as well as sign liability waivers. This is a safe, fun, and controlled environment for children to experience rock climbing.

- Open Wednesday-Friday, noon-11; Saturday, 11-8; Sunday, noon-8. Kid's Nite Class meets every Friday, 6:30-8 p.m.

- Kid's Night: $21 for 1½ hours for one child; second child in same family can be included for total cost of $33 for 1½ hours. Weekend afternoon "Open Belay" sessions (similar to Kids' Night): $5 per climb, equipment included. Basic Skills course for ages 14 and older: $33, includes two hours of climbing instruction and additional climbing time after work.

- Metrorail Blue line (Van Dorn Station) to the Alexandria location.

- Lockers available and controlled access.

- Recommended for children age ten and older.

- Birthday Parties.

Special activities include summer programs, membership discounts and specials. See website for more details.

Make Your Own Crafts

Clay Café Studio

*101 N. Maple Ave., Falls Church, VA (703-534-7600) - **www.claywire.com**. From the Washington Beltway (I-495) take exit Route 7 (Leesburg Pike) East. Continue on Route 7 (called W. Broad St. in Falls Church). Turn left onto N. Maple Avenue. Turn left into the first parking lot. The entrance to Clay Café Studios is from the parking lot.*

Select a ceramic piece, have fun painting it, and then pick up your glazed and fired piece about four days later.

- Cost includes the price of the ceramic piece you select, plus a $6 per hour studio fee for paints, materials and decoration tools, instruction, glazing and firing.
- Monday-Thursday, 11- 7; Friday-Saturday, 11- 9; Sunday, noon-4.

Made By You

*4923 Elm Street, Bethesda, MD (301-654-3206) - **www.madebyyou.com**. Other locations at: 3413 Connecticut Avenue, NW, Washington, DC (202-363-9590), 209 N. Washington Street, Rockville, MD (301-610-5496), 2319 Wilson Boulevard, Arlington, VA (703-841-3533).*

Use your creative talents to decorate and paint ceramic items ranging from animal figurines to cookie jars, mugs, platters, vases and bowls. Ceramics are glazed and fired on site and ready four days later. This is a great place for children to "make" gifts for relatives.

- Bethesda store open Monday-Friday, 10-9; Sunday, 10- 6. Call other sites for specific hours.
- Items range from $5-$65, most cost $15-$25.
- Metrorail Red line (Bethesda).
- Birthday Parties, Wheelchair Accessible.

Plaster, Paint and Party

*8511 Ziggy Lane, Gaithersburg, MD (301-527-0373) - **kidspaintparty.com**. Take the Beltway , ((I-495)) to I-270 north to Exit 8 (Shady Grove Road); turn right on Shady Grove Road (east). Cross over Rockville Pike (Route 355) and take the next left at Oakmont. Proceed .3 miles. Turn left at Ziggy Lane, third store on the right. Free parking.*

Feeling creative? Plan a party at Plaster, Paint and Party where all paints, smocks and finishes are supplied, and children take home their finished items the same day

- Open Thursday-Friday, noon-8; Saturday and MCPS early-release or no-school days, 10-6; Sunday, noon-6
- Wheelchair accessibility and stroller space is limited.

8. Day Trips in the Region
Baltimore Inner Harbor

Baltimore is a city that continues to do an excellent job of updating its image while preserving its historic heritage. There is a wealth of things to do and see in this nearby international port town with its rich cultural texture. Many attractions are within walking distance of the Inner Harbor. However, it is impossible to explore the rich offerings of Baltimore in a day, so come back often or consider staying the weekend. Spending a night in one of the city's convenient hotels is a real treat for the entire family. See Chapter 1, "Starting Out," for information on the Baltimore Area Visitors Center.

To reach Baltimore from Washington, DC, travel north about 40 miles on Route 95 or on the Baltimore-Washington Parkway. Follow the signs to the Inner Harbor. Many other Baltimore sights can be found from the Inner Harbor simply by following the signs. Pay particular attention to signs for commercial parking lots because on-street parking is very limited.

American Visionary Art Museum

*800 Key Highway, Baltimore, MD (410-244-1900) - **www.avam.org**. Take I-95 North to Exit 55. Bear left at first light onto Key Highway. Follow Key Highway two miles; Museum is on the left at the corner of Covington Street. Located within walking distance of the Inner Harbor. A pay-parking lot is located across the street from the main entrance, $3 per day. Metered on-street parking is also available.*

This national museum and education center is dedicated to extraordinary works of art created by intuitive, self-taught artists, many regarded as eccentric in their passionate pursuit of artistic expression. The 55-foot tall whirligig is an eye-catcher even before you enter the museum; inside, there are six art galleries, a wild flower sculpture garden, museum store, and restaurant.

- Open 10-6, Tuesday-Sunday; closed Christmas, Thanksgiving.
- Adults, $8; children, seniors, and students, $6; groups of ten or more, $3.
- Field Trips, Birthday Parties, Wheelchair Accessible.

Special activities include 4th of July Family Day.

Babe Ruth Museum

*216 Emory Street, Baltimore, MD (410-727-1539) -**www.BabeRuthMuseum .com**. Take I-95 north to I-395; follow the signs for Martin Luther King Jr. Blvd exit; turn right at second light on Pratt Street, then right on Emory.*

Here is an opportunity for fans of all ages to visit the house where baseball's number one slugger was born, and to view mementos and films of Babe Ruth. You will also get a feel for Maryland's baseball heritage and Orioles history. Exhibits change each year.

- Open daily, April-October, 10-5 (until 7p.m. on Oriole home game days); November-March, 10-4. Closed Thanksgiving, Christmas, and New Year's Day.
- Adults, $6; senior citizens, $4; children 5-16, $3; members and children under 5, free.
- Parking available in the museum lot on Pratt Street, just before Emory Street.
- Wheelchair access to first floor only.
- Field Trips, Birthday Parties.

The Baltimore Civil War Museum - President Street Station

*202 West Monument Street, Baltimore, MD (410-385-5188) - **www.mdhs. org**. Located at the end of I-83 north at the corner of Fleet and President, at the east end of the Inner Harbor.*

The museum tells the stories of Baltimore's role in the Civil War, especially the Pratt Street Riot which accounted for the first bloodshed of the War. The museum also explains the link between this railroad station and the Underground Railroad, as well as the story of the Philadelphia, Wilmington and Baltimore Railroads.

- Open daily, 10-5.
- Adults, $3; seniors and students, $2; under 12 free.
- Wheelchair Accessible.

Baltimore Maritime Museum

*Piers 3 and 5, Pratt Street, Baltimore, MD (410-396-3453) - **www.Balto maritimemuseum.org**. Take the Washington Beltway (I-495) to I-95 north towards Baltimore/New York. Take the BWI Airport (I-95)/Baltimore Beltway(I-695) and keep to the right on I-395 North ramp. Continue on I-395 North towards downtown Baltimore and the Inner Harbor. Continue on South Howard Street, turn right onto West Pratt Street and then continue on East Pratt Street to Pier 3 and 5.*

This is a great favorite for children. They always love the tours of these three vessels, even if they aren't old enough to truly understand the different naval technologies presented.

The **Taney** is the last surviving warship from the attack of Pearl Harbor, and the Torsk sank the last two Japanese combatant ships of WWII. **Lightship Chesapeake**, a floating lighthouse, marked entrance ways to harbors when other navigational devices were impractical. The seven-foot Knoll Lighthouse marked the mouth of the Patapsco River for 133 years before being moved to Pier 5 in Baltimore's Inner Harbor.

- Open daily, 10-5:30; until 6:30, Friday-Saturday; 10:30-5 Sunday. In winter, open only on Friday-Sunday. Closed Thanksgiving, Christmas, and New Year's Day.

- Adults, $6; senior citizens, $5; children 6-15, $3; children five and under, free. Group rates available for ten or more.

- Lightship Chesapeake, USS Torsk, and USCGC Taney, and the Seven-foot Knoll Lighthouse.

- Restaurants and food stalls at adjacent Harborplace.

- No wheelchair access; no strollers.

- Overnight Programs, Field Trips.

Baltimore Public Works Museum

751 Eastern Avenue, Baltimore, MD (410-396-5565, 410-396-1509) - **www.ci.baltimore.md.us/government/dpw/museum**. *Take the Washington Beltway (I-495) to I- 95 north to the Inner Harbor exit; turn right on Pratt Street and right on President Street; follow President Street through the intersection with Eastern Avenue. The museum entrance is on Falls Way, facing the Inner Harbor. Museum is situated on the edge of "Little Italy", and is a two-block walk from the National Aquarium over pedestrian bridges. Parking in nearby commercial lots at President and Fleet Streets.*

This is a hands-on museum that should easily draw young children and teens into understanding public works. The museum is a 90-year-old red brick sewage pumping station completed in 1912. Children are introduced to the museum with a 15-minute child-oriented video. A "construction site" filled with puzzles, blocks and books is popular with young children. If weather permits, the outdoor "streetscape" is compelling. It is a two-level exhibit that features a fire hydrant, public telephone, parking meter, manhole, and alarm box, with a "peel back the pavement" look at the network of pipes and connections below. A stairway joins both levels for a closer look.

- Open Tuesday-Sunday, 10-4. Closed Good Friday, Thanksgiving, Christmas, New Year's Day, Martin Luther King's Birthday, and other Baltimore City holidays.

- Adults, $2.50; senior citizens, $2; children 6-17, $2; children under six, free.
- Call to arrange tours or field trips. Group rate of $1.25 per person applies for ten or more.
- Wheelchair and stroller accessible.

Federal Hill Park

800 Battery Avenue, Baltimore, MD (410-396-0814, 410-396-7946). Take the Washington Beltway (I-495) to I-95 to Key Highway; proceed 2.5 miles to park.

Located in the heart of downtown Baltimore, historical Federal Hill Park offers a beautiful country setting with a picnic area and playground and an excellent view of the Inner Harbor!

- Open dusk to dawn.
- Free Admission
- Limited on-street parking.
- Wheelchair accessibility on main circular path.
- Picnicking, Playgrounds.

Harborplace and The Gallery

*Inner Harbor at corner of Pratt and Light Streets, Baltimore, MD (410-332-4191) - **www.harborplace.com**. Just off of Interstate 95 and 83.*

Harborplace and **The Gallery** are located in the heart of Baltimore's financial and business district, overlooking its Inner Harbor. Its three main buildings offer an exciting range of more than 200 shops, restaurants, stalls, and harbor-side terraces, as well as easy access to several main attractions, such as the National Aquarium and the Maryland Science Center. You can take a ride in paddleboats or travel on the Water Taxi to the various sights on the Inner Harbor. The outdoor promenades are perfect for strolling, skipping, pushing a stroller, or people watching. In good weather, you may be lucky and run into street performers who will keep you and your children amused.

- Stores open Monday-Saturday, 10-9; Sunday, 10-6. Restaurants close later.
- Valet parking now available weekdays after 5 p.m. and all day on weekends. Parking available in the Gallery Garage and numerous commercial lots. Also accessible by Metro, train, bus or water taxi.
- Stroller and wheelchair accessible.
- Boating, Picnicking.

Special activities include over 200 free events annually with street performers, concerts, and seasonal celebrations. For example, Christmas at Harborplace has featured petting zoos, choral competitions, celebrity Santas, ice-skating, and a Santa House from Thanksgiving to New Year's Eve. Events calendar online.

Maryland Science Center

601 Light Street, Baltimore, MD (410-685-5225, 410-962-0223 TDD) - www.mdsci.org.

You can easily spend a whole day in this excellent museum with its permanent exhibits on energy, the Chesapeake Bay, space, structures, and the Hubble space telescope. Many hands-on exhibits will keep your children involved. Temporary exhibits change every three months, so it is a place you can visit often.

- Open weekdays, 10-5; Saturday, 10-6, Sunday noon-5. Extended summer hours. Closed Thanksgiving and Christmas.

- Live demonstrations daily. Davis Planetarium and IMAX Theater presentations changes several times throughout the year

- Memberships in the Maryland Science Center also provide members access to more than 200 science centers and children's museums in North America.

- Restaurant/Snack Bar.

Maryland Tours

Inner Harbor, Baltimore, MD (410-685-4288, tickets, April-Oct., 410-745-9216, November-March).

Experience the Inner Harbor on one of several narrated harbor cruises on the Baltimore Patriot and Fort McHenry Shuttles. Pass sites such as Fells Point, where the USS Constellation was launched and Federal Hill, site of Union fortifications during the Civil War.

- The Baltimore Patriot offers three cruises daily in April, May, September, and October; it departs hourly June-August. The Fort McHenry Shuttle operates Memorial Day-Labor Day every half hour; in May and September, departures are every hour.

- Rates vary. Call for information.

National Aquarium In Baltimore

*Pier 3, 501 East Pratt Street, Baltimore, MD (410-576-3800, 410-576-3833, reservations) - **www.aqua.org**. Take the Washington Beltway (I-495) to I-95 north to I-395-downtown. Follow signs for Inner Harbor to Pratt and Gay Streets. The Aquarium is on the corner.*

The National Aquarium is a spectacular, seven-level structure that houses fascinating and sophisticated aquatic exhibits. Children especially like the children's cove where they can hold horseshoe crabs, sea stars, and other small animals. A favorite is the marine mammal pavilion. Watch bottlenose dolphins and their trainers! But be careful, you could get wet! In the surrounding education arcade, kids can learn humpback whale songs, create bubbles to help humpbacks engulf their meals, and play "Whales in Jeopardy." Be sure to visit the Exploration Station, Atlantic Coral Reef, large shark exhibits, and rain forest. A complete tour will take about two and a half hours.

The Aquarium is one of Baltimore's most popular attractions, so it is best to visit in late afternoon or evening to avoid the crowds. If you think your family will visit the Aquarium more than once a year, you may save money by becoming a member.

- November-February: Fridays, 10-8; all other days, 10-5; March-June, September-October: Fridays, 9-8; all other days, 9-5; July-August: Monday-Thursday, 9-6 and Friday-Sunday, 9- 8. Visitors should note that the museum is the *least crowded during January.*

- Adults, age 12-59, $14; senior citizens, $10.50; children, age 3-11, $7.50; children under three, free. Advance timed tickets are available through Ticketmaster in Washington, D.C., 202-432-SEAT, and it is possible to pick up advance tickets at the museum itself. Tickets can be purchased online - see the Aquarium's website.

- Food court

- Wheelchair access through Seal Pool entrance. Call to make arrangements. The rain forest area is not accessible to wheelchairs. Strollers are not permitted in the building, but the Aquarium will provide back-packs for babies and toddlers.

Port Discovery Children's Museum

*35 Market Place, Baltimore, MD (410-727-8120) - **portdiscovery.com**.
Take the Washington Beltway (I-495) to I-95 north to I-395 - Baltimore (Inner
Harbor) past Camden Yards to Pratt Street and make a right. Once past the
Aquarium, get into the far left lane to make a left onto Market Place. After
crossing Lombard Street, Port Discovery will be on the right. Nearby
parking sites: Lombard and Market Place, Market Place and Frederick
Streets, Gay and Water Streets, Baltimore and Holliday Streets, Commerce
and Water Streets.*

Port Discovery, designed in collaboration with Walt Disney Imagineering, offers three floors of interactive fun for the whole family. A wonderfully innovative, powered experience, the Port Discovery Children's Museum was voted fourth **best children's museum in the United States** in Child Magazine, 2002.

Take Note...

Stay close to younger children - or keep your eyes on them as they go through the tube mazes because they come out at different levels!

80,000 square feet of interactive exhibits cater to children ages 6-12, although children of all ages will find something to spark their interest. The central core of the museum is a three-story climbing structure... why take the stairs when there's a more challenging way to the top floor? Each floor is filled with fabulously creative exhibits and hand-on activities. Try to find the missing family members of Miss Perception's Mystery House or star in a kid-geared game show; create and build a project to take home in the R&D Dream Lab or challenge yourself to a memory game of colors and lights.

- Open daily, 10-5:30.
- $8.50 per child; $11 per adult; children under 3, free
- Field Trips, Birthday Parties, Restaurant/Snack Bar, Wheelchair Accessible.

Special activities include traveling exhibits, cool workshops, and special events.

U.S.S. Constellation

*301 E. Pratt Street, Pier One, Baltimore, MD (410-539-1797) -
www.constellation.org.*

The U.S.S. Constellation is another guaranteed favorite for kids. This 1854 ship-of-war was the last sailing ship of the U.S. Navy. It is the oldest American warship the only Civil War era vessel still afloat. The U.S.S. Constellation has hands-on activities and demonstrations for visitors as they explore life on board and see how thousands of sailors lived at sea.

- Open May 1-October 14, 10- 6; October 15-April 30, 10-4. Closed Thanksgiving, Christmas & New Year's Day.

- Adults, $6.50; senior citizens, $5; youth 6-14, $3.50; children 5 and under are free. Group rates are adults, $5; senior citizens, $4; youth, $2.50. Last tickets for the day are sold 30 minutes before closing.

- Every Saturday and Sunday: "Powder Monkey Tour" for Kids from 1-3 p.m., where kids can be a member of Constellation's crew, try on uniforms and learn about life on board through hands-on activities.

- Every Saturday "Ship Shape Days" are from 8-noon. Volunteers help to preserve one of America's great historic treasures

- Group tours available by appointment.

- Wheelchair accessible.

Special activities include historical reenactments in the summer featuring Will, the ordinary "Jack Tar" sailor, who entertains with tales of life at sea in the 1800s; Navigating Through History; "A Living History" series.

Around Baltimore

Baltimore and Ohio Railroad Museum

*901 West Pratt Street, Baltimore, MD (410-752-2490) - **www.borail.org**. Take I-95 north to I-395; exit at Martin Luther King, Jr. Boulevard; go three blocks to left turn on Lombard Street; turn left at first light on Poppleton; cross over Pratt Street to museum entrance.*

This old roundhouse contains the world's largest collection of locomotives, cabooses, freights, and other cars dating back to 1829. Children can go through a caboose and the back of a mail car. The large model railroad station is always a hit. Enter the museum through Mt. Claire Station, the oldest railroad station in the United States.

- Open daily, 10-5. Closed all major holidays.

- Adults, $9; senior citizens (60+), $8; children 2-12, $6. Children under 2, free. Train rides are $2 with admission fee. Call for family and group rates, 410-752-2463.

- Lunch café and snack bar is in a diner car.

Special activities include train excursions to Western Maryland and West Virginia in the fall. Programs schedules are available on the website.

Baltimore Museum of Art

*Art Museum Drive, Baltimore, MD (410-396-7100) - **www.artbma.org**.
Take I-95 north to I-395; follow the signs for Martin Luther King Jr.
Boulevard exit; turn left on Howard Street; continue north (past 29th Street);
veer right at the fork on Art Museum Drive. Metered parking lots on the east
side of the museum and some metered on-street parking.*

This exceptional museum features the Cone Collection of
early 20th century art. Matisse and Picasso are particularly
well represented. Children of all ages are invited to sample
the colorful palette of workshops, performances, and
education programs presented by the BMA. Each program is
designed to educate and fascinate by introducing young
people to the world of art.

- Open Wednesday-Friday, 11-5; Saturday-Sunday, 11-6.
  Closed Thanksgiving, Christmas, New Year's Day, and
  July 4th.

- Adults, $7; senior citizens (65+) and students, $5; free
  to children age 18 and younger. The first Thursday of
  the month free to all visitors.

- Be sure to make reservations for lunch at the
  restaurant at least a day ahead.

Special activities include children's art classes and
workshops throughout the year. Families are encouraged to
discover what's inside the BMA by dropping in during
Freestyle, the BMA's festive, free-for-all evening the first
Thursday of each month from 5-8 p.m. The evening includes
live music, performances, tours, and a relaxed atmosphere to
view art.

Baltimore Museum of Industry

*1415 Key Highway, Inner Harbor South, Baltimore, MD (410-727-4808) -
www.thebmi.org. Take I-95 north to Key Highway/Fort McHenry National
Monument; turn left at light; go under overpass; left on Key Highway;
Museum is immediately on the right; look for the big red crane.*

Voted "Best Hands-On Museum for Kids" by Baltimore
Magazine. This hands-on museum, located in the heart of
industrial south Baltimore, contains a print shop, a machine
shop, a garment loft, and an assembly line where youngsters
learn how parts become finished products. This museum is a
great "find." Housed in a harbor-side cannery that was used
during the Civil War to send oysters off to the soldiers, the
building itself bears testimony to the working life the museum
recreates.

- Monday-Saturday 10-4. Closed Thanksgiving,
  Christmas Eve and Christmas Day.

- Adults, $7; senior citizens, $3.50; and students, $5. Group and family rates available.
- Free parking available on site. Also accessible via Seaport Taxi.
- Field Trips, Birthday Parties, Scouts.

Special activities include special programs for birthday parties, senior tours, scouting programs and large groups.

Baltimore Streetcar Museum

1901 Falls Road, Baltimore, MD (410-547-0264, 410-298-5034) -
www.baltimoremd/streetcar. *Take I-95 north to I-395; exit at Martin Luther King, Jr. Boulevard to left on Howard Street; turn right on North Avenue; turn right on Maryland Avenue; turn right at Lafayette; turn right on Falls Road to museum.*

A rolling history of the streetcars of Baltimore, the museum houses a collection of Baltimore streetcars, horse-drawn and electric, covering the 104-year history of this type of transportation in the city. Enjoy unlimited streetcar rides, tours, exhibits, and a slide show in addition to a collection of Baltimore streetcars from 1859-1963.

- Open June-October, Saturday and Sunday, noon-5; November-May, Sunday, noon-5.
- Adults, $5; children, ages 4-11 and senior citizens, $2.50; children under age 4, free. Admission includes streetcar rides.
- Tours for grades K and up. Call 410-298-5034 to schedule a tour and to get reduced school group rates.
- Wheelchair accessibility on some of the streetcars.
- Birthday Parties, Picnicking.

Special activities include a museum's birthday celebration the first Sunday in July; Antique Auto Meets three times a year; a Big Band Concert in the summer; Phantom Trolley for Halloween; and Holly Trolley in December. Call or write the museum for a complete listing.

The Baltimore Zoo

Druid Hill Park, Baltimore, MD (410-366-LION, 410-396-7102) - ***www. baltimorezoo.org***. *Take I-95 north, take I-695 west towards Towson; take Route 83 south (Exit 23) to Exit 7; follow signs. Or take I-88 south to exit 7. Parking is free.*

Rated as having the best children's zoo in the country by "The Zoo Book: A Guide to America's Best," the Baltimore Zoo is home to over 2,200 exotic animals and wildlife. The **Children's Zoo** has 48 interactive exhibits where kids can experience what it is like to burrow underground like woodchucks or hop on a lily pad like a frog. Travel to the **African Watering Hole**, a spectacular six-acre home for zebras, pelicans, white rhinos, lions, cheetahs, extraordinary birds, and visit a habitat for African black-footed penguins, the Chimpanzee Forest, and the Leopard Lair!

- Open daily, 10-4. Extended summer hours. Closed Thanksgiving Day, Christmas and one day in June for an annual fundraiser.

- Adults, $10; senior citizens, $8, and children 2-15, $6. Children admitted free with a paying adult the first Tuesday of each month between 10-noon.

- Trams are available to take passengers to the main areas of the zoo.

- Group permits and tours by appointment. Maryland school groups, free.

- A free zoo shuttle picks up visitors at the MTA (Mass Transit Administration) Woodberry stop. Call for times.

- Rental strollers, wheelchairs and scooters are available.

Special activities include a Spring Event; Zoo Booo!, a Howl-o-ween Spectacular in October; Keeper Encounters, where guest can learn what goes on behind the scenes, and summer education camps.

Fire Museum

*1301 York Road, Lutherville, MD (410-321-7500) - **www.firemuseummd .org**. Take the Washington Beltway (I-495) to I-95 North towards Baltimore. Take the Baltimore Beltway (I-695) west to York Road / Lutherville exit north (exit 26B). Go one block north, Museum is located behind the Heaver Plaza Office Building. Free on-site parking.*

America's premier collection of fire-fighting apparatus awaits you at the Fire Museum. More than 40 fire engines are on display. See hand-pulled trucks that required 40-50 men to pull them, horse-drawn trucks, and the motorized trucks of the 1950's. This museum helps children learn the history of fire fighting. Experience the thrill of sending an alarm over an antique fire alarm system, visit the dress-up corner where kids can put on fire fighter boots and turnaround coats, explore the Children's Discovery Room and shop in the Museum store.

- Open Saturdays, 11-4. Closed July 4.

- $6 for adults; $5 firefighters and senior citizens 62+; $3 for children ages 3-18; under 3 free. Family membership is $35

- Stroller and wheelchair accessible.

Special activities include story time Fridays at 11:30 a.m., June-August. Group and Educational programs: March-November; facility rentals year-round; special winter events.

Fort McHenry National Monument and Historic Shrine

*2400 East Fort Avenue, Baltimore, MD (410-962-4290) - **www.nps.gov/ fomc**. Take the Washington Beltway (I-495), take 95 North. Exit at Key Highway, the last exit before the Harbor Tunnel (you will see signs for Fort McHenry), and bear left. At third traffic light, make left on Lawrence Street; at first light, turn left on E. Fort Avenue. Located at the end of E. Fort Avenue.*

From a ship in Baltimore's outer harbor, Francis Scott Key saw the *Star-Spangled Banner* still flying from the ramparts of Fort McHenry after a 25-hour bombardment by the British in the War of 1812. There is a movie at the Visitor Center about the battle and the writing of the national anthem. Children are interested in the cannons and enjoy the soldiers in period uniforms on summer weekends.

- Open daily, 8-4:45; summer hours (1st weekend in June through Labor Day) 8 a.m-7:45 p.m. Closed Christmas and New Year's Day.
- Free admission to movie and grounds. Admission to historic area: adults age 17 and over, $5; children, free.
- Audio tour is available in different languages.
- Braille Map is available upon request.
- Security Information: Reserves the right to check bags.
- Picnicking, Wheelchair Accessible.

Special activities include ranger-guided activities offered June through Labor Day, military demonstrations, drills, and special ceremonies presented by "soldiers" dressed in period uniforms, Saturday and Sunday afternoons, June through August. In the evening on Flag Day (June 14) and Defenders' Day (the second Saturday in September), there are commemorative celebrations with band concerts and fireworks.

Ladew Topiary Gardens

*3535 Jarrettsville Pike, Monkton, MD - **www.ladewgardens.com**. From the Baltimore Beltway (I-695) take I-83N via exit 24. Exit 20A Shawan Road East - toward Cockeysville. Right on Shawan Road to right on York Road (MD-45). Left onto Ashland Road (MD-145). Left onto Jarrettsville Pike (MD-146).*

Self-taught gardener Harvey Ladew created 15 gardens "rooms"- each with its own theme - on part of his Maryland estate. His creation has been called "the most outstanding garden in America." A 1½ mile nature walk leads through woods, fields and across a wetland board walk.

- Open mid-April though October 10-4, Monday-Friday; Saturday and Sunday 10:30-5.
- Adults, $8; seniors and students, $7; children, $2.

Lexington Market

400 West Lexington Street, Baltimore, MD (410-685-6169) -
www.Lexington Market.com. *Take I-95 north to I-395 to Russell Street exit; continue on Paca Street five blocks north. You can enter the market from Paca or Lexington Streets. There are additional small markets sprinkled throughout downtown Baltimore. Parking adjacent to market.*

This world-famous market has been in operation since 1782 and is one of the oldest markets in the United States. Ralph Waldo Emerson referred to it as the "gastronomic capital of the universe." Over 130 merchants can be found selling food from all around the world. The market bustles and offers a multitude of sights, sounds, smells, and tastes. A great place to stop for lunch or a snack – you may sample food from a variety of food stalls.

- Open Monday-Saturday, 8:30-6. Closed Sunday, Memorial Day, July 4, Labor Day, Thanksgiving, Christmas, and New Year's Day.

Special activities include a Preakness Crab Derby in mid-May, Lunch with the Elephants in mid-March and a Chocolate Festival in October.

Maryland Historical Society

201 West Monument Street, Baltimore, MD (410-685-3750) –
www.mdhs.org. *Take I-95 to I-395; exit at Martin Luther King, Jr. Boulevard; turn right on Druid Hill Avenue; left on Howard Street; turn right on West Monument Street.*

Museum highlights include a Hands-On-History Room with a rope bed, cast iron cook stove, butter churns, try-on clothing and "A Child's world", featuring 300 years of toys and games.. Dioramas trace Maryland history in the Darnall Young People's Museum. The original manuscript of the "Star-Spangled Banner" is housed here in an exhibit on the War of 1812. Another exhibit focuses on the history of the Civil War in Maryland.

- Closed for renovation June-November 2003
- Open Wednesday-Friday, 10-5; Saturday, 9-5; Sunday, 1-5. Closed major holidays and Sunday in July-August.

- Adults, $4; children under 12, free; senior citizens and children 13-17, $3. Family rate: $12 for two adults and children under 17.

- Call in advance for group tours (no charge for school and scout groups).

- Wheelchair access to all except Pratt House and the library. Strollers permitted, but it is preferred that they be left at the door.

Special activities include a summer children's series; and family programs with performances, crafts, & treasure hunts.

National Museum of Dentistry

31 South Greene Street, Baltimore, MD (410-706-0052, 410-706-8314) - www.dentalmuseum.org. Take I-95 to I-395 (downtown Baltimore) and exit onto Martin Luther King Jr. Boulevard, staying in the right lane. At the fourth traffic light, turn right onto Baltimore Street. Turn right at the first traffic light onto Greene Street. Look for NMD banners on left.

The Dr. Samuel D. Harris National Museum of Dentistry, an affiliate of the Smithsonian Institution, gives an educational overview of the history of dentistry and the importance of good oral care. This is done through exciting interactive exhibitions and the careful preservation and creative presentation of dental artifacts. Experience the amazing feats of an "iron jaw" performer, play a tune on the tooth jukebox, and view George Washington's "not-so-wooden" teeth.

- Open Wednesday-Saturday, 10-4; Sunday, 1-4. Closed Monday, Tuesday, and major holidays.

- Adults (age 19-59), $4.50; youths (age 7-18), $2.50; senior citizens, students with I.D., and children age six and under, free. Group rates are available.

- Light Rail (Campden Yards).

- Limited on-street metered parking, as well as a parking garage located on Paca Street and another just north of Oriole Park at Camden Yards. You may enter the museum from Paca or Pratt Streets.

- Call for school tours 410-706-0510.

- Stroller and wheelchair accessible.

Special activities include a George Washington celebration in February.

Star-Spangled Banner Flag House

*844 East Pratt Street, Baltimore, MD (410-837-1793) - **www.flaghouse.org**. Take I-95 north to I-395 to downtown Baltimore; follow signs for Inner Harbor to Pratt Street; go east on Pratt Street; cross over President Street (six blocks from Inner Harbor) to corner of Albemarle; turn left and make a U-turn to parking spaces in front of the house. Parking available on the street in front of the house on Albemarle Street. Ask for a parking permit to place on your windshield.*

This is the home of Mary Pickersgill, the young woman who sewed the 30' x 42' flag that flew over Fort McHenry during the Battle of Baltimore. This is the flag that inspired Francis Scott Key to write our National Anthem. Step back to the early 1800's and learn how Mary and her family lived and worked. The house is furnished with antiques of the Federal period, and the adjacent 1812 Museum houses a collection of artifacts from the War of 1812 and features a video program where you will hear the stirring story of the Battle of Baltimore.

- Open Tuesday-Saturday, 10-4. Closed Monday, Sunday, and major holidays.
- Adults, $5; senior citizens, $4; children $3.
- Close to "Little Italy," where there are many restaurants.
- The 1812 Museum and garden are wheelchair accessible. The Flag House is accessible on the first floor.
- Recommended for children age ten and older.

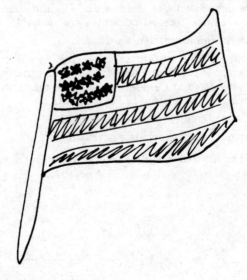

Walters Art Gallery

*600 North Charles Street, Baltimore, MD (410-547-9000) - **www.thewalters .org**. Take I-95 north to I-395 to Martin Luther King, Jr. Boulevard north; continue for one mile; turn right on Druid Hill Avenue (which becomes Center Street). Museum is on the left five blocks down at the corner of Center and Cathedral Streets.*

This gallery is considered one of America's great public museums, with a collection that spans 5,000 years of artistic achievement, ranging from its well-known ancient Egypt collection to the French Impressionists. Children typically enjoy the collection of arms and armor, as well as the Egyptian mummy exhibit. The museum provides many hands-on workshops, concerts, storytelling, and docent-led tours for children.

- Open Tuesday-Sunday, 10-5. Closed Monday, New Year's Day, Fourth of July, Thanksgiving, Christmas Eve, and Christmas Day.
- Adults, $8; senior citizens (60+), $6; young adults (18-25) $5; children 17 and under free.
  Free admission hours for all on Saturdays, 10-1.
- Troia, The Walters restaurant, is open for lunch, Tuesday-Saturday, 11:30 a.m.-3:30 p.m.; dinner, Friday-Saturday and first Thursday of the month, 5:30 p.m.-9:30 p.m.
- Call 410-547-ARTS for information on special exhibitions and programs featured throughout the year.
- Wheelchair access through entrance at corner of North Charles Street and West Mt. Vernon Place.

Annapolis

The waterfront area of Historic Annapolis is the center of activity in this charming city. Here you can enjoy Annapolis yachting facilities, water tours, restaurants, summer theater, specialty shops, galleries, Market House, and strolling areas. Tour the harbor by boat. Day trips to other nearby locales operate from May to September. Schedules and fees are posted at the dock, or call Chesapeake Marine Tours, 410-268-7600 or 301-261-2719. The Annapolis Sailing School, 800-638-9192, offers weekday and weekend sailing lessons. For tours of Annapolis, call 410-267-7619; to receive a **free kiddie kit**, call 410-280-0445.

Special activities include Annapolis Arts Festival in June, Sailboat and Power Boat Shows in October, and the festive New Year's Eve celebration, First Night, with entertainment and fireworks.

Take Note...

Just along the City Dock a sculptural tableau depicts Alex Haley reading to a group of children near the place where his ancestor, Kunte Kinte arrived in Annapolis in 1767. The memorial, dedicated in 2002, incorporates the statues of Haley and Kunte Kinte, along with 10 markers dedicated to diversity, family, love, forgiveness and other values.

The Chesapeake Children's Museum

*25 Silopanna Road, Annapolis, MD 21403 (410-990-1993) - **www.theccm .org**. Route 50 east to Exit 22, Aris T. Allen Blvd. Stay on this (don't get off at Riva Road) as it becomes Forest Drive. Turn left at the 4th traffic light, Hilltop Lane. Turn left at the first traffic light, Spa Road. Pass Gentry Court and Spindrift Way on your right. Take the next right, Silopanna Road. Look for the CCM sign on your left at the stop sign. Plenty of parking in the lot.*

The Chesapeake Children's Museum offers a hands-on experience for children of all ages — but is especially appropriate for preschool and early elementary age children. The mission of the museum "is to create an environment of discovery about oneself, the peoples, the technologies, and the ecology of the Chesapeake Bay area for all our children and for the children in us all."

Highlights include a "Bay Window" exhibit of live aquatic and land-dwelling animals, the seven-foot-tall human replica "Stuffee", which can be taken apart to see the internal organs, and a stage with dress-up costumes and audience seating for impromptu performances. An art and science workshop space is available for exploration by reservation. The museum's new facility provides outdoor areas including an herb garden and the Harriet Tubman Walk — a simulated walk along the Underground Railroad.

- Open daily 10 a.m. – 4 p.m. except Wednesdays.
- Wednesdays are reserved for groups of 10 or more; group reservations available other times.

Historic Annapolis Foundation Welcome Center and Museum Store

*77 Main Street, Annapolis, MD (410-268-5576) - **www.Annapolis.org**.*

Housed in the old Victualling Warehouse, this museum offers an interesting diorama of the port of Annapolis as it was 200 years ago when Annapolis was the principal seaport of the Upper Chesapeake Bay.

- Open Monday-Sunday, 10-5. Closed holidays.
- Self-guided tours for individuals are available: "Walk with Walter Cronkite," an African-American History Tour, and a rental audiotape tour of Annapolis. Group tours by appointment.

Quiet Waters Park

*600 Quiet Waters Park Road, Annapolis, MD (410-222-1777, 410-280-1423, skating information) - **www.aacpl.net/rp/parks/quietwaters/index.htm**. From I-695 Beltway to I-97. Follow I-97 south to US-50 east and immediately take exit 22 (I-665 - Aris T. Allen Blvd.). Stay on I-665 until it ends and merges with Forest Drive. Follow Forest Drive for 2 miles. Turn right onto Hillsmere Drive. The park entrance is 100 yards on the right side.*

Scenically located on the South River and Harness Creek near Annapolis Maryland, this 336-acre park offers natural beauty and a variety of recreational activities. The park has over six miles of hiking/biking trails, six picnic pavilions available by reservation, open picnic areas (some with grills), scenic South River overlook, formal gardens, a large children's playground and a cafe. Visitors can rent bicycles, sailboats, pedal boats, rowboats, kayaks, and canoes. There is an outdoor ice skating rink open from November to March. Two art galleries are located in the Visitor's Center. Juried sculpture from across the country is displayed throughout the park as part of the Sculpture in the Park program.

- Open daily 7 a.m. to dusk except Tuesday. Outdoor ice rink open November-March. Boat rentals available Spring- Fall. Visitor Center open from 9-4 on weekdays and 11-4 on weekends.
- $4 per vehicle, handicapped plate $2 per vehicle, buses $20 per bus, school bus (school hours only Monday - Thursday) free with pavilion rental (all other vehicles

must pay), walkers, runners, bikers, roller blades, free. Annual vehicle entry permits and Senior Citizen lifetime passes are available. There is also a fee to enter the two art galleries in the Visitor Center.

- Ramp access to the Visitor Center is at the main level in the rear.
- Biking, Boating, Fishing, Hiking, Picnicking, Playgrounds, Restaurant/Snack Bar, Skating.

Special activities include Earth Day; Summer Concert Series in June - August; Environmental Lecture Series on Thursday nights, monthly May through October; Bridal Celebrations and Open House in mid-March; Arts Festival in mid-November and Friends of Quiet Waters Park Volunteer Appreciation Banquet in mid-December.

State House Visitor Center

*91 State Circle, Annapolis, MD (410-974-3400) - **mdisfun.org**. From the Washington Beltway (I-495) take Route 50 east and follow the signs to the State House.*

The State House is the oldest State Capitol in continuous legislative use. On the first floor is the Old Senate Chamber where George Washington resigned his commission as Commander-in Chief before the Continental Congress on December 23, 1783. The State House in Annapolis was the first peacetime Capitol, from November 1783 to August 1784. Maryland Legislature meets for 90 days, second Wednesday in January to April. Maryland school groups can arrange meetings with members of their county's senators or delegates during this time.

- Visitor Center is open daily.
- State House open Monday-Friday, 9-5. Saturday and Sunday 10-4. Closed Christmas. No tours on Thanksgiving and New Year's Day.
- Tours daily at 11 and 3. For large groups, special times may be arranged.
- Wheelchair access from the back of the building.
- Security Information: Photo ID required.

Special activities include State House by Candlelight program the first weekend in December (Friday and Saturday evenings), featuring musical orchestras, bands, and choral groups.

U.S. Naval Academy

*Armel-Leftwich Visitor Center, 52 King George Street, Annapolis, MD (410-263-6933) - **www.usna.edu**.*

This is the part of Annapolis that many youngsters really want to see. Favorites are the Armel-Leftwich Visitor Center and U.S. Naval Academy museum, the crypt of John Paul Jones, and the statue of Tecumseh. The Rogers Ship Model Collection contains 108 ship models dating from 1650 - 1850, and includes models of British Ships constructed by French prisoners of war during the Napoleonic conflict. At noon on some days, you may be lucky to see the midshipmen line up in front of Bancroft Hall and march with bugles and drums. Try *not* to visit during graduation (third week in May) because it is extremely crowded.

- Grounds open daily, 9-5. Museum open Monday-Saturday, 9-5; Sunday, 11-5. Visitor Center is open March-December, 9-5; January-February, 9-4; closed Thanksgiving, Christmas, and New Year's Day. Public walking tours are available daily.
- Admission is $6 for adults; $5.50 for seniors; $4.50 for students in grades 1-12.
- Wheelchair access to most areas.
- Restaurant/Snack Bar.

Special activities Enter Gate 1, King George Street. Photo ID required for 16 and older. No vehicles except those with DOD stickers or handicapped tags.

Watermark Cruises

*P.O. Box 3350; City Dock, Slip 20, Annapolis, MD (410-268-7600, 410-268-9749, group sales) - **www.watermarkcruises.com**. Take the Washington Beltway (I-495) to Route 50 east towards Annapolis. Take the Rowe Boulevard exit to the right and follow signs to Annapolis. Stay on Rowe Boulevard to the end; turn right and enter traffic circle; exit onto Duke of Gloucester Street; proceed through one traffic light and turn left onto Green Street. Turn right on Dock Street; the boat is at the end of the dock.*

Take advantage of this wonderful way to see such sights as the U.S. Naval Academy, Historic Annapolis Harbor, the scenic Severn River, the Chesapeake Bay, or even a trip to St. Michaels on the Eastern Shore of Maryland. Cruises depart from and return to the City Dock, located in the heart of historic downtown Annapolis. Various cruises are available, from 40 minutes to seven and one-half hours. Choose the cruise that's right for you!

- March-October, weekdays from 11-4 and weekends until 7.
- Ticket prices vary depending on the cruise.
- Wheelchair accessibility on the Harbor Queen.
- Boating, Snack Bar.

William Paca House and Garden

*186 Prince George Street, Annapolis, MD (800-603-4020, 410-267-7619) - **www.Annapolis.org**.*

This 37-room, five-part mansion was built by William Paca, a signer of the Declaration of Independence and three-term governor of Maryland. The two-acre terraced garden behind the house, hidden for many years, was uncovered through archaeological excavation. The garden includes roses, boxwoods, flowerbeds, hollies, a Chinese trellis bridge, domed summer house, and fish-shaped pond.

- Open daily, 10-5; Sunday, noon-4. In January and February, open Friday-Sunday and Federal holidays.
- House and garden: adults, $8; seniors, $7; children 6-18, $5.
- Children's group tour on colonial life, call for information.
- Wheelchair access to garden. Strollers are not permitted in the house.

Special activities include children's colonial activities and a garden event in the spring.

Harper's Ferry

Harper's Ferry National Historical Park

Shenandoah Street, P.O. Box 65, Harpers Ferry, WV (304-535-6029, 304-535-6298) - **www.nps.gov/hafe/home.htm**. *Follow signs on Route 340 to the National Historical Park entrance where you will find the Visitors Center parking lot; shuttle buses will take you to the Information Center and to the restored town.*

As you begin your tour of Harpers Ferry, look for the Information Center where you will get an overview of the six main park themes: local industry, John Brown's raid, the Civil War, African-American history, transportation, and environment. In addition to the museums listed below, there are hiking trails accessible from the town and fishing in the river nearby (licenses are required).

Black History Museum: This museum is devoted to the history of slaves and their struggle to gain freedom. It includes information before the Civil War and afterwards.

Storer College Museum: Learn the history of the college that educated freedmen after the Civil War.

John Brown's Fort: This was the armory's fire-engine house, used by John Brown as a refuge during his 1859 raid. Located at the corner of Shenandoah and Potomac Streets.

John Brown Museum: On Shenandoah Street, look for this museum relating the events of John Brown's raid. Video presentations describe the events leading to the raid and its immediate effects on the country.

Civil War Museum: Located on High Street, the museum depicts the way that the Civil War affected the town of Harpers Ferry. During the war, the town was occupied by either the Union or Confederate Armies.

Harper House: Built in 1782, this is the oldest surviving structure in the park. Climb the stone steps leading uphill from High Street to reach this historic site.

Dry Goods Store, Provost Marshall's Office, Blacksmith Shop: On Shenandoah Street, there are good places to visit to appreciate the social and economic history of the times. In the summer, the office and shops are staffed with people in period clothing.

- Visitors Center open daily, 8-5; Memorial Day-Labor Day, until 6. Closed Thanksgiving, Christmas, and New Year's Day.

- An entrance fee of $5 per vehicle secures a 3-day pass to everything offered by the National Park Service. For those entering the park on foot, bicycle, or tour bus, the entrance fee is $3 per person, but children 17 and under, bus drivers, and escorts are free. A variety of annual passes can be purchased at the Visitors Center for senior citizens and others.

■ Public walking tours are offered Memorial Day-Labor Day. During the rest of the year, tours are available by reservation only.

■ Some wheelchair access; wheelchairs are available for loan. Strollers are permitted, but the ride is bumpy.

■ Field Trips, Fishing, Hiking, Restaurant/Snack Bar.

Gettysburg

Eisenhower National Historic Site

*97 Taneytown Road, Gettysburg, PA (717-338-9114) - **www.nps.gov/eise**. Take the Washington Beltway (I-495) to I-270 north to U.S. 15 north Business Route (Steinwehr Avenue Exit); follow for six miles to National Park Service Visitor Center on the right.*

During the Eisenhower presidency from 1955-1961, the farm now known as the Eisenhower National Historic Site served as a weekend retreat, a refuge in times of illness, and a relaxed setting in which to meet with world leaders like Premier Khruschev and President Charles de Gaulle.

It was a working farm as well with fertile cropland and a show herd of black Angus cattle. While in retirement, President Eisenhower spent his time on the farm enjoying his hobbies, tending his cattle, and often advising Presidents Kennedy and Johnson. The Eisenhowers deeded the farm to the National Park Service in 1967.

A visit to the farm includes a tour of the Eisenhower home which retains all its original furnishings. Self-guided walks throughout the site's 690 acres allow for exploration of the skeet range, putting green, rose gardens, guest house, black Angus herd, and barns still housing Eisenhower vehicles and farm equipment. In season, living history and park ranger programs are offered. A reception center features a video and exhibits on Eisenhower's life, including his military career.

- Open daily, April 1-October 31, 9-4; November 1-March 31, open Wednesday-Sunday. Closed Thanksgiving, Christmas, New Year's Day, and four weeks in January-February.
- Adults, $5.25; children 13-16, $3.25; children 6-12, $2.25.
- All visits are by shuttle bus from the Visitor Center.
- Wheelchair users may drive to site; strollers are carried on shuttle bus; good accessibility on the grounds.

Explore & More ⁱⁿⁿ

*70 East High Street, Gettysburg, PA (717-337-9151) - **www.exploreandmore.com**.*

This hands-on children's museum and playhouse is designed for ages 4-8 and includes a Civil War playhouse with general store and battlefield encampment, a construction zone, giant bubbles and an art room.

- Daily from 10- 5.

Gettysburg National Military Park

*97 Taneytown Road, Gettysburg, PA (717-334-1124) - **www.nps.gov/gett**. Located in Gettysburg, PA, off Route 15.*

This park is the site of a major battle of the American Civil War. The three days of fighting on July 1, 2, and 3, 1863, are considered a turning point in the war and marked the second and final invasion of the North by Confederate forces. The Gettysburg National Cemetery adjoins the park and is where Abraham Lincoln delivered his famous Gettysburg Address.

The **Visitor Center** is located south of the town of Gettysburg and is accessible from Routes 15 and 134. If you begin here, you will get tour information, see the Rosensteel Collection of Civil War artifacts, and see an electronic map of the battle. The first show starts at 8:15 am and is held every 45 minutes until closing.

The **Cyclorama Center**, adjacent to the Visitor Center, contains the Famous Cyclorama painting of "Pickett's Charge" by Paul Philippoteaux in 1884. The painting is displayed with a dramatic sound and light program. There are no advance reservations. Groups are admitted in order of arrival. This center also contains a number of free exhibits.

- Visitor facilities open daily except Thanksgiving, Christmas, and New Years Day. Hours are 8-5. Park roads are open from 6 a.m. to 10 p.m. year-round. See www.gettysburgtourguides.org
- Free admission. Fees for the Electric Map and Cyclorama Program.
- Licensed Battlefield Guides are available for a personal two-hour guided tour in the visitor's vehicle. The cost for a guide is: $40 for 1-5 people, $60 for 6-15 people, and $90 for 16-49 people.
- Camping is available for organized youth groups only.
- Security Information: Backpacks, daypacks, large handbags and large containers are prohibited in the Visitor and Cyclorama Centers.
- Biking, Camping, Hiking.

Special activities include guided tours, historical demonstrations, and programs.

Ghosts of Gettysburg
Candlelight Walking Tours

*271 Baltimore Street, Gettysburg, PA (717-337-0445) - **www.ghostofgettys
burg.com**. Located two blocks south of the traffic circle in downtown
Gettysburg on Business Route 15 (Baltimore Street), on the corner of
Breckenridge Street.*

These tours are popular evening destinations. They are based
on the "*Ghosts of Gettysburg*" trilogy by Mark Nesbitt.
Trained guides in 19th century garb take stories from
Nesbitt's best-selling books and turn them into a fascinating
hour and fifteen-minute stroll through the darkened streets of
Gettysburg. Each tour covers about a mile of leisurely
walking and contains about ten different "haunted" sites.

- Open daily during the summer, 12-10 p.m. Tours are
  Baltimore Street Tour, $6; Carlisle Street Tour, $6.50;
  Children seven and under, free. Group rates available.

- Tours are conducted on sidewalks through town, and
  are offered from 7:30-9:45 p.m.

Maryland

Breezy Point Beach

5230 Breezy Point Road, Chesapeake Beach, MD (410-535-0259) -
www.co.cal.md.us/ccpr/breezy_point.html. *Located 6 miles south of Chesapeake Beach, MD. I-495 to Exit 11A/Route 4 South/East. MD 260 nine miles to Chesapeake Beach. Turn right on MD 261; left on Breezy Point Road to beach.*

Visit the Chesapeake Bay! Spend the day exploring the beach, swimming, fishing or picnicking in the shade. Spend the night at a bay-front campsite. Collect fossils and search for shark teeth!

- Open daily, May 1-October 31.
- Ages 12 - Seniors, $5; Ages 3-11, $3; Ages 2 and under, free; Seniors, $3.00.
- Daily camping - $25 per night for to 4 people
- Bathhouses, playground, and swimming area.

Calvert Marine Museum

14200 Solomons Island Road, Solomons, MD (410-326-2042, 410-326-6691). Take I-95 to Route 4 south. Follow signs to Solomons Island.

Located at the confluence of the Patuxent River and the Chesapeake Bay, the Calvert Marine Museum offers a hands-on opportunity to learn about maritime history, paleontology, and the unusual biology of the estuary (when salt and fresh water mix). The museum has 15 tanks which display the amazing diversity of life found in the Chesapeake Bay and Patuxent River. There are boats, models, paintings, and woodcarvings that showcase the lives of watermen, cannery workers, and shipbuilders. Outside, river otters frolic in the water next to a salt marsh that is home to crabs, herons and egrets. Take a walk to the Drum Point Lighthouse, just behind the museum, that dates back to 1883. Another great way to experience the area is to board an **old oyster boat** built in 1899.

- Open daily, 10-5.
- Adults, $5; seniors, $4; children age 5-12, $2; children under five, free.
- Guided group visits, field trips, art classes, educational programs, and a summer camp offered. Website features an on-line tour.
- Field Trips, Boating, Picnicking, Wheelchair Accessible.

Special activities include Sharkfest in July, Meet the Lighthouse Keeper in April, Winter Lights Festival in January, Patuxent Family Discovery Day in May, Cradle of Invasion in August, and Patuxent River Appreciation Day in October.

Chesapeake Beach Railway Museum

4155 Mear's Avenue, Chesapeake Beach, MD (410-257-3892). Take the Washington Beltway (I-495), to Route 4 south into Calvert County; at the cross county line, take a left onto Route 260. Proceed five miles to Chesapeake Beach. Turn right onto Route 261; left onto Mear's Avenue.

Chesapeake Beach was a popular resort destination for many years prior to World War II. This museum tells the history of the resort and of the railroad that connected it to DC and Baltimore from 1900-mid 1930s. Although there are no full-size trains to see, children will enjoy the model trains, photos from the early railroad days, and an old-fashioned toy locomotive. The museum is housed in a turn-of-the-century railroad station, the last surviving station of the Chesapeake Railroad. At the museum, visitors can see artifacts, photographs, a model of the early boardwalk, and share stories with old timers from the beach. One of the treasures of the museum is a stenciled kangaroo from a Dentzel carousel, as well as a 1914 Ford station wagon. That kangaroo and the carousel are now located at Watkins Regional Park in Prince George's County.

- Open May 1-September 30, 1-4; in April and October, open weekends only from 1-4. Groups and individuals are encouraged during winter months by appointment.
- Wheelchair Accessible.

Special activities include special children's summer programs, Thursday mornings, mid-June to mid-August, 10-11:30 a.m.; Bay Breeze summer concert series, June-September, the second Thursday evening of the month at 7:30 p.m.; antique car show, the third Sunday in May; and a Christmas open house, the first Sunday in December.

Chesapeake Beach Water Park

*4079 Gordon Stinnett Drive, Chesapeake Beach, MD (301-855-3803, 410-257-1404) - **www.chesapeak-beach.md.us**. Located 25 minutes from I-95 and 30 minutes from Annapolis; take Exit 11 via Route 4 to 260. Turn right on Bay Side Road (Route 261) to Water Port.*

This water park is a great place to take a break from the heat and humidity of a Washington summer. Located at the Chesapeake Bay, this park offers eight water slides of varying thrill levels, including one that is wheelchair accessible. There is a separate pool for very little ones and a children's activity pool where kids can wrestle an alligator or swim with a giant serpent. Dreamland River, waterfalls, and fountains add to the fun! Parents with older kids can pass the time swimming laps or playing water volleyball. Families can also watch the action while relaxing in the beach area.

- Open daily, 11-8.
- Daily admission $11.50 - $14 for non-residents; season passes available.
- Birthday Parties, Picnicking, Restaurant/Snack Bar, Swimming, Wheelchair Accessible.

The Children's Museum of Rose Hill Manor Park

*1611 North Market Street, Frederick, MD (301-694-1650, 301-694-1646 group tours) - **www.co.frederick.md.us/parks/rosehill**. Take the Washington Beltway (I-495) to I-270 north to Route 15 north at Frederick; take Motter Avenue exit; left onto Motter; next left onto 14th Street; two blocks left on North Market Street; Rose Hill Manor Park is next left just past the Governor Thomas Johnson Schools.*

This delightful children's museum is located on a 43-acre historic park. The staff prides itself on making the 19th century come to life for its visitors. Children and adults may participate in hands-on activities. Make sure you visit more than the manor house. Follow your child's interest to the carriage museum, blacksmith shop, log cabin, icehouse, and herb and flower gardens. Costumed interpreters conduct the tours and encourage children to make stitches on a quilt, card wool, grind herbs, operate toy banks, and more.

- Open April-October, 10-4 Monday-Saturday, and 1-4. Sunday; weekends only in November. Closed January-February.
- Adults, $4; seniors, $3; children 3-17, $3.
- Wheelchair access to 6 exhibit buildings except for 2nd floor of the manor and log cabin.
- Field Trips, Children's Museums, Picnicking.

Special activities include special events each year featuring children's historic games, colonial craft demonstrations, hands-on crafts, and holiday programming: Opening weekend, the first weekend of April; Farm and Family Festival, the last weekend of April; Museum Discovery Weekend and Fall Festival, the first weekend in October; Autumn Campfire, the third Sunday in October; Children's Holiday Programs, the first weekend in December; and an Antique Car Show and Children's Summer Social, the third weekend in August.

Deep Creek Lake State Park

898 State Park Road, Swanton, Maryland, (301) 387-4111- **www.dnr. state.mdus/publiclands/western/deepcreeklake.html**. *Directions: From 495, take 270 north to I-70 west to I-68 west, to exit 14A/Route 219 South/ Deep Creek Lake. Continue on Route 219 South for 18 miles. Turn left onto Glendale Road. Continue on Glendale Road for one mile. Just after crossing the Glendale Bridge, turn left onto State Park Road to the information sign—approximately 1 mile.*

Deep Creek Lake State Park and the surrounding resort areas are nestled into Maryland's beautiful western mountains, in the Alleghany Highlands. Deep Creek Lake, Maryland's largest, was the result of a 1920's hydroelectric project on Deep Creek. The area gets 100-200 feet of snow in winter, summer nights are cool, and the autumn foliage is impressive. Swimming, fishing and picnicking are available along the shoreline in Deep Creek Lake State Park. Hiking and canoeing are available at Meadow Mountain and Meadow Mountain Cove in the park.

- Family campsites in the park may be reserved by calling 1-888-432-2267. Private campgrounds as well as bed and breakfast accommodations can be found throughout the area.

- Information also available at Garrett County Chamber of Commerce, 15 Visitors Center Drive, McHenry, MD 21541, (301) 387-4386 – **www.garrettchamber.com/ visiting_findingus.asp.**

Greenbrier State Park

*21843 National Pike, Boonsboro, MD (301-791-4767) - **www.dnr.state.md. us/publiclands/western/greenbrier.html**. Take the Washington Beltway (I-495) to I-270 north to I-70 west; follow signs for Greenbrier State Park.*

Greenbrier State Park is a 1,288 acre park ten miles east of Hagerstown and less than an hour's drive from Washington. The park's picnic area overlooks a 42-acre man-made lake, with a swimming area marked off with buoys and ropes. A lifeguard is on duty daily from 11-7. The peaceful, wooded setting makes this spot a nice swimming alternative to the noisy neighborhood pool. A small sandy beach slopes up to the tree-shaded picnic area, with picnic tables, barbecue grills and a pleasant view of the water. There is a small concession stand and a bathhouse with restrooms, changing rooms and showers. You can fish from the pier and rent a rowboat or canoe. You pay a day-use fee when you enter the park, allowing you access to the beach as well as other areas. Campsites are available.

- Open Memorial Day to Labor Day from 8 a.m. to sunset
- $3 per person on weekends and holidays; $2 per person weekdays; children in car seats are free; $2 per vehicle.
- Boating, Camping, Fishing, Hiking, Picnicking, Restaurant/Snack Bar, Swimming.

National Museum of Civil War Medicine

*48 E. Patrick Street, Frederick, MD (301-695-1864) - **www.civilwarmed. org**. Take I-270 to the Jefferson Street exit, #5. Turn right on Route 144, South Street; make a left on Carroll Street and then a left on E. Patrick. Museum is on the left. Public parking garage entrance is on the left, just after the museum.*

For Civil War buffs and children curious about medicine and nursing, this unique museum offers a fascinating picture of wartime health care over 100 years ago. The museum is an official site on the Civil War Discovery Trail. It is valuable to combine this site with a visit to the Battleground at Antietam.

The museum is dedicated to telling the medical story of the American Civil War. Photographs, drawings, and displays of all kinds of Civil War-era medicine bring to life the treatment available to soldiers. The museum may not be appropriate for young children, but if you can call ahead at least two weeks, the staff can tailor a tour that is age-appropriate for your family or group.

In addition to the permanent exhibits, the museum has special events scheduled each month. Some examples: living historians portray nurses and doctors in period dress, a Union drummer boy talks about the role of children in the Civil War, and an exhibit of African-American contributions to Civil War medicine.

- Monday-Saturday, 10-5; Sunday, 11-5. Closes 1 hour earlier mid-November to mid-March.
- Call for information about tours offered.
- Adults, $6.50; seniors age 60 and above, $6; children ages 10-16, $4.5; children under ten, free.
- Kids' Corner.
- Recommended for children age ten and older.
- Wheelchair Accessible.

Rocky Gap State Park 16

*12500 Pleasant Valley Road, Flintstone, MD (301-777-2139, 888-432-2267 for reservations) - **www.dnr.state.md.us/publiclands/western/rocky gap.html**. Take the Washington Beltway (I-495) to I-270 north towards Frederick for about 30 miles to I-70 west. Stay on I-70 for 60 miles to I-68 west. You will be on I-68 for approximately 40 miles to Rocky Gap State Park on exit 50. Make a right off of the exit.*

A beautiful place to vacation, Rocky Gap State Park features a 243-acre lake surrounded by mountains, and inexpensive lodgings at the 220-room lakeside lodge - Rocky Gap Lodge and Golf Resort. Take a swim in the lake, rent canoes, go fishing, and enjoy the 18-hole Jack Nicklaus Signature golf course. Two boat ramps are available in the park along with rentals. Hiking trails from ¼-5 miles are throughout the park.

- Open year round. Boats are allowed on Lake Habeeb 24 hours a day, seven days a week. (Gasoline powered motors are prohibited.)
- Fishing is permitted 24 hours a day, seven days a week. Children's fishing programs are available throughout the summer season.
- Enjoy a ride on the Western Maryland Scenic Railroad.
- See web site for camping season dates and the Chalet, campground, mini cabin, and pavilion rates.
- Wheelchair access for the mobility impaired is available at the fishing dock, amphitheater, picnic tables and campgrounds. The park also offers free of charge two all-terrain cars. There is also programs available for interpretive pontoon boat rides,
- Golf Course, Field Trips, Biking, Boating, Camping, Canoe and Kayak Rentals, Fishing, Hiking, Picnicking, Playgrounds, Restaurant/Snack Bar, Swimming, Wheelchair Accessible.

Special activities include white sandy beaches, whitewater rafting, fishing for trout and largemouth bass, fitness room, outdoor swimming pool, tennis and volleyball courts, a gazebo dock with paddle and electric boats, and a fire pit. Adventure packages are available for guided kayaking, rappelling, canoeing, biking and hiking.

Sideling Hill Exhibit Center

*3000 Sideling Hill, Hancock, MD (301-678-5442, 301-842-2155) - **www.dnr.state.md.us**. Take the Washington Beltway (I-495) to I-270 west to I-68 west; go six miles past Hancock. Open parking on I-68 east and west bound.*

View a geological tour of rocks and fossils dating as far back as 200 million years ago at the Sideling Hill Exhibit Center. Highway construction of I-68 here cut through the mountain and exposed an 85-degree vertical foot trough of stratified rock. There are four floors of exhibits: the first floor presents a children's mountain art gallery and auditorium; the second, travel information, mountain vistas, and stuffed wildlife; and the third and fourth floors offer geological exhibits explaining the construction of the cut and the formation of the rocks.

- Open daily 9-5.
- To schedule a guided tour, call Fort Frederick State Park at 301-842-2155.
- Wheelchair Accessible.

South Mountain Recreation Area

U.S. Route 40, seven miles east of Hagerstown, Boonsboro, MD (301-791-4767). Take the Washington Beltway (I-495) to I-270 north to I-70 West at Frederick. Take exit 42 through Myersville to U.S. Route 40. Turn left (west) and continue 3 miles to park entrance.

This recreation area encompasses four state parks. Greenbrier State Park is a multi-use park with picnic sites, swimming, boating, hiking, fishing, and camping available. Washington Monument State Park features the first monument built in honor of George Washington (1827). Other features include hiking, day-use area, picnic sites, and pavilions for rent. Guthland State Park was the site of the Battle of South Mountain (September, 14, 1862) as part of Lee's Maryland campaign. South Mountain is the site where Lee decided to end his first attack on the North and set the stage for the Battle of Antietam, three days later. This site was also the estate of George Alfred Townsend, writer and civil war correspondent and includes the War Correspondents Memorial. South Mountain State Park runs the length of South Mountain on the border between Washington and

Frederick Counties. It is mostly wooded and features the 38 mile section of the Appalachian Trail.

- Open daily, 8 a.m.-sunset.
- Admission: $2 per person, weekdays from Memorial Day to Labor Day; $3 per person weekends and holiday; all other times, $1 per vehicle.
- Field Trips, Boating, Camping, Fishing, Hiking, Picnicking, Playgrounds, Swimming, Wheelchair Accessible.

Special activities include campfire programs, Living History, and a Junior Ranger Program.

Western Maryland Scenic Railroad

*13 Canal Street, Cumberland, MD (800-872-4650, 301-759-4400) - **www. wmsr.com**. Take I-70 west to I-68 west (at Hancock). In Cumberland, taken exit 43C; at the bottom of the ramp, turn left directly into parking lot.*

From Cumberland, take a three-and-a-half hour trip through the Allegheny Mountains on Mountain Thunder. The 1916 Baldwin steam engine chugs through rugged countryside, climbing 1,300 feet over 16 miles of track through a 900-foot tunnel and around horseshoe curves, to the Old Depot for a layover in Frostburg for lunch at the historic freight depot, and a visit to the Thrasher Carriage Museum.

- Train departs daily at 11:30 a.m. in May-October, and on weekends, November-December.
- May-September: adults, $19; senior citizens, $17; children (12 and under), $10. First class tickets and group rates are also available.
- Restaurant/Snack Bar, Wheelchair Accessible.

Special activities include dinner, comedy and murder mystery train rides, fall foliage excursions.

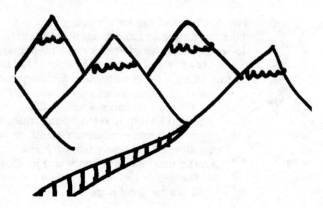

Virginia

Flying Circus Air Show ⚹16⚹

*Route 644 and Route 17, Bealeton, VA (540-439-8621) – **flyingcircusair show.com**. From the Washington Beltway (I-495) take I-66 west towards Front Royal. Take Highway 15 South to US-29 / 211. Turn left onto Meetze Road and right onto VA-28. In about a mile and a half turn right onto Germantown Road which becomes VA-610/Midland Road.*

The Flying Circus Air Show in Bealeton has 200 acres of Antique Airfields and performs every Sunday at 2:30 from May through October. From parachute jumpers to wing walkers, audiences are thrilled and amazed. Gates open up at 11 a.m.

- Every Sunday May-October; 11 a.m.-dusk.
- Adults, $10; children 12-3, $3; children under three are free; group rates available
- Grassy open area.
- Picnicking, Snack Bar.

Special activities include an Annual Balloon Festival, in August. Please check at the Gift Shop for prices and availability of Hot Air Balloon Rides. Model-T Antique Car, Hot Rod Car, Motorcycle and Mazda Sports Car days throughout the Summer. Armed Forces Appreciation Day in May and Women in Aviation Day in June. See web site for details and dates.

Lake Anna State Park ⚹16⚹

*VA (540-854-5503) - **www.dcr.state.va.us/parks/lakeanna**. Take the Washington Beltway (I-495) to I-95 South. Two exits past Fredericksburg is the Lake Anna/Thornburg exit. Follow signs to the State Park. The park is adjacent to route 601 off of Route 208, 25 miles SW of Fredericksburg, 60 miles NW of Richmond.*

For families looking for a fun day-trip to a lake, an outing to Lake Anna State Park located just south of Fredericksburg is just the answer. Only 90 minutes from D.C., Lake Anna offers a fresh water lake for swimming, boating, fishing and water-skiing. The state park features a sandy, life-guarded beach, wooded hiking trails, playground and concession stand, as well as a stocked kids-only fishing pond. Nearby marinas rent boats and jet skis by the day or half day. Bring a picnic and have a great day!

Luray Caverns

*Route 211 West, Luray, VA (540-743-6551) - **www.luraycaverns.com**.*
Located 90 minutes from Washington on U.S. 211 off scenic Skyline Drive.
Take I-66 west to Gainesville; take Route 29 south to Warrenton; take Route
211 west to Luray Caverns.

Tour the largest and most
popular cavern in eastern
America. The profusion
of formations and the
variety of natural colors
make this an
underground
wonderland. Hear the
Great Stalagpipe Organ.
See monumental
columns, rooms with

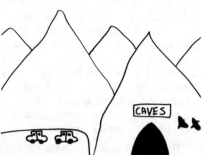

ceilings more than ten stories high, shimmering draperies,
crystal clear pools, and glittering, glistening stone. Children
will be amazed by the profusion of colorful formations.
Admission also includes **The Historic Car** and **Carriage
Caravan Museum**. Tours last about 45 minutes.

- Open daily, year-round. Guided tours are admitted to
  the caverns approximately every 10-20 minutes.

- Under 7 years of age, free; Children ages 7-13, $7;
  Adults, $16; Seniors, $14.

- Picnicking, Restaurant/Snack Bar.

Middleburg, VA Pink Box Visitor Center

12 N. Madison Street, Middleburg, VA (540-687-8888, 540-687-5152) -
***www.cr.nps.gov/nr/travel/journey/mid.htm**. Take the Washington*
Beltway (I-495) to I-66 west to Route 50 west (toward Winchester). Drive
approximately 25 miles to Middleburg. Turn right at the only traffic light in
town; the Pink Box will be on the left.

Middleburg is an historic, rural village in the heart of Virginia
Hunt Country. Antique shops, specialty stores, and great
restaurants abound. Three top wineries and the Glenwook
Park Race Course are just minutes away.

- The Visitor Center, open 11-3 daily, will provide
  brochures and maps on what to do in Middleburg and
  Loudoun County.

Special activities include the Middleburg Garden Tour in
the spring, Christmas in Middleburg in December, and scores
of special events at the Middleburg Community Center.

National Museum of the Marine Corps

*Marine Corps Heritage Foundation, P.O. Box 998, Quantico, VA (703-640-7965) - **www.marineheritage.org**.*

The National Museum of the Marine Corps will be located on a 135-acre site just off I-95 next to the Marine Corps Base at Quantico, VA, 30 miles south of Washington D.C. The architecture is inspired by the Flag Raising at Iwo Jima (see page 88), with a 210-foot tilted mast and glass atrium inspired by the Flag Raising at Iwo Jima and a 160-foot atrium housing the central gallery. Galleries will hold permanent and changing exhibits on Marine Corps history, an interactive Boot Camp exhibit, and other exhibits about the Marine Corps experience.

- Projected facilities include a restaurant, gift shop, IMAX theater, auditorium, classroom, and office spaces.
- Scheduled to open November 2005.

New Market Battlefield Military Museum

*9500 Collins Drive, New Market, VA (540-740-8065) - **www.newmarket militarymuseum.com**. Take the Washington Beltway (I-495) to I-66 west to I-81 south to Exit 264 (New Market). Take the first left after the exit onto Route 305.*

Atop this small hill is the actual New Market Battlefield and museum. The museum is a rendition of General Lee's famed Arlington House. The focus is primarily Civil War, however the collection of military memorabilia, relics, uniforms, flags, weapons, etc. from the American Revolution to the present is one of the largest on display. Fourteen marble and granite troop position markers dot the landscape and forever mark the Union and Confederate soldiers who fought and died here. There are walking paths and a wooded picnic area.

- Open 9-5 daily, from March 15 to October 31.
- Call for rates and for group reservations.
- Picnicking, Wheelchair Accessible.

Potomac West

*Mount Vernon Avenue, Alexandria, VA - **www.pwba.org**.*

Take a visit to Mount Vernon Avenue, an area known as Potomac West in DelRay, Alexandria. This lively business community is full of restaurants offering free samples of their cuisines and discounts, antique stores, and much more.

- The first Thursday in May through August.
- Free shuttle from the Metro.

Shenandoah National Park

3655 U.S. Highway, 211 East, Luray, VA (540-999-3500, 540-999-3481) - **www.nps.gov/shen**. *Take the Washington Beltway (I-495) to I-66 west to Front Royal, VA. The North entrance is in Front Royal.*

The Shenandoah National Park contains over 196,000 acres and lies across the crest of the Blue Ridge Mountains in Virginia. **Skyline Drive**, a winding road that runs through the park, provides vistas of the spectacular landscape. This land was previously used by mountain farmers for grazing sheep and cattle, and farming and hunting.

The park was established in 1935 to bring the National Park experience to the millions of people living "within a day's drive", along the east coast. Trails totaling more than 500 miles provide short or long hiking adventures. Visitors can see plants and animals and experience the beauty and peace of this vast national park.

- The park is open year round; however, Skyline Drive may be closed for ice or snow. Park facilities and services are available April through November
- Entrance fees vary.
- 101 miles of the Appalachian National Scenic Trail, waterfalls, high altitude meadow, Skyline Drive.
- Camping available spring through November. Call for reservations, 1-800-365-2267.
- Most facilities and one trail are wheelchair accessible.
- Field Trips, Fishing, Hiking, Picnicking, Restaurant/Snack Bar.

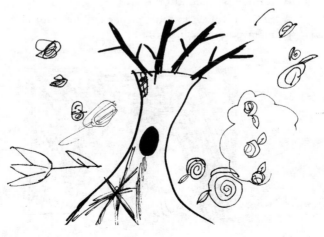

Skyline Caverns

*10344 Stonewall Jackson Street, Front Royal, VA (540-635-4545, 800-296-4545) - **www.skylinecaverns.com**. From Northern Virginia, follow I-66 west to Exit 13. At exit 13, follow Route 55 west to Route 340. Follow Route 340 south for two miles.*

When making a trip to Shenandoah National Park, don't miss the opportunity to visit the beautiful and unusual Skyline Caverns. These underground caves are filled with amazing geological formations that inspire the imagination while offering real life lessons about the physical history of the earth. The 60 million year old caverns remained a secret until 1937 when they were first discovered.

Bring along a sweater, as the temperature inside is 54 degrees all year round. The best way to see the caverns is on a guided walking tour conducted by a member of the knowledgeable staff. It lasts about an hour and covers just over one mile. The spectacular lighting brings to life the aptly named wonders beneath the earth: the Capitol Dome, the Rainbow Trail, the Wishing Well, the Shrine, and Fairyland Lake, to name a few. There are also three underground streams, one of which forms a lovely 37-foot waterfall. Amidst all this magic, the constant dripping of water throughout the caverns teaches children how the formations are made, and just how long it takes nature to do the work. Anchorites, call "orchids of the mineral kingdom," grow an inch every seven thousand years.

After the tour, enjoy a half-mile ride on the miniature train and have a picnic on the wooded grounds. Also be sure to visit nearby Dinosaur Land, see page 258.

- Open daily including holidays; hours vary by season; call for specific hours.
- Adults, $12; children (7-13), $6.
- Stairs involved in tour; please call for information.
- Field Trips, Picnicking.

Pennsylvania

Bedford Park and Museum

*Fort Bedford Drive, P.O. Box 1758, Bedford, PA (814-623-8891) - **www.bed fordcounty.net/attaract/fort**. Take the Pennsylvania Turnpike to exit 11; turn right onto Business Route 220. Go approximately three miles to the third traffic light; turn right to next light; turn right. You will see museum from there. Free parking available in park*

Tour this re-creation of a French 1758 stockade fort from the French and Indian War. Artifacts from the war are on display here. They include flintlock rifles, early clothing, and antique hand tools. Discover the history of Fort Bedford and the pioneer days on the frontier of western Pennsylvania.

- Open daily, 10-5. Closed Tuesdays in May, September and October.
- Adults, $3; senior citizens (60+), $2.50; children (6-18), $1.50. Group rates available.
- Stroller and wheelchair accessible.
- Field Trips, Fishing, Picnicking, Playgrounds.

Hershey Gardens

*170 Hotel Road, Hershey, PA (717-534-3492) - **www.hersheygardens.org**. Located 2 1/2 hours from Washington. Take the Washington Beltway (I-495) to I-95 north to I- 695 north; take Route 83 north to Route 322 E to Hersheypark Drive. Follow the signs for Hershey Gardens. Free parking.*

This 23-acre botanical garden, home to spectacular annuals and perennials, rare specimen trees and much more, was founded by Milton Hershey in 1937. Its award-winning rose garden has over 7000 roses and is one of the largest of its kind in the United States. Hershey Gardens has one of the largest outdoor butterfly houses in Pennsylvania, featuring 300 North American butterflies. The Children's Garden (open 2003) offers interactive learning experiences and fun with gardens and plants.

- Open 9-6, April-September; 9-5, October; 9-8 Friday, Saturday, and Sunday (Memorial Day-Labor Day); Butterfly House open daily mid-June to mid-September.
- Adults (ages 13-54), $5; youth (ages 3-12); $2.50; senior citizens (ages 55 and older), $4.50.
- Stroller and wheelchair accessible.

Old Bedford Village

220 Sawblade Road, Bedford, PA (800-238-4347, 814-623-1156) -
www.oldbedfordvillage.org*. Take the Pennsylvania Turnpike to exit 11;
turn right; Old Bedford Village is 1½ miles on the right.*

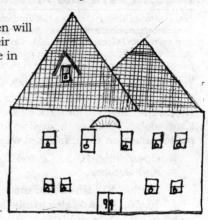

The butcher, the baker, the candlestick maker... children will find them all, practicing their crafts at Old Bedford Village in Bedford, Pennsylvania. Parents and kids alike will enjoy stepping back in time as they tour this pioneer-era village (1750-1850) featuring over 40 reproduction and authentic log, stone and frame structures. There are two schools, a church, a general store, and plenty of pioneers in period clothing cooking and farming. You can also see crafts people demonstrating the rigor of every day living or one of over 14 period crafts.

About a two-hour drive from the Washington metropolitan area, Old Bedford Village merits an all-day trip. In addition to the historical village, families can enjoy hiking, camping, fishing, and picnicking.

- Open Memorial Day - Labor Day, 9-5. Closed Wednesday. Labor Day-October open Thursday through Sunday 10-4.

- Adults, $8; students (age 6-college w/ID), $4; under age 6, free. Senior Citizen, AAA, and Group Discounts off the Regular Adult Admission are available. Admission for some events and programs are vary. Please call for rates.

- Guided tours are available to groups who book them in advance.

- Stroller and wheelchair accessible.

- Field Trips, Birthday Parties, Athletic Fields, Camping, Fishing, Hiking, Picnicking, Restaurant/Snack Bar.

Special activities include reenactments, Oktoberfest and Pioneer Days, 18th Century Christmas Celebration, Celtic Heritage Days, Bedford County Colonial Crafts Festival, and more. Adult workshops, field trips and hands-on workshops for groups are available.

Theme Parks

Catoctin Wildlife Preserve and Zoo

*13019 Catoctin Furnace Road, U.S. Route 15, Thurmont, MD (301-271-3180, 301-271-4922, office) - **www.cwpzoo.com**. Take I-270 North to Frederick; take Route 15 North towards Gettysburg; Zoo is 15 minutes north of Frederick on the right.*

Catoctin Wildlife Preserve and Zoo is a privately owned zoo that delivers fun, intimate, educational encounters with exotic animals. Covering 35 acres filled with natural wildlife, the zoo exhibits bears, boas, macaws, monkeys, big cats and small mammals in an up-close manner... perfect for children. Shows called "Encounters" are scheduled seasonally, where visitors can play with a baby animal, get the "bear facts" on grizzlies, rub and scrub the 575-pound tortoise, talk to a tiger, and hug a boa constrictor.

- Open weekends, March and November, 10-5; daily, April-October, 9-6.
- Adults, $10; seniors, $8; children ages 2-12, $6. Season passes and group rates are available.
- Paths are graveled.
- Field Trips, Birthday Parties, Picnicking, Restaurant/Snack Bar.

Special activities include Catfish Derby, overnight camps for kids, Family Sleepover, Earth Weekend, and Boo-in-the-Zoo in October.

Dinosaur Land

3848 Stonewall Jackson Highway, White Post, VA (540-869-2222). Take the Washington Beltway (I-495) to I-66 to Front Royal. Go North on Route 522/340 for six-seven miles. Located on the left at the intersection of Routes 227, 522, and 340.

- Open 9:30-5:30 daily; May 30-September 1, until 6:30.
- Children age 2-10, $3.00; age 11 and older, $4.
- Wheelchair Accessible.

After a visit to Skyline Caverns, be sure to plan a quick stop at Dinosaur Land. Children will love to romp amongst the 36 life-size fiberglass dinosaurs, prehistoric mammals and fanciful creatures in a shaded outside setting. Take a self-guided tour of the dinosaurs; there are explanatory signs beside each one. This is a great place for taking photos!

Hershey Park

*100 West Hersheypark Drive, Hershey, PA (800-437-7439) - **www.hershey park.com** and **www.hersheypa.com**. Located 2½ hours from DC. Take I-95 north to I-695 north; take Route 83 north to Route 322 at Harrisburg east; follow Route 322 east to Hershey. Free parking; Public transportation from Harrisburg PA.*

Hershey Park is a world-class theme park with more than 60 rides and attractions and more than six hours of live entertainment daily. "*Roller Soaker*" is the first interactive water coaster in the Northeast. With the addition of "Roller Soaker", Hershey Park is home to nine thrilling roller coasters and seven drenching water rides. In addition, there are more than 20 rides designed especially for younger guests. Admission to Zoo America North American Wildlife Park is also included in a one-price admission to Hershey Park.

Enjoy Hershey's Chocolate World visitors center, the official visitors center of Hershey Foods Corporation. Travel like a coca bean from a typical jungle though the factory manufacturing process and learn how chocolate is made and receive a free sample at the end of the tour. Also fun is "Hershey's Really BIG 3-D Show" - a three-dimensional musical adventure featuring the famous Hershey's product characters. While you're there, take a tour of the town on the Hershey Trolley or learn about the man behind the chocolate - Milton S. Hershey at the Hershey Museum, which features a Discovery Room especially for children.

- Open May-September, days and hours vary.
- Regular (ages 9-54), $34.95; Junior (ages 3-8) and Senior (ages 55-69), $19.95; Senior+ (70 and over),

$14.95; children two and under, free. Special Flex tickets, Preview plans, and Group Discounts.

- Wheelchair rental is available

Special activities include several seasonal celebrations; not all rides and attractions are available for the seasonal celebrations. "Springtime in the Park" (no admission-pay as you go) opens in mid April. "Halloween in Hershey" (no admission-pay as you go) is open late October weekends. "Christmas in Hershey (dates and hours vary-no admission-pay as you go) opens in November-January 1.

The Land of Little Horses

125 Glenwood Drive, Gettysburg, PA (717-334-7259, 717-334-9771) - www.littlehorses.com. From the Washington Beltway (I-495) take I-270 North to Frederick. Then take route towards Gettysburg.

Enjoy this animal park featuring performing Falabella miniature horses and a petting farm with many other animals. The little horses, originally bred in Argentina, stand as small as 26" high. Also see shows, a nature trail, barn displays and much more.

- Open 10-5, Saturday-Sunday, April-May and September-October; open daily, June-August.
- Admission $7 (under two, free). Rides are extra.
- Picnicking, Playgrounds, Restaurant/Snack Bar, Wheelchair Accessible.

Leesburg Animal Park

1228 Hunter Mill Road, Vienna, VA (703-669-0010) – www.Leesburg AnimalPark.com. Take the Washington Beltway (I-495) to the Dulles Toll Road. Greenway Toll Road (267 West). Exit Route 7 west/ 15 south, then exit 15 south toward Warrenton.

This petting zoo is home to farm animals such as cows, chickens, and goats, as well as to more exotic animals such as llamas, a zebra, and a tiger. Visitors can purchase food to feed the animals, enjoy a pony or elephant ride, and observe wild animals up close.

- Open weekends, 10-5. Closed in the winter.
- Adults, $7.95; senior citizens (age 55 and above) and children (age 2-12), $6.95.
- Field Trips, Birthday Parties, Picnicking, Playgrounds, Wheelchair Accessible.

Special activities include magicians, storytellers, singers, and animal shows; Pumpkinsville in October.

Paramount's Kings Dominion

Route 30 and I-95, Doswell, VA (804-876-5000) - ***www.kingsdominion.
com.*** *Located 75 miles south of Washington, on Interstate 95 at exit 98.*

Kings Dominion is a 400-acre theme park including Water
Works Water Park. Kidzville and Nickelode on Central provide
rides and activities for preschoolers through elementary age.
Concerts and special events are scheduled throughout the
season. Older children and teens will find a dozen coasters
and thrill rides.

- There is a fee for parking.
- Wheelchairs and strollers available for rental. Special
  boarding times for disabled riders are scheduled on
  some attractions. A special guidebook is available at
  Guest Services for guests with disabilities.
- Swimming.

Six Flags America
and Paradise Island Water Park

13710 Central Avenue, Largo, MD (301-249-1500) - ***www.sixflags.com.***
*Take the Washington Beltway (I-495) to I-95 south to Exit 15A, Route
214/Central avenue east. Six Flags America is five miles on the left.*

The park features eight roller coasters including the steel
theme coasters, "Batwing" and "Superman Ride of Steel", and
a water park. "Looney Toons Movie Town" features 12 rides
and attractions for younger children and parents.

- Open Memorial Day-Labor Day and selected weekends
  in May and October. Friday and Sunday nights in
  October, the park opens at 4 p.m. and on Saturday at
  noon for "Hallowscream."
- Adults, $35.99; senior citizens and children under 54",
  23.99; children three and under, free. Discounts to
  groups of 15 or more. Prices subject to change.
- Parking fee, $5.
- Food catering in the Pavilion is offered to groups of 75
  or more. Groups have access to volleyball, horseshoe,
  and softball facilities.
- Wheelchair access to almost all attractions, restrooms,
  and shows.
- Restaurant/Snack Bar, Swimming.

Special activities include Hallowscream, with haunted rides
and a Trick-or-Treat Trail in October.

ZooAmerica, North American Wildlife Park

*100 West Hersheypark Drive, Hershey, PA (717-534-3860) - **www.Hershey PA.com**. Take the Washington Beltway (I-495) to I-95 north; to I-83 north; to Route 322 east to Hershey.*

This 11-acre walk-through zoo features over 200 animals representing five regions of North America.

- Open year round. Hours change seasonally
- Adults (ages 13-54), $5.25; youth (ages 3-12), $4; senior citizens (ages 55 and over), $4.75; children ages two and younger, free.
- A visit to ZooAmerica is included in the admission price to Hershey Park when entered from within the park.
- Stroller and wheelchair accessible.
- Security Information: All persons are subject to search by security personnel.

Special activities include Creatures of the Night in October, a unique opportunity to see nocturnal creatures in their natural settings.

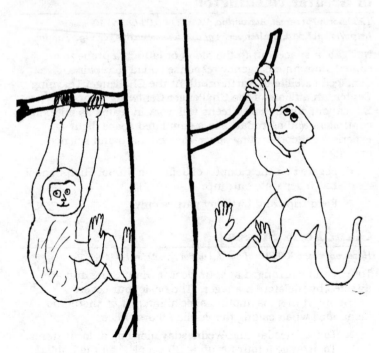

9. Field Trips

Most of the sites designated in this book are wonderful places to take groups of children for special outings. This chapter lists additional sites that offer worthwhile field trips.

Challenger Learning Center of Greater Washington

1250 North Pitt Street, Alexandria, VA 22314 (703-683-9740) -
http://launchpad.challenger.org/ *and* ***www.challenger.org.*** *Parking.*

Navigate a spacecraft to the moon or launch a probe to a comet! Join an emergency response squad to repair a damaged satellite in Earth orbit! At the Challenger Learning Center, an affiliate of the Challenger Center for Space Science Education, children and teens will work in teams as mission controllers and astronauts in a simulated space flight experience incorporating space-themed math and science exercises.

- Located on the campus of Jefferson Junior High School; has a separate entrance.
- Field trips and birthday parties only.

Giant Food Stores

Headquarters, 6300 Sheriff Road, Landover, MD (301-341-4100).

Tours can be arranged at your closest Giant Store and are directed by the store manager. The basic tour covers nutrition. If there is another special interest, it should be mentioned when calling the Public Affairs Office.

- Tours Tuesday and Wednesday morning at local stores. To arrange a tour for up to 25 people, call the Public Affairs Office at least two weeks in advance.
- Tours are for children in kindergarten through third grade only.

Montgomery County Humane Society

14645 Rothgeb Drive, Rockville, MD (301-217-5960, 301-279-1023-tours) -
www.mchumane.org. *Take the Washington Beltway (I-495) to I-270. Exit*
at West Montgomery Avenue/Darnestown (Exit 6B). Take 3rd right onto
Research Boulevard. Take a right at first light onto West Gude Drive.
Continue past the Route 355 Frederick Road intersection for about 2 miles.
Take left onto Rothgeb. Shelter is on the right. Free parking.

This shelter takes in over 10,000 animals per year. Visitors
view the animals and learn about pet overpopulation.

- Open Monday-Friday, 10-7 and Saturday, 10-5.
  Closed Sundays.
- Metrorail Red line (Rockville).
- Wheelchair Accessible.

Montgomery County Recycling Center

16105 Frederick Road, Derwood, MD (304-417-1433). Take the Washington
Beltway (I-495) to I-270 north towards Shady Grove Road exit. Take a
sharp right onto Redland Road. At the second light (Route 355), turn left.
At first light, turn right. The building is to the right. Parking is available.

At the recycling center, visitors observe the sorting process for
recyclables. They learn how recycling works and the
importance of recycling.

- Open Monday-Friday and most holidays, 9-3.
- Metrorail Red line (Shady Grove).
- Tours available Monday - Friday between 9:30-3. For
  groups of ten or more, call 301-417-1433 to arrange for
  a 30-minute presentation.
- Wheelchair Accessible.

National Public Radio

635 Massachusetts Avenue, NW, Washington, DC (202-414-2000).

Here visitors can see the studio where Morning Edition and
All Things Considered are produced. Because of the technical
nature of broadcast production, these 45-minute tours are
recommended for individuals who are familiar with NPR
programming and have a strong interest in radio. Visitors
may also see the satellite operations and some production
facilities.

- Tours Thursday, 11 a.m. Tours are for a maximum of
  eight people; call to confirm availability.
- Metrorail Red line (Gallery Place). Commercial parking
  lots are located nearby.
- Tours are recommended for children age 15 and older.

National Weather Service

44087 Weather Service Road, Sterling, VA (703-260-0107).

Virtual Tour of the office at http://weather.noaa.gov/lwx

The Pentagon

*OASD (PA), Directorate for Community Relations, Washington, DC (703-695-1776) - **www.defenselink.mil/pubs/pentagon**. Located in Virginia, just across the 14th Street Bridge off I-395. The tour office is at the top of the escalators on the Shopping Mall Concourse.*

The Pentagon, headquarters of the United States Department of Defense and the nerve center for command and control, is virtually a city within itself. The 60-year-old building is one of the world's largest office buildings, with approximately 23,000 military and civilian employees and about 3,000 non-defense support personnel.

> ## Take Note...
>
> Fact from the Pentagon website: Despite 17.5 miles of corridors it takes only seven minutes to walk between any two points in the building.

- Tours of the Pentagon are available to schools, educational organizations and other select groups by reservation only. Groups interested in touring the Pentagon should contact the Pentagon Tour Office at 703-695-1776.
- Metrorail Blue and Yellow lines (Pentagon).
- A 24-minute virtual tour is available on the Pentagon website.

Seneca Schoolhouse Museum

16800 River Road, Poolesville, MD (301-972-8588). Take the Washington Beltway (I-495) to I-270 north to Route 28 west (Darnestown Road). Bear left on Route 107 to Poolesville.

Incorporated in 1974, Historic Medley District, Inc., operates the **Seneca Schoolhouse Museum**, a one room school house built in 1866. Costumed docents teach history in this authentic setting to classes from area schools. While visiting this museum, stop by the **John Poole House**, a log house built in 1793 which was used as a trading post for merchants and families of the surrounding farms and plantations.

- Open Sunday, 1-5, mid-March to mid-December, and by appointment.
- Donations requested.

Voice of America

330 Independence Avenue, SW, Washington, DC (202-619-3919). Entrance is on the C Street side of the building, between 3rd and 4th Streets, SW.

During the 45-minute tour, visitors will view live broadcasts and learn about the U.S. government's international broadcast network. VOA transmits approximately 1000 hours per week in 52 languages (including English) to an estimated worldwide audience of 90 million regular listeners!

- Tours weekdays at 10:30, 1:30 and 2:30. Closed Federal holidays. Reservations are required.
- Metrorail Blue and Orange lines (Federal Center).
- Stroller and wheelchair accessible.

The Washington Post

*1150 15th Street, NW, Washington, DC (202-334-7969) - **washpost.com**.*

Tour includes a 14-minute video on the history of the Washington Post and how the newspaper is made, and a visit to the newsroom where the reporters work.

- No individual tours or walk-ins. Organized groups can arrange a tour with two weeks notice by calling the Public Relations Office. Tours offered Monday, 10-5. Individuals or groups can sign up for tours. Up to 40 people per tour can be accommodated. Children must be in the fifth grade or older.
- Metrorail Orange and Blue lines (McPherson Square); Red line (Farragut North).

WETA-TV, Channel 26

3620 27th Street South, Arlington, VA (703-998-2696). Take I-395 south to Shirlington/Glebe Road; follow signs for Shirlington; turn right at first light on Shirlington Road; make an immediate left on South 27th Street. WETA's studio is the first building on the left.

The tour of this Public Broadcasting System facility includes a look at the studios and control rooms, where such programs as *Newshour with Jim Lehrer* are produced, and an explanation of the technical equipment.

- Tours weekdays when volunteers and studios are available. Tours should be arranged two-four weeks in advance by calling or writing to the Volunteer Coordinator, Box 2626, Washington, DC 20013.
- Children must be ten or older.
- Maximum group size is 15.

Whole Foods Market

Corporate Office, 6015 Executive Boulevard, Rockville, MD (301-984-3737) -
www.wholefoodsmarket.com*. Locations and directions provided online.*

Tours usually cover all the departments, including produce, cheese and pasta, seafood, and bakery. Explanations are given about organic and non-organic foods that are sold at the store. Depending on the size and age of the group, some behind-the-scenes activities can be studied. Samples are often tasted and compared.

- Tours for groups of up to 20.
- Call the Community Affairs Representative of your local neighborhood Whole Foods Market Store to arrange a tour.
- Contact individual stores for their monthly calendar of events.

10. Quick Guide to Special Interests

Children (and adults) who are enthusiastic about their interests want to find all the places to go where they can nurture their enthusiasm. From toy trains to scenic railroads, from goldfish to sharks, special interests can grow from home to the wide world. Here is a list of frequently mentioned special interests and where to find them. We've included a short list of sites that specialize in birthday parties - and many of the other sites in these lists are great places for birthday celebrations.

New for the 16th Edition

The African-American Civil War Memorial   38

Alexandria Black History Resource Center   80

American Film Institute;
AFI Silver Theatre and Cultural Center   170

Barston's Child's Play   186

Brambleton Regional Park   129

City Museum   40

Clark Griffith Collegiate Baseball League   193

Croydon Creek Nature Center   146

Dickerson Conservation Area   108

Downpour at Algonkian Regional Park   206

Drug Enforcement Administration Museum
and Visitors Center   85

ESPN Zone   211

ExploraWorld   211

Explore and More   239

Flying Circus Air Show   250

Freedom Park   86

Galyan's Trading Company   213

International Spy Museum   48

Ladew Topiary Gardens 227

Lake Anna State Park 250

Maryland Museum of African American
History and Culture 78

McCrillis Gardens and Gallery 166

National Firearms Museum 93

National Museum of the American Indian 27

Radio-Television Museum 77

Rockville Skate Part at Welsh Park 203

Rocky Gap State Park 247

Round House Theatre 179

Rust Sanctuary (Audubon Naturalist Society) 153

Shadowland 213

South Germantown Recreational Park 140

Sullivan's Toy Store 189

U.S. Botanic Garden 28

Union Station 64

Walney Visitor Center - Ellanor C. Lawrence Park 160

Webb Sanctuary (Audubon Naturalist Society) 154

Whirligigs and Whimsies 191

White Flint Golf Park 199

Woodend Nature Sanctuary (Audubon Naturalist Society) 155

Appropriate for Preschoolers

A Likely Story Children's Bookstore 184

Borders Books 186

Bull Run Regional Park 130

Burke Lake Park 131

Cabin John Regional Park 131

Chuck E Cheese 210

ExploraWorld 211

Glen Echo Park and Carousel	73
Hadley's Park	136
Hidden Oaks Nature Center	147
Lake Accotink Park	137
Lake Fairfax Park	137
Locust Grove Nature Center	149
Montgomery Aquatic Center	207
Noyes Library for Young Children	187
Olney Indoor Swim Center	208
Oxon Hill Farm	159
Parenting Resource Centers	212
Puppet Company Playhouse	178
Smithsonian Discovery Theater	180
Watkins Regional Park	141
Wheaton Regional Park	142
Zany Brainy	191

Of Special Interest to Teens

African Art Museum of Maryland	68
Alexandria Archaeology Museum	80
Arlington House, the Robert E. Lee Memorial	81
Arthur M. Sackler Gallery	15
Baltimore Orioles	192
Beall-Dawson House and Stonestreet Museum of 19th Century Medicine	68
B'nai B'rith Klutznick National Jewish Museum	39
Brookside Gardens	165
Carlyle House Historic Park	83
Corcoran Gallery of Art	41
Dave and Buster's	210
Drug Enforcement Administration Museum and Visitors Center	85

Fairland Batting Cages 135

Folger Shakespeare Library 34

Fort Washington Park 125

Frederick Douglass Home (Cedar Hill) 46

Gadsby's Tavern Museum 86

Hirshhorn Museum and Sculpture Garden 17

The Kreeger Museum 51

Laser Quest 213

National Museum of Civil War Medicine 246

National Museum of Health and Medicine
of the Armed Forces 53

National Portrait Gallery 54

The Phillips Collection 59

Radio-Television Museum 77

Renwick Gallery 60

Sportrock Climbing Center 214

Star-Spangled Banner Flag House 230

Sully Historic Site 94

Tudor Place 61

U.S. Botanic Garden 28

U.S. Holocaust Memorial Museum 62

U.S. Navy Memorial and Naval Heritage Center 63

Washington Navy Yard 67

Airplanes/Space

College Park Aviation Museum 72

Flying Circus Airshow 250

Montgomery County Airpark 76

National Air and Space Museum 20

Aquariums

National Aquarium In Baltimore 221

National Aquarium, Washington 21

National Zoo 55

Arboretums/Gardens

Brookside Gardens 165

Constitution Gardens 15

Dumbarton Oaks Gardens and Museum 44

Green Spring Gardens Park 165

Hershey Gardens 255

Hillwood Museum and Garden 47

John Poole House 75

Kenilworth Park and Aquatic Gardens 166

Meadowlark Botanical Gardens 167

Morven Park 91

River Farm Garden Park 167

U.S. National Arboretum 168

William Paca House and Garden 236

Woodend Nature Sanctuary (Audubon Naturalist Society) 155

Batting Cages

Cameron Run Regional Park and Great Waves Water Park 132

Fairland Batting Cages 135

Occoquan Regional Park 138

Upton Hill Regional Park 141

Rocky Gorge 199

Battlefields/Forts

Antietam National Battlefield 124

Ball's Bluff Regional Park 124

Bedford Park and Museum 255

Federal Hill Park 219

Fort McHenry National Monument and Historic Shrine 227

Fort Ward Museum and Historic Site 85

Fort Ward Park 125

Fort Washington Park 125

Fredericksburg and Spotsylvania National Military Park 126

Gettysburg National Military Park 240

Manassas National Battlefield Park 126

New Market Battlefield Military Museum 252

Patapsco Valley State Park 111

South Mountain Recreation Area 248

Biking

Allen Pond Park 127

Black Hill Regional Park 103

Bluemont Park 129

Capital Crescent Trail 100

Cedarville State Forest 105

Chesapeake and Ohio (C&O) Canal
Historical Park Great Falls, MD 105

East Potomac Park 134

Fletcher's Boathouse 195

Fountainhead Regional Park 116

Gettysburg National Military Park 240

Lake Accotink Park 137

Lake Artemesia Park 109

Mount Vernon Trail 118

Occoquan Regional Park   138

Patapsco Valley State Park   111

Prince William Forest Park   120

Quiet Waters Park   233

Rock Creek Park   101

Rocky Gap State Park   247

Seneca Creek State Park   114

Sligo Creek Park   115

Swain's Lock   196

Thompson's Boat Center   196

Washington and Old Dominion (W&OD)
Railroad Regional Park   122

Watkins Regional Park   141

Wheaton Regional Park   142

White's Ferry   79

Whitetail Resort   205

Birthday Parties

Take Note!

Many park recreation buildings and picnic sites may be rented
for special events:

www.pgparks.com/places/permits.html

www.mc-mncppc.org/permits/index.shtm

www.fairfaxcounty.gov/parks/weddings.htm

www.co.fairfax.va.us/parks/picnic-r.htm

www.co.arlington.va.us/prcr/scripts/facitilties/facilities.htm

Bethesda Big Train   193

Cabin John Ice Rink   131

Capital Childrens Museum   32

Catoctin Wildlife Preserve   257

Challenger Learning Center of Greater Washington   262

College Park Airport Museum 72

Croyden Creek Nature Center 146

Discovery Creek 43

ExploraWorld 211

Imagination Stage 173

Made by You 215

Martin Luther King, Jr. Pool 207

National Aquarium in Baltimore 221

National Capital Trolley Museum 77

National Zoo 55

Now This Kids! 177

Potomac Horse Center 198

Splashdown Water Park 209

Sportrock Climbing Center 214

Boating

Algonkian Regional Park 127

Allen Pond Park 127

Anacostia Park 99

Black Hill Regional Park 103

Bull Run Marina 116

Burke Lake Park 131

Calvert Marine Museum 242

Chesapeake and Ohio (C&O) Canal at Great Falls, MD 105

Cosca Regional Park 107

Cunningham Falls State Park 107

Fletcher's Boathouse 195

Fountainhead Regional Park 116

Greenbrier State Park 244

Harborplace and The Gallery 219

Jack's Boats 195

Lake Accotink Park 137

Lake Fairfax Park 137

Lake Needwood Park 110

Mount Vernon Trail 118

Occoquan Regional Park 138

Patapsco Valley State Park 111

Patuxent River State Park, Jug Bay Natural Area 112

Piscataway National Park 113

Pohick Bay Regional Park and Golf Course 139

Quiet Waters Park 233

Riverbend Park 121

Rock Creek Park 101

Rocky Gap State Park 247

Seneca Creek State Park 114

South Mountain Recreation Area 248

Spirit Cruises 8

Swain's Lock 196

Theodore Roosevelt Island 122

Thompson's Boat Center 196

Watermark Cruises 235

White's Ferry 79

Canoe and Kayak Rentals

Bull Run Marina 116

Fletcher's Boathouse 195

Pohick Bay Regional Park and Golf Course 139

Quiet Waters Park 233

Rocky Gap State Park 247

Carousels

Burke Lake Park	131
Glen Echo Park and Carousel	73
Lake Accotink Park	137
Lake Fairfax Park	137
Lee District Park and Robert E. Lee Recreation Center	138
Smithsonian Information Center, 'the Castle'	27
Watkins Regional Park	141
Wheaton Regional Park	142

Children's Museums

Capital Children's Museum	32
The Children's Museum of Rose Hill Manor Park	244
Discovery Creek Children's Museum of Washington	43
Explore and More	239
Port Discovery Children's Museum	222

Disk Golf

Bull Run Regional Park	130
Pohick Bay Regional Park and Golf Course	139
Seneca Creek State Park	114

Equestrian

Bluemont Park	129
Bull Run Marina	116
Bull Run Regional Park	130
Meadowbrook Stables	198
Patapsco Valley State Park	111
Potomac Horse Center	198

Riverbend Park 121

Rock Creek Park Horse Center 198

Rocky Gap State Park 247

Shenandoah National Park 253

Wheaton Regional Park 142

Fishing

Algonkian Regional Park 127

Allen Pond Park 127

Anacostia Park 99

Ball's Bluff Regional Park 124

Bedford Park and Museum 255

Black Hill Regional Park 103

Bluemont Park 129

Bull Run Marina 116

Burke Lake Park 131

Calvert Cliffs State Park 103

Cameron Run Regional Park and
Great Waves Water Park 132

Catoctin Mountain Park 104

Cedarville State Forest 105

Chesapeake and Ohio (C&O) Canal
Historical Park Great Falls, MD 105

Cosca Regional Park 107

Cunningham Falls State Park 107

Dickerson Conservation Area 108

Fort Washington Park 125

Fountainhead Regional Park 116

Great Falls Park 117

Greenbrier State Park 244

Harpers Ferry National Historical Park 237

Lake Accotink Park 137

Lake Anna State Park 250

Lake Artemesia Park 109

Lake Fairfax Park 137

Lake Frank 109

Lake Needwood Park 110

Martin Luther King, Jr. Swim Center (MLK) 207

Mount Vernon Trail 118

National Wildlife Visitor Ctr., Patuxent Research Refuge 151

Occoquan Regional Park 138

Old Bedford Village 256

Oxon Hill Farm 159

Patapsco Valley State Park 111

Patuxent River State Park, Jug Bay Natural Area 112

Pohick Bay Regional Park and Golf Course 139

Quiet Waters Park 233

Riverbend Park 121

Rocky Gap State Park 247

Seneca Creek State Park 114

Shenandoah National Park 253

South Mountain Recreation Area 248

Swain's Lock 196

Theodore Roosevelt Island 122

Wheaton Regional Park 142

White's Ferry 79

Whitetail Resort 205

Golf Courses

Algonkian Regional Park 127

Anacostia Park 99

Brambleton Regional Park 129

East Potomac Park 134

Jefferson District Park   136

Lake Needwood Park   110

Pohick Bay Regional Park   139

Rock Creek Park   101

Rocky Gap State Park   247

Sligo Creek Park   115

Wisp   205

Miniature Golf

Algonkian Regional Park   127

Bohrer Park at Summit Hall Farm   206

Bull Run Regional Park   130

Cameron Run Regional Park & Great Waves Water Park   132

East Potomac Park   134

Fountainhead Regional Park   116

Jefferson District Park and Golf Course   136

Lake Accotink Park   137

Pohick Bay Regional Park and Golf Course   139

Rocky Gorge   199

South Germantown Recreational Park   140

Upton Hill Regional Park   141

Watkins Regional Park   141

White Flint Golf Park   199

Nature Centers

Brookside Nature Center   145

Clearwater Nature Center   145

Cosca Regional Park   107

Croydon Creek Nature Center   146

Gulf Branch Nature Center   147

Hidden Oaks Nature Center   147

Hidden Pond Nature Center   148

Little Bennett Regional Park   110

Locust Grove Nature Center   149

Long Branch Nature Center   150

Meadowside Nature Center   150

Potomac Overlook Regional Park   119

Riverbend Park   121

Rock Creek Nature Center and Planetarium   152

Rust Sanctuary (Audubon Naturalist Society)   153

Watkins Regional Park   141

Woodend Nature Sanctuary (Audubon Naturalist Society) 155

Observatories/Planetarium

Arlington Public Schools Planetarium   144

Howard B. Owens Science Center and Planetarium   149

Maryland Science Center   220

National Air and Space Museum   20

Rock Creek Nature Center and Planetarium   152

U.S. Naval Observatory   153

University of Maryland Observatory   154

Railroads

Baltimore and Ohio Railroad Museum   223

The Baltimore Civil War Museum   217

Baltimore Streetcar Museum   225

Burke Lake Park   131

Cabin John Regional Park   131

Chesapeake Beach Railway Museum   243

Lake Fairfax Park   137

National Capital Trolley Museum   77

Rocky Gap State Park   247

Skyline Caverns   253

W&OD Railroad Regional Park   122

Watkins Regional Park   141

Western Maryland Scenic Railroad   249

Wheaton Regional Park   142

Ships

Baltimore Maritime Museum   217

Calvert Marine Museum   242

Maryland Tours   220

The Navy Museum   56

U.S.S. Constellation   222

Swimming

Algonkian Regional Park   127

Anacostia Park   99

Audrey Moore / Wakefield Park and Recreation Center   128

Bohrer Park at Summit Hall Farm   206

Breezy Point Beach   242

Bull Run Regional Park   130

Calvert Cliffs State Park   103

Cameron Run Regional Park & Great Waves Water Park   132

Chesapeake Beach Water Park   244

Chinquapin Center and Park   133

Cunningham Falls State Park   107

Downpour at Algonkian Regional Park   206

East Potomac Park   134

Fairland Regional Park   135

Greenbrier State Park   244

Lake Fairfax Park   137

Lee District Park and Robert E. Lee Recreation Center   138

Martin Luther King, Jr. Swim Center (MLK)   207

Montgomery Aquatic Center   207

Olney Indoor Swim Center   208

Paramount's Kings Dominion   260

Pohick Bay Regional Park and Golf Course   139

Prince William Forest Park   120

Rockville Municipal Swim Center   208

Rocky Gap State Park   247

Six Flags America and Paradise Island Water Park   260

South Germantown Recreational Park   140

South Mountain Recreation Area   248

Splash Down Water Park   209

Upton Hill Regional Park   141

Tennis

Audrey Moore/Wakefield Park and Recreation Center   128

Bluemont Park   129

Cabin John Regional Park   131

Candy Cane City   133

Chinquapin Center and Park   133

Cosca Regional Park   107

East Potomac Park   134

Fort Ward Park   125

Hidden Pond Nature Center   148

Jefferson District Park and Golf Course   136

Lee District Park and Robert E. Lee Recreation Center   138

Martin Luther King, Jr. Swim Center (MLK)   207

Mason District Park   118

Montrose Park   138

Rock Creek Park 101

Rockville Municipal Swim Center 208

Sligo Creek Park 115

Splash Down Water Park 209

Tuckahoe Park and Playfield 140

Watkins Regional Park 141

Wheaton Regional Park 142

VA TimeTravlers Site

Alexandria Archaeology Museum 80

Carlyle House Historic Park 83

Claude Moore Colonial Farm at Turkey Run 157

Fort Ward Museum and Historic Site 85

Fredericksburg and Spotsylvania National Military Park 126

Gadsby's Tavern Museum 86

George Washington Masonic National Memorial 87

Great Falls Park 117

Gulf Branch Nature Center 147

Gunston Hall Plantation 88

The Lee-Fendall House Museum 89

The Lyceum, Alexandria's History Museum 90

Manassas National Battlefield Park 126

Mount Vernon Estate and Gardens (George Washington's Home) 92

Oatlands Plantation 93

Stabler-Leadbeater Apothecary Shop and Museum 94

Sully Historic Site 94

Walney Visitor Center - Ellanor C. Lawrence Park 160

Woodrow Wilson House 67

Zoos

The Baltimore Zoo   225

Catoctin Wildlife Preserve and Zoo   257

Leesburg Animal Park   259

National Museum of Natural History   26

National Zoo   55

ZooAmerica, North American Wildlife Park   261

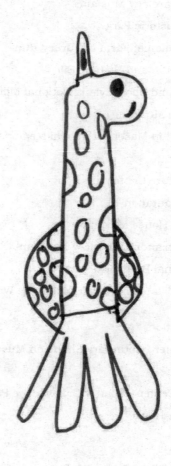

11. Annual Events for Children and Families

In every season of the year, special events take place throughout Washington and the surrounding areas. The events listed in this chapter are specifically geared towards children's and family interests. Events are free unless otherwise noted in the listing. Since only approximate dates are provided, it is best to call ahead or check the newspaper for more information.

Spring (March-May)

March

Chamber Music Concerts, The Phillips Collection	59
Daily Military Ceremonies And Outdoor Concerts, U.S. Navy Memorial and Naval Heritage Center	63
Group And Educational Programs, Fire Museum	226
Hayride In Bunnyland, Butler's Orchard	161
Kite Festival, Gunston Hall Plantation	88
Kite Festival, Washington Monument	30
Lunch With The Elephants, Lexington Market	228
Mad Hatters Tea Party, Marietta House Museum	75
Needlework Exhibit, Woodlawn Plantation Frank Lloyd Wright's Pope-Leighey House	98
Open House, Quiet Waters Park	233
Origami, National Building Museum	52
Seal Days, National Zoo	55
Shakespeare Festivals, Folger Shakespeare Library	34
St. Patrick's Day Open House, Arlington House, the Robert E. Lee Memorial	81
Wildlife Tram Tours, National Wildlife Visitor Center, Patuxent Research Refuge	151

April

African-American Family Celebration, National Zoo   55

Annual Easter Egg Roll, The White House
and White House Visitor Center   31

Farm And Family Festival, The Children's
Museum of Rose Hill Manor Park   244

Herb, Bread and Tea Festival, Montpelier Mansion   90

Living History Boat Charters, Chesapeake and Ohio
(C&O) Canal Historical Park Great Falls, MD   105

Marching Through Time-Multi Period Living History,
Marietta House Museum   75

Meet The Lighthouse Keeper, Calvert Marine Museum   242

Middleburg Garden Tour, Middleburg,
VA Pink Box Visitor Center   251

Jefferson's Birthday, April 13, Jefferson Memorial   18

Opening Weekend, The Children's
Museum of Rose Hill Manor Park   244

Point-to-Point Races, Oatlands Plantation   93

Shakespeare's Birthday Open House,
Folger Shakespeare Library   34

Springtime In The Park, Hershey Park   258

Tours Of The Gardens And The House,
The White House and White House Visitor Center   31

Weekday Lunchtime Concerts, Market Square/
Alexandria City Hall   90

May

18th Century Market Fair, Claude Moore
Colonial Farm at Turkey Run   157

Annual Open House And Heritage Festival,
Potomac Overlook Regional Park   119

Antique Car Show, Chesapeake Beach Railway Museum   243

Armed Forces Appreciation Day, Flying Circus Air Show   250

Blacksmith Days And Civil War Living History
Encampment, Carroll County Farm Museum   156

Cathedral's Flower Mart, Washington National Cathedral   65

Environmental Lecture Series, Quiet Waters Park   233

Guppy Gala, National Zoo   55

Irish Feis, Dance Competition,
Glen Echo Park and Carousel   73

Irish Festival, Wolf Trap Farm Park
for the Performing Arts/The Barns at Wolftrap   183

Mr. Lincoln's Soldiers, Featuring Civil
War Reenactments, Theodore Roosevelt Island   122

Patuxent Family Discovery Day, Calvert Marine Museum   242

Preakness Crab Derby, Lexington Market   228

Preservation Garden Party, Woodrow Wilson House   67

Sheep Dog Trials, Oatlands Plantation   93

Steeplechase Races, Morven Park   91

Wreath-Laying Ceremonies, Vietnam Veterans Memorial   29

Summer (June-August)

June

4th Of July Family Day, American Visionary Art Museum 216

A Civil War Camp Day,
Fort Ward Museum and Historic Site 85

Arts And Crafts Festival, Morven Park 91

Bay Breeze Summer Concert Series,
Chesapeake Beach Railway Museum 243

Big Band Concert, Baltimore Streetcar Museum 225

Bowiefest, Allen Pond Park 127

British Car Day, Allen Pond Park 127

Candlelight Open House In October,
Arlington House, the Robert E. Lee Memorial 81

Celebrations Of Textile Day, Textile Museum 61

Children's Games, Marietta House Museum 75

Corn Maze, Homestead Farm 162

Daily Military Ceremonies And Outdoor Concerts,
U.S. Navy Memorial and Naval Heritage Center 63

Drill Team, U.S. Navy Memorial and Naval Heritage Center 63

Earth Day Summer Concert Series, Quiet Waters Park 233

Family Free Day, The Phillips Collection 59

Hayrides, Frying Pan Park, Kidwell Farm 158

History Tour, Beall-Dawson House and
Stonestreet Museum of 19th Century Medicine 68

Junior Golf Tournament,
Jefferson District Park and Golf Course 136

Marine Sunset Parades, Iwo Jima Memorial 88

Military Band Concerts, Sylvan Theater 181

Military Band Concerts, Washington Monument 30

Military Concerts, The Capitol 32

Model-T Antique Car, Hot Rod Car, Motorcycle and
Mazda Sports Car Days, Flying Circus Airshow 250

Museum Walk Weekend, Woodrow Wilson House 67

Native American Indian Festival, American Indian
Cultural Center/Piscataway Indian Museum   68

Ranger-guided Activities, Fort McHenry National
Monument and Historic Shrine   227

Silver Spring Outdoor Movie Series, "Silver Screen
Under The Stars,", American Film Institute; AFI Silver
Theatre and Cultural Center   170

Spring Muster of Antique Fire Equipment and Fiddlers'
Convention, Carroll County Farm Museum   156

Storytime Every Friday at 11:30, Fire Museum   226

Summer Twilight Concerts, Cabin John Regional Park   131

Sunset Serenades Concert Series, National Zoo   55

Twilight Concerts, Fort Ward Park   125

Washington Folk Festival, Glen Echo Park and Carousel   73

Weekday Lunchtime Concerts, Market Square/
Alexandria City Hall   90

Women In Aviation Day, Flying Circus Air Show   250

July

4th of July Celebration, Allen Pond Park   127

Archaeology Summer Camp,
Alexandria Archaeology Museum   80

Fireworks, Lee District Park and Robert E. Lee
Recreation Center   138

History Days, Marietta House Museum   75

Montgomery County Farm Tour, Phillips Farm   163

Museum's Birthday Celebration,
Baltimore Streetcar Museum   225

Old-Fashioned July 4th Celebration,
Carroll County Farm Museum   156

Sharkfes, Calvert Marine Museum   242

Summer History Camp, Beall-Dawson House
and Stonestreet Museum of 19th Century Medicine   68

Twilight Tattoos, The White House and White House
Visitor Center   31

Waterlily Festival, Kenilworth Park and Aquatic Gardens   166

August

A Ship's Company: Navy Living History,
Fort Ward Museum and Historic Site 85

Annual Balloon Festival, Flying Circus Air Show 250

Antique Car Show And Children's Summer Social,
The Children's Museum of Rose Hill Manor Park 244

Antique Car Show, Allen Pond Park 127

Butterfly Show, Brookside Gardens 165

Children's Needlework Workshop, Woodlawn
Plantation/Frank Lloyd Wright's Pope-Leighey House 98

Corn Maize, Temple Hall Farm Regional Park 159

Cradle Of Invasion, Calvert Marine Museum 242

Fairfax County 4-H Fair,
Frying Pan Park, Kidwell Farm 158

Fall (September-November)

September

"Happy Birthday, Montgomery County", Beall-Dawson
House and Stonestreet Museum of 19th Century Medicine   68

Annual Open House, Washington National Cathedral   65

Arts Festival, John F. Kennedy Center
for the Performing Arts   174

Building Arts, National Building Museum   52

Chamber Music Concerts, The Phillips Collection   59

Children's Chautauqua Day, A Free Workshop
for Kids, Glen Echo Park and Carousel   73

Children's Day, Brookside Gardens   165

Civil War Encampment, Chesapeake and Ohio
(C&O) Canal Historical Park Great Falls, MD   105

Fall Festival, American Indian Cultural Center/
Piscataway Indian Museum   68

Fiesta Musical, National Zoo   55

Harvest Festival, Gunston Hall Plantation   88

Hayrides, Frying Pan Park, Kidwell Farm   158

Irish Folk Festival, Glen Echo Park and Carousel   73

Kalorama House And Embassy Tour,
Woodrow Wilson House   67

Living History Boat Charters, Chesapeake and Ohio
(C&O) Canal Historical Park Great Falls, MD   105

Mason Days, Mason District Park   118

Naturalization Ceremony, Constitution Gardens   15

Pumpkin Patch, Cox Farms (Market and Pumpkin Patch)   161

Rock Creek Park Day, Rock Creek Park   101

Shaker Forest Festival, Seneca Creek State Park   114

Steamshow Days, Carroll County Farm Museum   156

The International Children's Festival, Wolf Trap Farm
Park for the Performing Arts/The Barns at Wolftrap   183

Traditional American Trails Fair, Montpelier Mansion   90

Train Excursions To Western Maryland and
West Virginia, Baltimore and Ohio Railroad Museum　　223

Twilight Concerts, Fort Ward Park　　125

October
"In Search Of Ghosts", A Halloween Ghost Tour,
Beall-Dawson House and Stonestreet Museum
of 19th Century Medicine　　68

"Picking' In The Glen" Bluegrass Music Festival,
Glen Echo Park and Carousel　　73

Arat Expo, Allen Pond Park　　127

Autumn Campfire, The Children's Museum
of Rose Hill Manor Park　　244

Boo-in-the-Zoo, Catoctin Wildlife Preserve and Zoo　　257

Chocolate Festiva, Lexington Market　　228

Creatures Of The Night, ZooAmerica,
North American Wildlife Park　　261

Fall Garden Day, Tudor Place　　61

Fall Harvest Days, Carroll County Farm Museum　　156

Ghostly Tours, Woodlawn Plantation/
Frank Lloyd Wright's Pope-Leighey House　　98

Halloween In Hershey, Hersheypark　　258

Halloween Train Ride, Lee District Park
and Robert E. Lee Recreation Center　　138

Hallowscream, Six Flags America
and Paradise Island Water Park　　260

Harvest Days, Patapsco Valley State Park　　111

Hayride, Jefferson District Park and Golf Course　　136

Kids On The Bay, Baltimore Visitor Center　　4

Medieval Fair, Marietta House Museum　　75

Museum Discovery Weekend And Fall Festival,
The Children's Museum of Rose Hill Manor Park　　244

Patuxent River Appreciation Day, Calvert Marine Museum　242

Phantom Trolley, Baltimore Streetcar Museum　　225

Pumpkin Festivals, Butler's Orchard　　161

Pumpkin Harvest Days, Butler's Orchard　　161

Pumpkin Patch, Phillips Farm   163

Seasonal Riverboat Cruises, Mount Vernon
Estate and Gardens (George Washington's Home)   92

St. Patrick's Day Open House, Arlington House,
the Robert E. Lee Memorial   81

Steeplechase Races, Morven Park   91

The Blessing Of The Pets, Christ Church   83

Theodore Roosevelt Birthday Celebration,
Theodore Roosevelt Island   122

Tours Of The Gardens And The House,
The White House and White House Visitor Center   31

Zoo Booo!, A Howl-o-ween Spectacular,
The Baltimore Zoo   225

November

Arts Festival, Quiet Waters Park   233

Choose And Cut Christmas Trees, Butler's Orchard   161

Christmas In Hershey, Hersheypark   258

Garden Of Light, Brookside Gardens   165

Holiday Festivals, John F. Kennedy Center
for the Performing Arts   174

Wildlife Tram Tours, National Wildlife
Visitor Center, Patuxent Research Refuge   151

Wreath-Laying Ceremonies, Vietnam Veterans Memorial   29

Winter (December-February)

December

"Holiday Decorations", Beall-Dawson House
and Stonestreet Museum of 19th Century Medicine   68

"Old-Fashioned Ornament Workshop",
Beall-Dawson House and Stonestreet Museum
of 19th Century Medicine   68

19th Century Valentines And Crafts,
Surratt House Museum   95

A Christmas In Camp Open House,
Fort Ward Museum and Historic Site   85

Annual Christmas Display,
Washington Dolls' House and Toy Museum   64

Annual Christmas Lighting Ceremony,
Market Square/Alexandria City Hall   90

Annual Christmas Open House,
Frederick Douglass Home (Cedar Hill)   46

Annual Family Festivals, National Museum
of Women in the Arts   54

Candlelight Tours Of Historic Homes
In Old Town Alexandria, Alexandria Convention
and Visitors Bureau   3

Candlelight Tours, Carlyle House Historic Park   83

Candlelight Tours, Marietta House Museum   75

Candlelight Tours, The White House
and White House Visitor Center   31

Candlelight Tours, Tudor Place   61

Chamber Music Concerts, The Phillips Collection   59

Children's Holiday Programs, The Children's
Museum of Rose Hill Manor Park   244

Christmas At Harborplace, Harborplace and The Gallery   219

Christmas Candle-light Program, Old Stone House   58

Christmas Candlelight Tours, Montpelier Mansion   90

Christmas Carol Sing-a-Long, Wolf Trap Farm Park for
the Performing Arts, The Barns at Wolftrap   183

Christmas In Middleburg, Middleburg,
VA Pink Box Visitor Center   251

Christmas On S Street, Woodrow Wilson House   67

Christmas Open House,
Chesapeake Beach Railway Museum   243

Christmas Tour, Morven Park   91

Country Christmas, Colvin Run Mill Historic Site   84

Drive-through Animated Holiday Lights Show,
Bull Run Regional Park   130

Family Fun Day, B'nai B'rith Klutznick
National Jewish Museum   39

Festival Of Lights, Washington Temple
Visitors' Center (known as the "Mormon Temple")   79

Friends Of Quiet Waters Park Volunteer
Appreciation Banquet, Quiet Waters Park   233

Gaithersburg's Winter Lights, Seneca Creek State Park   114

Holiday Events, Decatur House Museum   43

Holiday Exhibit, Woodlawn Plantation Frank Lloyd
Wright's Pope-Leighey House   98

Holiday Fair, Woodend Nature Sanctuary
(Audubon Naturalist Society)   155

Holiday Theme Tour, Carroll County Farm Museum   156

Holly Trolley Feast, National Capital Trolley Museum   77

Holly Trolley, Baltimore Streetcar Museum   225

In June; And A , Arlington House, Robert E. Lee Memorial   81

Memorial Illumination, Antietam National Battlefield   124

National Christmas Tree Lighting and Pageant of Peace,
The White House and White House Visitor Center   31

Plantation Christmas, Gunston Hall Plantation   88

Scottish Christmas Walk, Alexandria Convention
and Visitors Bureau   3

Victorian Yuletide, Surratt House Museum   95

Winter Festival Of Lights, Watkins Regional Park   141

January
"Dr. Stonestreet Holds Office Hours", Beall-Dawson
House and Stonestreet Museum of 19th Century Medicine   68

"Winter Pastimes Afternoon: Make Old-fashioned Toys",
Beall-Dawson House and Stonestreet Museum of 19th
Century Medicine   68

Annual Oratorical Contest For Area Students,
Frederick Douglass Home (Cedar Hill)   46

BMA's Festive, Free-for-all, Baltimore Museum of Art   224

Holiday Events, Decatur House Museum   43

Winter Lights Festival, Calvert Marine Museum   242

Wreath-laying Ceremony in Honor
of Martin Luther King, Jr., Lincoln Memorial   19

February
African-American History Month, Arlington House,
the Robert E. Lee Memorial   81

Black History Month,
Frederick Douglass Home (Cedar Hill)   46

Exploring Engineering, National Building Museum   52

George Washington Birthday Parade,
Alexandria Convention and Visitors Bureau   3

Groundhog Day Celebration, Brookside Gardens   165

Maple Sugaring Festival, Brookside Nature Center   145

Wreath-laying Ceremony And Reading
of The Gettysburg Address, Lincoln Memorial   19

Wreath-Laying Ceremony, Washington Monument   30

A

A Likely Story Children's Bookstore, 184
A Tour de Force, 6
Adventure Theatre, 169
AFI Silver Theatre and Cultural Center, see American Film Institute, 170
American Film Institute, 170
African Art Museum of Maryland, 68
African Heritage Center for African Dance and Music, 170
Aladdin's Lamp Children's Books and Other Treasures, 184
Alexandria Archaeology Museum, 80
Alexandria Black History Resource Center, 80
Alexandria Convention and Visitors Bureau, 3
Algonkian Regional Park, 127
Allen Pond Park, 128
American Indian Cultural Center/Piscataway Indian Museum, 68
American Visionary Art Museum, 216
Anacostia Museum & Center for African American History & Culture, 38
Anacostia Park, 99
Anecdotal History Tours, 6
Annapolis Conference Center and Visitors Bureau, 3
Antietam National Battlefield, 124
Arboretum, see U.S. National Arboretum, 168
ARC IceSports of Rockville, 200
Arena Stage, 170
Arlington House, the Robert E. Lee Memorial, 81
Arlington National Cemetery, 82

Arlington Public Schools Planetarium, 144
Arthur M. Sackler Gallery, 15
Audrey Moore / Wakefield Park and Recreation Center, 128
Audubon Naturalist Society, see Audubon Naturalist Woodend Bookshop, 185
Audubon Naturalist Society, see Webb Sanctuary (Audubon Naturalist Society), 154
Audubon Naturalist Society, see Woodend Nature Sanctuary (Audubon Naturalist Society), 155
Audubon Naturalist Woodend Bookshop, 185

B

Babe Ruth Museum, 217
Ball's Bluff Regional Park, 124
Baltimore and Ohio Railroad Museum, 223
Baltimore Civil War Museum, see Baltimore Civil War Museum - President Street Station, The, 217
Baltimore Maritime Museum, 217
Baltimore Museum of Art, 224
Baltimore Museum of Industry, 224
Baltimore Orioles, 192
Baltimore Public Works Museum, 218
Baltimore Streetcar Museum, 225
Baltimore Visitor Center, 4
Barnes and Noble, 185
Barston's Child's Play, 186
Basilica of the National Shrine of the Immaculate Conception, 39
Battery-Kemble Park, 100
Beall-Dawson House and Stonestreet Museum of 19th Century Medicine, 69
Bedford Park and Museum, 255
Belair Mansion, 70

Belair Stable, 70
Beltsville Agricultural Research
    Center, 144
Bethesda Academy of
    Performing Arts, see
    Imagination Stage - Bethesda
    Academy of Performing Arts
    (BAPA), 173
Black Hill Regional Park, 103
Blackrock Center for the Arts,
    171
Bluemont Park, 129
B'nai B'rith Klutznick National
    Jewish Museum, 39
Bohrer Park at Summit Hall
    Farm, 206
Borders Books, 186
Bowie Baysox Baseball, 192
Bowie Train Station and
    Huntington Museum, 71
Boyds Negro School House, 71
Brambleton Regional Park, 129
Breezy Point Beach, 242
Brookside Gardens, 165
Brookside Nature Center, 145
Bull Run Marina, 116
Bull Run Regional Park, 130
Bureau of Engraving and
    Printing, 40
Burke Lake Park, 131
Butler's Orchard, 161

C

C&O Canal Historical Park
    Great Falls, MD, see
    Chesapeake & Ohio (C&O)
    Canal Historical Park Great
    Falls, MD, 105
Cabin John Regional Park, 131
Calvert Cliffs State Park, 103
Calvert Marine Museum, 242
Cameron Run Regional Park &
    Great Waves Water Park, 132
Candy Cane City, 133
Capital Children's Museum, 32
Capital Crescent Trail, 100
Capitol Concerts - Armed
    Forces Band and National
    Symphony, 171

Carlyle House Historic Park, 83
Carroll County Farm Museum,
    156
Castle, The Smithsonian, see
    Smithsonian Information
    Center, 'the Castle', 27
Catoctin Mountain Park, 104
Catoctin Wildlife Preserve and
    Zoo, 257
Cedarvale Farm, 157
Cedarville State Forest, 105
Chesapeake & Ohio (C&O)
    Canal Historical Park Great
    Falls, MD, 105
Chesapeake Beach Railway
    Museum, 243
Chesapeake Beach Water Park,
    244
Children's Theater, 172
Chinquapin Center and Park,
    133
Christ Church, 83
Chuck E Cheese, 210
City Museum, 40
Clara Barton National Historic
    Site, 71
Clark Griffith Collegiate
    Baseball League, 193
Claude Moore Colonial Farm at
    Turkey Run, 157
Clay Café Studio, 215
Clearwater Nature Center, 145
College Park Aviation Museum,
    72
Colvin Run Mill Historic Site,
    84
Comedy Sportz Arena, 172
Constitution Gardens, 15
Corcoran Gallery of Art, 41
Cosca Regional Park, 107
Cox Farms (Market and
    Pumpkin Patch), 161
Croydon Creek Nature Center,
    146
Cunningham Falls State Park,
    107

D

D.C. Duck Tours, 6

DASH, 10
Daughters of the American
  Revolution Museum, 42
Dave and Buster's, 210
Decatur House Museum, 43
Deep Creek Lake State Park,
  245
Dickerson Conservation Area,
  108
Dinosaur Land, 258
Discovery Creek Children's
  Museum of Washington, 43
Downpour at Algonkian
  Regional Park, 206
Drug Enforcement
  Administration Museum and
  Visitors Center, 85
Dumbarton Oaks Gardens and
  Museum, 44

E

East Potomac Park, 134
Eastern Market, 34
Eisenhower National Historic
  Site, 239
Ellipse Visitors Pavilion, 4
ESPN Zone, 211
ExploraWorld, 211
Explore & More, 239
Explorers Hall, National
  Geographic Society, 45

F

Fairfax Ice Arena, 201
Fairfax Symphony Orchestra,
  173
Fairland Recreational Park, 135
Fairland Regional Park, 135
Fairy Godmother, 187
Federal Hill Park, 219
Fire Museum, 226
Fletcher's Boathouse, 195
Flying Circus Airshow, 250
Folger Shakespeare Library, 34
Ford's Theatre/Lincoln
  Museum/Petersen House, 45

Fort McHenry National
  Monument and Historic
  Shrine, 227
Fort Ward Museum and Historic
  Site, 85
Fort Ward Park, 125
Fort Washington Park, 125
Fountainhead Regional Park,
  116
Franciscan Monastery, 46
Franconia Roller Skating Center,
  202
Franklin Delano Roosevelt
  Memorial, 16
Frederick Douglass Home
  (Cedar Hill), 46
Frederick Keys Baseball, 194
Fredericksburg and Spotsylvania
  National Military Park, 126
Freedom Park, 86
Freer Gallery of Art, 16
Friday Night in the Park
  Concerts, 173
Friendship Firehouse, 86
Frying Pan Park, Kidwell Farm,
  158

G

Gadsby's Tavern Museum, 86
Galyan's Trading Company, 213
Gardens IceHouse, 202
George Washington Masonic
  National Memorial, 87
Gettysburg National Military
  Park, 240
Ghosts of Gettysburg
  Candlelight Walking Tours,
  241
Giant Food Stores, 262
Glen Echo Park and Carousel,
  73
Glover-Archibold Parkway, 101
Good Knight Kingdom
  Museum, 74
Great Falls Park, 117
Green Spring Gardens Park, 165
Greenbelt Museum, 74
Greenbelt Park, 108
Greenbrier State Park, 246

Gulf Branch Nature Center, 147
Gunston Hall Plantation, 88

H

Hadley's Park, 136
Harborplace and The Gallery, 219
Harpers Ferry National Historical Park, 237
Hemlock Overlook Regional Park, 136
Hershey Gardens, 255
Hersheypark, 258
Hidden Oaks Nature Center, 147
Hidden Pond Nature Center, 148
Hillwood Museum and Garden, 47
Hirshhorn Museum and Sculpture Garden, 17
Historic Annapolis Foundation Welcome Center and Museum Store, 233
Holocaust Museum, see U.S. Holocaust Memorial Museum, 62
Homestead Farm, 162
Howard B. Owens Science Center and Planetarium, 149
Huntley Meadows Park, 117

I

Imagination Stage - Bethesda Academy of Performing Arts (BAPA), 173
Imagination Station, 187
Interior Department Museum, 48
International Spy Museum, 48
Islamic Center, 49
Iwo Jima Memorial, 88

J

Jack's Boats, 195
Jeepers, 212
Jefferson District Park and Golf Course, 136
Jefferson Memorial, 18
John F. Kennedy Center, 50

John F. Kennedy Center for the Performing Arts, 174
John Poole House, 75

K

Kenilworth Park and Aquatic Gardens, 166
Kennedy Center, 50
Korean War Veterans Memorial, 19

L

Ladew Topiary Gardens, 227
Lake Accotink Park, 137
Lake Anna State Park, 250
Lake Artemesia Park, 109
Lake Fairfax Park, 137
Lake Frank, 109
Lake Needwood Park, 110
Larriland Farm, 163
Laser Quest, 213
Lee District Park and Robert E. Lee Recreation Center, 138
Leesburg Animal Park, 259
Lexington Market, 228
Liberty Mountain Resort, 204
Library of Congress, 35
Lincoln Memorial, 19
Little Bennett Regional Park, 110
Locust Grove Nature Center, 149
Long Branch Nature Center, 150
Luray Caverns, 251

M

Made By You, 215
Manassas National Battlefield Park, 126
MARC Trains, 10
Marietta House Museum, 75
Marine Barracks Evening Parade, 176
Marine Corps Historical Center, 51
Market Square/Alexandria City Hall, 90

Martin Luther King, Jr. Swim
Center (MLK), 207
Maryland Hall for the Creative
Arts, 176
Maryland Historical Society,
228
Maryland Science Center, 220
Maryland Tourism, 4
Maryland Tours, 220
Mason District Park, 118
McCrillis Gardens and Gallery,
166
Meadowbrook Stables, 198
Meadowlark Botanical Gardens,
167
Meadowside Nature Center, 150
Metrorail and Metrobus, 11
Middleburg, VA Pink Box
Visitor Center, 251
Montgomery Aquatic Center,
207
Montgomery County Airpark,
76
Montgomery County Humane
Society, 263
Montgomery County Recycling
Center, 263
Montpelier Mansion, 90
Montrose Park, 138
Mormon Temple, see
Washington Temple Visitors'
Center, 79
Morven Park, 91
Mount Vernon Community
Children's Theatre, 176
Mount Vernon Estate and
Gardens (George
Washington's Home), 92
Mount Vernon Trail, 118
Museum of Man, see National
Museum of Natural History,
26

N

NASA/Goddard Space Flight
Center, 76
National Air and Space
Museum, 20

National Aquarium In
Baltimore, 221
National Aquarium,
Washington, 21
National Archives, 22
National Building Museum, 52
National Capital Trolley
Museum, 77
National Firearms Museum, 93
National Gallery of Art, 22
National Geographic Society,
see Explorers Hall, National
Geographic Society, 45
National Museum of African
Art, 24
National Museum of American
Art, see Smithsonian Art
Museum, 60
National Museum of American
History, 24
National Museum of Civil War
Medicine, 246
National Museum of Dentistry,
229
National Museum of Health and
Medicine of the Armed
Forces, 53
National Museum of Natural
History, 26
National Museum of the
American Indian, 27
National Museum of the Marine
Corps, 252
National Museum of Women in
the Arts, 54
National Park Service - National
Capital Region, 4
National Portrait Gallery, 54
National Postal Museum, 36
National Public Radio, 263
National Weather Service, 264
National Wildlife Visitor Center,
Patuxent Research Refuge,
151
National Zoo, 55
Navy Art Gallery, 56
Netherlands Carillon Concerts,
177
New Market Battlefield Military
Museum, 252

Newseum, 57
Northern Virginia Transportation Commission, 12
Now This! Kids!, 177
Noyes Library for Young Children, 187

O

Oatlands Plantation, 93
Occoquan Regional Park, 138
Old Bedford Village, 256
Old Post Office Pavillion, 58
Old Stone House, 58
Old Town Trolley Tours of Washington, DC, 7
Olney Indoor Swim Center, 208
Olney Theater Center for the Arts, 177
Olsson's Books & Records, 188
Oxon Hill Farm, 159

P

Paramount's Kings Dominion, 260
Parenting Resource Centers, 212
Patapsco Valley State Park, 111
Patuxent River State Park, Jug Bay Natural Area, 112
Peace Park/ Kunzang Palyul Chöling, 151
Phillips Farm, 163
Piscataway National Park, 113
Plaster, Paint and Party, 215
Pohick Bay Regional Park and Golf Course, 139
Politics and Prose, 188
Port Discovery Children's Museum, 222
Potomac Horse Center, 198
Potomac Overlook Regional Park, 119
Potomac Riverboat Company Cruises, 7
Potomac Vegetable Farms, 164
Potomac West, 252

Prince George's Publick Playhouse for the Performing Arts, 178
Prince William Forest Park, 120
Puppet Company Playhouse, 178

Q

Quiet Waters Park, 233

R

Radio-Television Museum, 77
Ratner Museum, see Dennis and Philip Ratner Museum, The, 72
Red Rock Wilderness Overlook Regional Park, 120
Reginald F. Lewis Museum of Maryland African American History and Culture, 78
Renwick Gallery, 60
Reston Ice Skating Pavilion, 202
Ride-On Buses, Montgomery County, MD, 12
River Farm Garden Park, 167
Riverbend Park, 121
Rock Creek Nature Center and Planetarium, 152
Rock Creek Park, 101
Rock Creek Park Horse Center, 198
Rockville Municipal Swim Center, 208
Rockville Roller Skating Center, 203
Rockville Skate Part at Welsh Park, 203
Rocky Gap State Park, 247
Rocky Gorge 4 Seasons Golf Fairway, 199
Round House Theatre, 179
Roundtop, 204
Rust Sanctuary (Audubon Naturalist Society), 153

S

Sackler, see Arthur M. Sackler Gallery, 15

Samuel D. Harris, MD, see National Museum of Dentistry, 229
Saturday Morning at The National & Monday Night at The National, 179
Scotts Run Nature Preserve, 121
Second Story Books, 189
Senate and House Visitors Galleries, 5
Seneca Creek State Park, 114
Seneca Schoolhouse Museum, 264
Shadowland, 213
Shenandoah National Park, 253
Sideling Hill Exhibit Center, 248
Six Flags America and Paradise Island Waterpark, 260
Skate-N-Fun Zone, 203
Skyline Caverns, 254
Sligo Creek Park, 115
Smithsonian Art Museum, 60
Smithsonian Discovery Theater, 180
Smithsonian Information Center, 'the Castle', 27
South Germantown Recreational Park, 140
South Germantown Recreational Park - Splash Playgound and Miniatuure Golf, 209
South Mountain Recreation Area, 248
Spirit Cruises, 8
Splash Down Water Park, 209
Splash Playground, see South Germantown Recreational Park - Splash Playground and Miniatuure Golf, 209
Sportrock Climbing Center, 214
Stabler-Leadbeater Apothecary Shop and Museum, 94
Star-Spangled Banner Flag House, 230
State House Visitor Center, 234
Strathmore Hall Arts Center, 180
Sugarloaf Mountain, 115
Sullivan's Toy Store, 189
Sully Historic Site, 94

Summitt Hall Farm Park, see Bohrer Park at Summit Hall Farm, 206
Sunset Serenades at the National Zoo, 181
Supreme Court, 37
Surratt House Museum, 95
Swain's Lock, 196
Sylvan Theater, 181

T

Temple Hall Farm Regional Park, 159
Textile Museum, 61
The African-American Civil War Memorial, 38
The Baltimore Civil War Museum - President Street Station, 217
The Baltimore Zoo, 225
The Capitol, 33
The Children's Museum of Rose Hill Manor Park, 244
The Dennis and Philip Ratner Museum, 72
The Kreeger Museum, 51
The Land of Little Horses, 259
The Lee-Fendall House Museum, 89
The Lyceum, Alexandria's History Museum, 90
The National Colonial Farm, 158
The Navy Museum, 56
The Octagon, 57
The Pentagon, 264
The Phillips Collection, 59
The Sandy Spring Museum, 78
The Very Special Arts Gallery, 64
The Washington Post, 265
The White House and White House Visitor Center, 31
Theodore Roosevelt Island, 122
Thomas Jefferson Memorial, 18
Thompson's Boat Center, 196
Toby's Dinner Theatre, 182
Torpedo Factory Art Center, 96

Tourmobile Sightseeing
    Incorporated, 9
Toys... Etc., 190
Treetop Toys and Books, 190
Tuckahoe Park and Playfield,
    140
Tudor Place, 61

U

U.S. Botanic Garden, 28
U.S. Geological Survey National
    Visitors Center, 97
U.S. Holocaust Memorial
    Museum, 62
U.S. National Arboretum, 168
U.S. Naval Academy, 235
U.S. Naval Observatory, 153
U.S. Navy Memorial and Naval
    Heritage Center, 63
U.S.S. Constellation, 222
Union Station, 64
University of Maryland
    Observatory, 154
Upton Hill Regional Park, 141

V

Vietnam Veterans Memorial, 29
Virginia Railway Express, 12
Virginia Tourism Corporation, 5
Voice of America, 265

W

Wakefield District Park and
    Recreation Center, see
    Audrey Moore / Wakefield
    Park and Recreation Center,
    128
Walney Visitor Center - Ellanor
    C. Lawrence Park, 160
Walters Art Gallery, 231
Washington and Old Dominion
    (W&OD) Railroad Regional
    Park, 122
Washington Dolls' House and
    Toy Museum, 64
Washington Monument, 30

Washington National Cathedral,
    65
Washington Navy Yard, 67
Washington Navy Yard -
    National Museum of the
    Marine Corps, 252
Washington Navy Yard - Navy
    Art Gallery, see Navy Art
    Gallery, 56
Washington Sailing Marina, 197
Washington Temple Visitors'
    Center (known as the, 79
Washington Walks, 9
Washington, DC Convention
    and Visitors Association, 5
Watermark Cruises, 236
Watkins Regional Park, 141
Webb Sanctuary (Audubon
    Naturalist Society), 154
West End Dinner Theater, 182
Western Maryland Scenic
    Railroad, 249
WETA-TV, Channel 26, 265
Wheaton Regional Park, 142
Whirligigs & Whimsies, 191
White Flint Golf Park, 199
White's Ferry, 79
Whitetail Resort, 205
Whole Foods Market, 266
William Paca House and
    Garden, 236
Wisp at Deep Creek Mountain
    Resort, 205
Wolf Trap Farm Park for the
    Performing Arts/The Barns at
    Wolftrap, 183
Woodend Nature Sanctuary
    (Audubon Naturalist Society),
    155
Woodlawn Plantation/Frank
    Lloyd Wright's Pope-Leighey
    House, 98
Woodrow Wilson House, 67

Z

Zany Brainy, 191
Zoo, see National Zoo, 55
ZooAmerica, North American
    Wildlife Park, 261

Notes

Going Places With Children
in Washington, DC
16th Edition

$20 per book
(includes tax & 1st class mail)

Order Form

Name:_____

Street:_____

City:_____ State:_____ Zip:_____

Telephone Number:_(____)_____

Also mail to:

Name:_____

Street:_____

City:_____ State:_____ Zip:_____

Telephone Number:_(____)_____

___ Please send me _____ copies at $20 per book.

___ Please send me a brochure about Green Acres School.

Total enclosed: $_____

Please make checks payable to:
Green Acres School, *Going Places*
11701 Danville Drive, Rockville, Maryland 20852-3717

Books are also sold in area bookstores. Quantity discounts
are available. Please call 301-881-4100 for more information.